Nicholas Jones

Strikes and the Media
Communication and Conflict

Basil Blackwell

© Nicholas Jones 1986

First published 1986

Basil Blackwell Ltd
108 Cowley Road, Oxford OX4 1JF, UK

Basil Blackwell Inc.
432 Park Avenue South, Suite 1505,
New York, NY 10016, USA

British Library Cataloguing in Publication Data
Jones, Nicholas
Strikes and the media.
1. Mass media and industrial relations –
Great Britain
I. Title
070.4'49331'0941   P95.82.G7

ISBN 0–631–14697–0

Library of Congress Cataloging in Publication Data
Jones, Nicholas.
Strikes and the media.
Includes index.
1. Strikes and lockouts — Miners — Great Britain.
2. Mass media and business — Great Britain. I. Title.
HD5365.M6J66   1986   331.89'2941   85–30687
ISBN 0–631–14697–0

HD
5365
M6
J66
1986

Typeset by Oxford Publishing Services, Oxford
Printed in Great Britain by Page Bros (Norwich) Ltd

Contents

Acknowledgements

The author and publisher are most grateful for permission to reproduce material as follows: *Plate 1* Neil Libbert/*The Observer*, *Plate 2* BBC Enterprises, *Plate 3* British Railways Board, *Plate 4* Associated Society of Locomotive Engineers and Firemen, *Plate 5* British Steel Corporation, *Plate 6* Express Newspapers, *Plate 7* Express Newspapers, *Plate 8* Campaign for Press and Broadcasting Freedom, *Plate 9* Express Newspapers, *Plate 10* Press Association, *Plate 11* Express Newspapers, *Plate 12* Syndication International, *Plate 13* Les Gibbard, *Plate 14* National Coal Board, *Plate 15* National Coal Board, North Derbyshire Area, *Plate 16* National Coal Board, *Plate 17* Raymonds, Derby.

ONE

Introduction

The media of mass communications have been used increasingly – and to increasing effect – by both employers and trade unions during British industrial disputes since the late 1970s. In some strikes the presentation of the opposing arguments, both to employees and to the public, became a crucial factor in deciding the final outcome. Several nationalised industries challenged the industrial strength of the trade unions by attempting to manage the way the news was reported, and on occasion this process revealed the extent of government involvement, as ministers were forced to take their place at the very forefront of the battle for publicity.

The disputes of this period happened at a time when major changes in the news media and in techniques of communication were taking place. Managers were discovering ways to bypass the trade unions in order to speak directly to their employees; a rapid expansion in the broadcasting services provided new opportunities for both sides to communicate with the public. In the course of some bitter strikes the electronic news media provided the only means of instant contact between the participants, particularly on those occasions when normal relations had broken down, and union leaders and employers often found they had to struggle to come to terms with the immediacy of radio and television reporting.

The strikes themselves had also altered in character. Sometimes they involved not wage claims, but workers' protests at the rate and scale of the industrial change which was accompanying the substantial restructuring of British industry and the drive for efficiency encouraged by government. Journalists and broadcasters found that they in turn were being subjected to the pressures arising both from prolonged industrial conflict and from the faster transmission of news and information, which had in itself led to a wider readjustment of traditional roles in the news media.

Many of the industrial disputes of the late 1970s and early 1980s saw the emergence of strong managements which were determined to persuade strikers to return to work. Trade union leaders found themselves being bypassed by sophisticated techniques which had become available through the modernisation and expansion of traditional channels of communication. When faced with difficult industrial disputes, instead of relying on the expertise of their own industrial relations departments, employers turned increasingly to consultants in the communications and advertising industry, which had developed new ways of taking advantage of the postal and telephone services. Several of these consultants were to become the closest advisers to the chairmen of nationalised industries and major companies as well as to the government. The techniques deployed by management included extensive advertising in national and local newspapers; personal letters from the chairman to the home of each worker; recorded telephone messages giving employees advice on how to break a strike; and sometimes opinion surveys among the staff which were carried out in secret and used by management to help work out policy objectives. Some disputes saw the full panoply of such counter measures in use.

It was the use that both trade unions and employers made of broadcasting, especially at times when negotiations had failed and normal discussions could not continue, that had the greatest impact on the public. Radio and television services were instantly available to both sides, who found they could respond to each other through interviews which could be transmitted live from a studio or broadcast within a few hours of being recorded. In some disputes union leaders and management became so preoccupied with the presentation of their case through the news media that the need to make statements and give interviews appeared to assume a greater priority than the task of trying to negotiate a settlement.

The ability to broadcast, sometimes within minutes, the news of a decision to call or end a strike had given the electronic media a considerable advantage over the national newspapers. Radio and television news organisations were anxious to develop this service, believing that the fast transmission of such information was in the public interest. Technical advances were to allow even more live broadcasts from remote locations, which speeded up the process still further.

The willingness of some trade unions and employers to allow industrial disputes to be negotiated through the news media coincided with a considerable expansion in the radio and television services. The growth in the number of local radio stations and the introduction in 1983 of breakfast programmes by BBC television and TV–AM provided, morning, noon and night, a non-stop national and local arena of news bulletins and discussion programmes. The broadcasting services were eager to participate directly in what were often major news stories, by providing the protagonists with the opportunity to negotiate face-to-face. They knew that direct negotiation in a studio could provide compulsive listening or viewing, especially during controversial disputes when there might already be a heightened sense of confrontation. They also believed that studio discussions could help to clear up the misunderstanding and confusion that might be preventing a settlement.

As union leaders and management struggled to come to terms with a new era in industrial relations, they found it hard to resist the microphones, television cameras and bright lights of broadcasting. Although some saw the danger in over-exposure, and were not prepared to see their own credibility undermined by it, the new concept of instant negotiation through the news media was to prove irresistible to a number of nationalised industry chairmen and union general secretaries and presidents. Their readiness to allow the discussion of a dispute to be conducted in public fuelled the enthusiasm of those who worked not only in radio and television but also in the national and local press. The point was reached in some disputes where the news media found that they were doing more than merely reporting what had happened – they seemed on some occasions to be even helping to create the news. One of the subjects this book will discuss is whether confrontation in the news media between union leaders and management could have the effect of prolonging a dispute.

My own interest in investigating the way radio and television are used by unions and employers began in 1982 during a series of rail strikes. This was perhaps the first dispute that saw a sustained attempt at negotiating through the electronic news media. As the dispute progressed it became noticeable that when management or union leaders sought justification for a particular decision they began to refer back to the latest broadcast that the other side had given. There always seemed a ready store of provocation in the answers to the questions that had been asked in news bulletins or current affairs programmes.

A journalist assigned to cover any long-running dispute has an unrivalled opportunity to observe not only the progress of events but also changes in the conduct of the participants. Frequently this involves standing outside the headquarters of unions and employers waiting for the latest news on the outcome of wage negotiations or the result of discussions over the calling or settling of strikes. There is usually a large group of reporters, photographers and television cameramen waiting on the doorstep. As a union leader or member of the management emerges the newsmen will often jostle with each other as they try to get the best possible position for hearing, recording or filming the statement or interview about to be given. A radio reporter has to get as near to the front as possible, which often means pushing through other people to stretch out an arm with the microphone. Similarly, when journalists are invited inside for a news conference a radio reporter occasionally needs to crouch on the floor, again trying to get the microphone as close as possible to the person speaking, while staying out of shot for the television cameramen and newspaper photographers.

The very nature of this work provides an opportunity to see at close range how union leaders and management react to the news media and to the questions they are asked. When tape recorders and television lights are

3

switched off, there is sometimes a moment or two left for some friendly gossip or an opportunity to ask an extra question away from the cut and thrust of a news conference or the formalities of a recorded interview.

In the course of everyday work a reporter specialising in labour and industrial affairs has innumerable interviews and conversations with union leaders, employers and politicians. I hope that the events I relate here, and my record of the comments made at the time, will help explain the relationship between those who work in the news media and those who seek or attract publicity during industrial disputes. This book is based on my own observation, and on information that was either volunteered or obtained as a result of my inquiries. Most of the conversations I refer to took place before or after meetings and negotiations, often in the presence of other journalists. The information I record was offered freely to a working journalist in the knowledge that it might or might not be used, and in reproducing such comments and conversations I do not believe I am breaking any confidences.

During a bitter industrial dispute many things are said in the heat of the moment; the participants frequently seek to provoke each other while at the same time criticising the news media for printing or broadcasting what has been said. Journalists and broadcasters often have a difficult task trying to disentangle fact from propaganda. I attempt to illustrate the pressures that can arise and the effect those pressures can have on the course of negotiations and on those who work for newspapers, radio and television.

Much of my book is devoted to one industrial dispute: the 1984–5 miners' strike. The year-long stoppage in the pits was to illustrate more than any other the need for good communications with the workforce, the importance of public presentation, and the trend towards arguing out major industrial disputes – and even negotiating them – on radio and television. Throughout the strike repeated attempts were made to exploit the news media. The National Union of Mineworkers, the National Coal Board and the government all tried with varying degrees of success to obtain publicity and to manage the way the dispute was reported by newspapers and the broadcasting services.

As the months went by the coal board and the government became increasingly dependent on the advice and expertise of advertising consultants and those well versed in the art of news management. They were having to compete with the publicity skills of one man – Arthur Scargill. As president of the miners' union and its official spokesman, Mr Scargill managed, single-handed, day after day, to set the agenda for Fleet Street and the radio and television newsrooms. However, Mr Scargill's skill in projecting himself masked the failure of the miners' union to devise a communications strategy. In the final weeks of the strike, as the return to work gathered pace, news management reigned supreme: the coal board and the government held the advantage and the NUM slid to defeat.

The phenomenon of unions and employers negotiating industrial disputes through radio and television became more apparent after the election of the Conservative government in 1979. The new Prime Minister was determined to modernise British industry and particularly, to increase the efficiency of the nationalised industries. Mrs Thatcher and her ministers wanted to end what they believed were decades of compromise by management. Major industrial disputes were no longer simply about wages and conditions; they became increasingly a fight against industrial change, to which there was organised resistance by a succession of powerful groups including car workers, steelworkers, railwaymen and miners.

Another change that had followed the 1979 general election was the Prime Minister's refusal to let the government be used as a final court of appeal for settling major strikes. Mrs Thatcher said she would not allow No. 10 Downing Street to become an escape route, as it had in the days of Labour prime ministers. Trade union leaders would not be invited in for beer and sandwiches as a prelude to a possible compromise with management. The government wanted the employers, especially in the public sector, to regain the right to manage. In this way Mrs Thatcher and her ministers had in effect changed the rules for industrial disputes. Gone were the days of compromise and negotiation. Government and management would henceforward take a decision and then stick to it. There would be no retreat in the face of trade union power. In these struggles propaganda would become an essential weapon against industrial muscle. The radio and television services would find themselves in the forefront of the battle for publicity, as unions and employers tried to control the way disputes were presented through the news media.

In previous years the protagonists had often been able to work out a last-minute deal with the relevant minister, but by removing that option the government had left management and union leaders with no choice but to fight it out. This change was hardest of all on the public sector, because the government was intent on breaking up the concentrations of trade union power that existed in the nationalised industries and public services. Mrs Thatcher and her ministers were known to be highly critical of much of management for allowing over-manning and poor productivity to have continued for so long. If British industry was to be made efficient and the private sector encouraged, management would have to take on the public sector unions. The state monopolies would either have to put their own house in order or they would be broken up and sold off to private industry. In this atmosphere the union leaders soon discovered that there was no point in asking the government to intervene. Nor were cabinet ministers ready to be seen offering a hand of friendship to state industry chairmen and managers who were not prepared to stand firm in the face of what was often described as Luddite trade unionism; and the government often encouraged public discussion of the background to industrial disputes because it provided an opportunity to drive home the case for efficiency.

In the early 1980s the nationalised industries were drawn, one after another, into a series of confrontations; there were several recurrent themes in the propaganda war that developed during these major strikes. The public sector employers, backed by government ministers, would emphasise repeatedly the need for efficient work practices. Wherever possible this appeal was made through the news media direct to the workforce, over the heads of local and national trade union leaders. Another message that the government was anxious to convey was the need for employers to regain the right to manage, but it was sometimes difficult for ministers to get the balance correct and keep public opinion supporting the need for change.

One priority for the government was to avoid criticism, and thus the possible electoral damage, that might result from a policy of non-intervention, especially when a dispute might be inconveniencing the public through disruption to services. This meant that while Mrs Thatcher and her ministers would insist that industrial disputes were for management to settle, they knew they would have to keep in close touch with what was happening. Therefore the government departments responsible for public services and the nationalised industries worked behind the scenes. But although ministers were often largely in control of what was happening, the impression given in public was that the government had distanced itself from the confrontations that were taking place between the unions and the state-owned industries and services.

This new era of industrial change was not introduced without a fight. The policy of seeking to make the public services and nationalised industries more efficient brought the government into conflict with a number of formidable alliances. In some areas of the public sector, management and union leaders had built up an effective working relationship. Over the years they had seen that their common enemy was often the government of the day, and that one of a nationalised industry's strongest weapons was the ability to make an effective joint approach to government. The two sides were often able to exercise influence over the government by synchronising their opposition to a particular policy. If some service or duty was to be removed from an industry's sphere of influence the trade unions might warn of industrial action, while management would leak information explaining why the change would be against the public interest; sometimes management would appear to be taking the initiative, but senior union leaders would be playing the equally important role of refraining from public comment.

Media presentation had become all-important on such occasions, which partly explains why for some time the nationalised industries had employed large staffs of public relations advisers. Senior management had to understand politics as well as their own industries – and that required a readiness to lobby through the news media, as one way of influencing public and parliamentary opinion. On the whole the nationalised industries believed they were good at publicity.

Close personal relationships often developed between the two sides, especially when a nationalised industry chairman and a senior union leader were in office together for some years and had to deal with frequent alterations in government policy. Two men who had a decade to establish their working relationship were the former chairman of the National Coal Board, Sir Derek Ezra, later Lord Ezra, and the former president of the National Union of Mineworkers, Joe Gormley, later Lord Gormley. Both held office from 1971 to 1982, saw two changes in government resulting from general election defeats, and served under four prime ministers.

After the miners' strikes of 1972 and 1974 there was relative peace in the pits for the rest of the Ezra–Gormley era. In their public statements the two men seemed to know the limitations of each other's position. They appeared both willing and able to co-operate when a publicity offensive was required, but they could also pull in the reins if they felt the propaganda was running out of control. There were the tell-tale signs of fine-tuning behind the media image of the blunt, no-nonsense union leader and the tough head of a nationalised industry. This warm management–union relationship reached its peak as the two men began their final years in office, which coincided with the start of the period of change that followed the Conservative Party's 1979 general election victory.

A good illustration of this cordial relationship was the traditional get-together on the last evening of the mineworkers' annual union conference when the National Coal Board would be host and all were welcome – management, union delegates and journalists. The first conference I attended as labour correspondent for BBC radio news, at Eastbourne in 1980, was the last but one for Sir Derek and Mr Gormley, and on this last evening the two leaders were comperes. After a meal at the Grand Hotel, beer began arriving by the jugful, and the tables were cleared ready for a singsong. The NCB management and press officers did a turn; then it was the moment for the Fleet Street journalists. But it was the miners' leaders and their wives who helped to make it such an unforgettable occasion, with songs from Sid Vincent, general secretary of the Lancashire NUM, and Cathy McGahey, wife of Mick McGahey, president of the Scottish union.

The friendships that could develop during these social occasions were invaluable, particularly when union leaders and management identified a common threat. But within months of the 1980 conference at Eastbourne, the coal industry was under pressure from the new Conservative government to start reducing the subsidies that were needed for uneconomic pits. The NCB announced plans to cut up to ten million tons from the coal industry's capacity, and the threat of up to twenty pit closures led to unofficial strike action in South Wales, which spread to other coalfields. A national stoppage seemed imminent.

Sir Derek and Mr Gormley knew that by doing all they could to work together they could probably take on the government and perhaps minimise the extent of any cutback. They might even win the day and secure new public investment for the industry. While the threat of industrial action was to intensify during February 1981, the two men were to make a joint approach to the government. This resulted in a meeting with David Howell, then Secretary of State for Energy. When Sir Derek and Mr Gormley emerged from their discussion with the minister, they announced to the waiting newsmen that the government had given way and would add another £300 million to the coal industry's cash limit, which in turn meant more in subsidies to the loss-making pits. Earlier that afternoon during a lobby briefing at No. 10 Downing Street, the Prime Minister's press office had indicated to political journalists that Mr Howell would be standing firm that evening when he met leaders of the miners' union. On the strength of the lobby guidance the *Daily Express* had prepared a leading article for the next day's paper praising Mrs Thatcher for her refusal to be swayed in the face of unofficial strike action by the miners. Therefore, when Mr Gormley emerged from his meeting at the Department of Energy to announce that the government would be providing extra money to prevent pit closures, there was surprise and consternation among the waiting journalists – and in a dash for the telephones, especially by those who had to tell their newsdesks to 'kill' their first edition stories. 'For "No" read "Yes"!' shouted Barrie Devney, industrial editor of the *Daily Express*, down the phone to his news editor.

There was little official guidance that evening from either Mr Howell's department or the National Coal Board over the precise extent of the government's retreat. Mr Gormley was the first to speak to the waiting reporters, and his interpretation of what had been agreed was the version that was carried in radio and television news bulletins and that appeared next morning in the national newspapers. Some time afterwards there were suggestions that the NUM president had exceeded his brief, by announcing a commitment on behalf of the government that was firmer than Mr Howell had intended. Indeed, one of the negotiators told me afterwards that as soon as Mr Howell had made his statement to the NUM leaders, Mr Gormley had asked to be excused from the meeting. The next Mr Howell's advisers saw of the president he was in the entrance hall of the Department of Energy telling newsmen that the government had given way.

The final outcome of a strike often rests on the initial presentation of what trade union leaders achieve in negotiation. If the workers believe there has been a positive outcome a dispute can be over in days, because they are satisfied that their efforts and sacrifices have been worthwhile. So it fell out in 1981: the success of Mr Gormley and Sir Derek in obtaining more money for the coal industry brought the miners' strike of that year to a swift conclusion.

The Prime Minister did not appear to enjoy what some sections of the news media described as her government's first 'U-turn' over industrial policy. There were indications at the time that Mr Gormley and Sir Derek had been on the point of settling for less, but that Mr Howell had misjudged the position, having failed to realise that away from the glare of publicity there was every prospect of an unofficial understanding between the NCB and NUM which could have resulted in a settlement on terms less humiliating for the government. Mrs Thatcher gave the impression of being in no mood to forgive. The following year Sir Derek was not invited to stay on for another term as NCB chairman. Mr Howell, in a ministerial reshuffle that September, was switched to Transport and replaced at Energy by Nigel Lawson. He in turn initiated the moves to build up record stocks of coal at the power stations, which were to be well in place for the 1984–5 miners' strike.

The final years of the Ezra–Gormley era illustrated the resistance that the Conservative government faced when it sought to reduce the power of the well established nationalised industries. Managements appeared secure in the belief that their industries were there not simply to make a profit, but also to fulfil a public service – a conviction often reflected in the degree of personal commitment shown by senior staff. There was also security for the trade unions, most of which had closed shop agreements guaranteeing membership and influence. In the coal industry, the closed shop was maintained not by a formal agreement but by the traditional solidarity of the mineworkers. However, the government was soon to start encouraging the nationalised industry chairmen to challenge these established trade union practices.

TWO

Communication or Conflict?
British Leyland and British Rail

One of the overriding industrial objectives of the 1979 Conservative government was to increase efficiency through securing changes in the attitudes of workers and management. The new administration believed that Britain could only prosper if its industries were made as competitive as those of the rest of the world. That process would involve major alterations in the scope of the nationalised industries: some were to be sold off to private shareholders, and others were slimmed as part of a wider drive to reduce the size of the state sector by bringing in private contractors. Industrial managers who shared the enthusiasm for the proposed fundamental changes were encouraged by the government, who acknowledged from the start that they would meet opposition, for the changes they were seeking were so far-reaching that they could not be achieved without weakening or breaking up the entrenched trade union power concentrated in the state-owned industries and public services. The government's determination to improve Britain's industrial performance had coincided, as we have noted, with the development of new and improved forms of communication, which were to be used increasingly by management to communicate directly with large groups of workers, often numbering several hundred thousand, at times of strike or industrial dispute.

In some sections of British industry it had become the established practice for trade union leaders rather than the employers to supply the workforce with information about pay increases, new working practices or advances in technology that affected the shop floor. First, management would convey the information to national or local trade union leaders; they in turn communicated the details to the workforce at mass meetings or through union shop stewards, who then spoke directly to the groups of workers for whom they were responsible. The possession of vital information that could affect the livelihood of workers reinforced the power and importance of individual union leaders or shop stewards, who could exercise considerable influence in the way they communicated what management had told them.

The Conservatives blamed weak managements in the past, as well as previous Labour governments, for often allowing trade unions to control, and in some cases to dictate, the flow of information to the workforce. This only encouraged a trade union stranglehold over the introduction of new technology, said the new government ministers. In a number of nationalised industries, management's failure to communicate effectively was considered to be one reason for inadequate productivity. There was general agreement among the new managers who hoped to speed up industrial change, that once managerial decisions had been taken they should be kept to, and that the task of communicating these decisions to the labour force was the responsibility of the employer. These managers were determined to win back control over communications with their employees, even though here was one factor that increased the trade union resistance that was already developing to the government's industrial policies.

Some senior industrial relations directors believed that a strategy for communicating directly with the workforce was the only way to improve competitiveness and speed up the introduction of new products and work practices. They had found that their employees were not always being given an opportunity to understand or adapt because local union representatives controlled the channels of communication. The traditional machinery of trade union consultation could be used effectively to block change, but the new techniques would ensure that employees received the facts directly from those employed to manage and motivate them.

The process of change began with a gradual reduction in the amount of advance information given to trade union leaders and shop stewards. This was accompanied by the development of new systems for communicating directly with the workers, who received information, sometimes in their own homes, about what the employer thought was important. Managements were careful, except during strikes, not to bypass the trade unions completely, by giving information to employees before it had been received by national leaders or shop stewards. In order to avoid antagonising the unions unnecessarily, some employers tried to run the two communication systems in parallel, but this rarely proved satisfactory, especially during disputes, and the government openly encouraged managements in the nationalised industries to adopt unilaterally the practice of talking directly to their employees. The flow of information at work was increased by training senior staff in the skills needed to communicate to groups of workers. By transferring responsibility for communications from shop stewards to supervisors and foremen, the employers believed that those members of management responsible for shop-floor workers would find their own authority had been strengthened – which was seen as an essential first step towards improving productivity.

Thus a number of employers began to rethink their whole approach to both internal and external communications. In previous years state-owned industries and major private employers had used their public relations departments largely to influence public and parliamentary opinion, as they had not seen the same need to devote resources to the task of conveying information to their workers. Once the pace of technological change quickened and major restructuring became necessary in order to survive, managements realised that they had to find ways to counter trade union resistance: external relations were no longer the sole priority. In some cases the 'public relations director' was replaced by a 'communications director', who was responsible for both internal and external communications systems. The techniques which had been built up by the public relations industry were slowly transferred and applied to communications with the workforce. Some employers moved quickly to take full advantage of both the expansion in radio and television and the improved services which were being offered by other traditional means of communication.

In some industries where managements were making a concerted attempt to improve efficiency, disagreements over restructuring and new work practices began to replace the issue of pay as the main source of conflict. This change in the character and emphasis of industrial disputes became noticeable in the final years of the Labour government, well before the 1979 general election, as the then National Enterprise Board struggled to come to terms with the task of improving the competitiveness of British Leyland, the one remaining British-controlled mass-producer of cars, trucks and buses. British Leyland, in which the government was the majority shareholder, had been losing money, and had a long record of industrial disputes and poor productivity rates. The crisis over what to do about BL reached its peak during 1977, when over 250,000 vehicles were lost through strike action, despite a strong demand for the group's medium-sized cars. In June of that year management had stepped up its efforts to reform pay bargaining procedures, in order to make way for the introduction of a common wage structure throughout the cars group.

One member of the National Enterprise Board who had, 'with some apprehension', observed BL's problems looming up was Michael Edwardes, later Sir Michael, who had been chairman of the Chloride Group for the previous three years. After a change in the leadership of the NEB, Sir Michael was asked if he would like to take on British Leyland – as chief executive, under a new chairman, Ian MacGregor. He replied immediately that he was against a split function at the top, and would not accept less than the combined role of chairman and chief executive. After a meeting between the two men at Kennedy Airport, Mr MacGregor agreed to serve as deputy chairman under Sir Michael, who began work at BL's headquarters in Piccadilly on 1 November 1977.

Sir Michael identified poor communications with the workforce as one factor responsible for the 'state of chaos' that he found, he said, on taking over as chairman. In some plants he discovered that managers had abdicated major functions to the shop stewards: all communication with employees was being effected by the unions, not by management. Within sixteen days of his appointment he announced a major reorganisation of the group and a new management structure. His team then began preparing plans for the group's recovery. Soon after the Conservatives were elected in 1979 he introduced what became known as the 'BL Recovery Plan', which required the complete or partial closure of thirteen factories, with the loss within two years of 25,000 jobs. Sir Michael's determination to improve the efficiency of BL's factories was fully endorsed by the new government, even though it was to lead to further industrial conflict.

Despite considerable opposition from local union leaders, Sir Michael went to great lengths to consult national officials in the major unions. He was encouraged by the knowledge that whatever might be said in public by certain union leaders, he could rely on at least a degree of co-operation from the then president of the Amalgamated Union of Engineering Workers, Terry Duffy. In the years before his death in October 1985, Mr Duffy explained to me that he had been prepared to back BL on what were, for his union, some difficult decisions, because he was convinced by the sincerity of Sir Michael's commitment to the industry and to the need to maintain BL as a volume car manufacturer.

During the protracted disputes that were to ensue Sir Michael proved that the chairman of a state-owned industry could use newspapers, radio and television to help secure fundamental change. He showed how management could exploit the news media to the employer's advantage, and the effectiveness of his approach was to be demonstrated by the seven to one majority vote for the Edwardes recovery plan that British Leyland obtained when the Electoral Reform Society conducted a secret ballot among all BL employees.

The central objective for BL was to get the company's message across as effectively and as quickly as possible. This meant acknowledging the importance of the early evening broadcasts on radio and television. A news item transmitted at tea-time could give BL an opportunity to speak directly to the car workers as they drove home from the factories, or sat down for their evening meal and watched or listened to the news. The company wanted to ensure that whenever possible they heard the latest announcement at first hand from the chairman at a time when it would have maximum impact, not only on the workers themselves but also on their families, who might be watching or listening too. An equal priority for management was to make contact with the workforce before local union leaders had a chance to hold a mass meeting.

The need to meet the deadlines of radio and television news was often considered more important than an extensive briefing for the national press, especially on those days when major announcements could not be made until the afternoon or later. On such occasions a news conference for

13

the media had to be tightly controlled. After making an initial statement to the journalists present, Sir Michael would spend some minutes answering general questions, but if at all possible he would avoid getting involved in lengthy discussions with individual Fleet Street reporters, because these could make a news conference confusing and might delay the proceedings.

Sir Michael was anxious to keep his press conferences as short and businesslike as possible because in the adjoining rooms radio and television reporters and technicians would be waiting to film or record face-to-face interviews with him. If there was time he would do individual interviews with each reporter, as he knew that this was likely to get maximum exposure on the radio and television networks. On some occasions he might have to do half a dozen or more separate interviews for use by national and local radio and television. He showed equal skill in handling radio and television interviews that had to be conducted later in the day, when there was not time to arrange a press conference. On some occasions he was intent on making only a brief statement that would not be followed up by too many supplementary questions from reporters. Short interviews, though requiring some degree of stage-management, could create a sense of immediacy and provide an opportunity to present the chairman in an everyday setting, away from the formal surroundings of a news conference.

The technique adopted by the public relations advisers at British Leyland was to make discreet telephone calls to the appropriate radio and television newsdesks, informing them that Sir Michael would shortly be leaving his London office in Portman Square and would speak briefly on his way out of the car park. Sir Michael would then appear at the appropriate moment, wind down the window of his Rover, with the engine still running. This was the moment for a stern warning from the chairman or some bullish words of encouragement, depending on the day's developments. As soon as a reporter tried a probing or unwelcome question, he would wind up the window and drive away. Here was the equivalent of a photo-call for newspapers: a talking picture for television, one that showed the chairman on the move, and not stuck in the office or trapped answering awkward questions at a news conference.

As a confident radio and television performer, Sir Michael was also quite prepared to be interviewed in the studio, though he was against appearing in a discussion with union leaders and made it a condition whenever possible that the interview be broadcast live rather than pre-recorded. For some years previously senior politicians had been expressing a strong preference for live interviews, as they believed that this ensured the least possible editorial interference by programme makers. The studio discussions that involved British Leyland were frequently preceded by pre-recorded films giving details of the latest development in each dispute or strike, and by appearing live Sir Michael had the opportunity to make the points that he thought were important,

Plate 1   Sir Michael Edwardes, in a well publicised pose as chairman of British Leyland, in November 1979. His communications staff thought it better if he was interviewed and photographed on the move: once he had delivered his message, he would wind up the car window and drive away.

usually ensuring in the process that he had the last word on the subject; he was adept at controlling his media appearances in such a way as to cause the least possible damage to his credibility. But he did not always play an active part in the presentation of BL's case in the news media, especially during pay disputes or local strikes, when he would delegate radio or television interviews to other members of management.

When news of a major decision was to be given to the news media, BL preferred its announcement to be published or broadcast before union leaders had an opportunity to respond with a counter-statement. If management was to seize and then hold the news initiative, it was essential that they reach an agreed view early in the morning. There was every chance that it could then dictate the way the day's events at the car factories would be viewed and reported by the news media.

British Leyland's public relations staff realised that if they were to be successful they had to work closely with the news media, taking care to satisfy the varying demands of the different news outlets. In long-running disputes, industrial correspondents are often asked by their newsrooms to provide a new angle on what might have become a rather familiar story. The reporters under the greatest pressure are those working for local evening newspapers, radio and television stations, because they have the earliest deadlines, with lunchtime news bulletins to prepare and newspapers that have to be printed mid-afternoon. So, once management had agreed on what they would be saying that day, they would contact these journalists. An early statement could be reinforced later, when a briefing would be given to reporters on the national papers, whose deadlines would be late in the afternoon or early evening. By being the first each day to volunteer information, the company hoped its statement would provide the new angle that journalists were looking for, thus forcing the trade union leaders on to the defensive in making them reply to what by then could well have become the established version of that day's events.

Whenever possible the lunchtime and afternoon radio and television news reports would be monitored by the management's public relations department to see if the company's statements were being correctly reported or whether they might be interpreted in a way that could be harmful to British Leyland. If, for example, a radio news bulletin at 1 or 5 p.m. was making what the company thought was a mistake or putting the wrong emphasis on an important development, the journalist responsible would be telephoned immediately. The public relations staff then monitored all subsequent news bulletins to make sure that the alterations had been made. It was important to stop radio and television news bulletins repeating what the company believed were mistakes because, as well as the immediate danger of staff being misinformed, there was also the possibility that 'inaccuracies' in those early news reports might be repeated next day by the national and local newspapers. Occasionally journalists working for radio, television and the evening papers felt under some pressure to reflect management's interpretation of 'the facts', as they relied on BL's co-operation in providing information in time for their news deadlines.

British Leyland was able to develop an aggressive stance with the news media because the public relations department knew that management would not go back on a decision once it had been taken. In other state-owned industries policies frequently changed, but if BL announced in a press statement that it would not be giving way to the trade unions, that decision would not be altered. As a result the press officers who were responsible for speaking to journalists could adopt a confident manner, safe in the knowledge that statements they issued would not have to be modified or withdrawn. Strict adherence to agreed policies enabled BL to synchronise its communications strategy so that the same unrelenting theme could be maintained in press releases, interviews and advertisements. An equally consistent approach was adopted in communications with workers in the car factories, largely because of the close working relationship which had developed between the press officers and one of the industrial relations managers, Geoffrey Armstrong, who was determined that the company should regain the responsibility for communicating with the workforce. Mr Armstrong was at British Leyland during the major disputes of the 1970s and early 1980s, becoming personnel director for Austin Rover and employee relations director for the BL cars group.

During the mid-1970s there had been attempts by a number of major companies to develop new ways of talking to their employees, especially when managements were faced with the problem of trying to communicate simultaneously with large groups of workers at different locations all over the country. Imperial Chemical Industries was one of the first to start posting letters outlining company policy to the homes of workers – a technique used by them during a number of local disputes in the late 1970s– and many firms relied on their company newspapers and journals to disseminate information.

BL began direct communications shortly before Sir Michael's appointment in 1977, when on several occasions letters were sent to the homes of car workers at Cowley. Then, in 1978, BL started mailing copies of its free newspaper *Leyland Mirror* to employees. Previously copies of the newspaper had been handed out at each factory, but at some plants management suspected that when the company made important announcements, militant shop stewards were disrupting its distribution. Bundles of the newspaper had been discovered by management piled up behind equipment or hidden in waste bins.

Efforts to develop new techniques were intensified by BL after a strike over bonus payments in February 1979 at the Longbridge car factory in Birmingham, which had involved the plant's Communist shop stewards' convenor, Derek Robinson. The company believed that during the dispute Mr Robinson was 'wilfully misleading' the workforce – which so infuriated Sir Michael that he decided BL would retaliate. At that time the practice of communicating directly with a worker at his or her home had rarely been used during a major industrial crisis, for fear of provoking further disruption. Sir Michael later recalled in his autobiography how the Longbridge strike and Derek Robinson's conduct had brought home to him the need to develop the skill of 'putting across the facts' direct to those who worked on the shop floor:

> From that time onwards we made sure that on each occasion when an important issue was at stake the company view was communicated directly to employees as well as through normal union channels. This often meant sending letters to employees' homes (where they could calmly and deliberately consider the situation with their families), the issuing of factory briefing sheets, and posters. We used newspaper advertisements where we felt a particular issue had wider significance, and they seemed to be effective for the militants invariably called 'foul'. On many occasions we were accused of peddling propaganda and 'going over the heads' of the shop stewards. In reality, our new policy was only a threat to those stewards who had something to hide, for a balanced and fair account of the issues defeated their purpose.

(Sir Michael Edwardes, *Back from the Brink*, Collins, March 1983)

BL stepped up direct communications in the summer of 1979, when it produced a ninety-two-page document setting out the details of new work practices and incentive payments. The document was reprinted in full in the form of a twelve-page newspaper, which was posted to the home of every worker. By sending each employee a copy of the new working practices the payments, the company had provided the labour force with exactly the same information as the trade union leaders; management hoped this might lessen disputes, since workers could check for themselves if they had doubts or disagreements with the interpretations given by the shop stewards.

Another letter was sent out in September of the same year outlining details of the BL Recovery Plan. These proposals were accepted the following month by an overwhelming majority, when just over 87 per cent of the workers voted 'yes'. In previous years BL had held workplace ballots, asking employees to vote at each factory under independent supervision. But after a successful postal ballot in December 1978 when BL car workers had accepted new pay parity proposals, management saw that voting by post could reduce the opportunities for pressure by union leaders, and might encourage an employee's wife or other members of the family to exercise some influence over the way the vote was cast. Although not much was known about the degree of participation by an employee's family, BL thought there was every likelihood that wives might be influenced by the company's consistent, unrelenting theme in both internal communications and statements to the news media. For the Recovery Plan ballot BL issued 151,557 ballot papers, of which almost exactly 80 per cent were returned in pre-paid envelopes to the Electoral Reform Society (the organisation called in to supervise the vote). The level of participation was high for a management ballot. Of the 121,679 voting papers which were returned, 106,062 (87.22 per cent) were in favour of restructuring. When the Longbridge convenor Derek Robinson challenged this majority vote to accept the streamlining of the company, by calling on his fellow workers to occupy the factories, he was dismissed.

If necessary Sir Michael was prepared to dispense with the niceties of the traditional industrial relations ritual, especially when he considered the trade unions were using the negotiating machinery to block progress. His priority throughout these early years was to ensure a consistent approach, so that what the industrial relations staff were communicating to the workforce corresponded exactly with the briefings being given to the news media by the public relations advisers.

Another of the new communication techniques developed while he was chairman was the use of private opinion polls. On two occasions polls were commissioned by management to test the workforce's reaction to particular developments. A high priority, during wage negotiations, was to prevent confusion or misunderstandings over the likely impact of a pay increase on individual earnings. Full details had to be provided by management as quickly as possible, before the workforce heard a different interpretation from the local union leaders and shop stewards. If pay talks were completed by early evening, staff worked overnight to prepare a letter setting out precise examples of the difference the increase would make to weekly wage rates. Each employee was then handed a copy of the letter on arriving for work next morning. BL prided itself on being able to deliver a message to 150,000 employees within twenty-four hours. The speed of the communications process ensured that the workers had all the relevant information before the shop stewards had time to organise a mass meeting to give their own report on the outcome of the negotiations.

In later years, after Sir Michael left British Leyland, management continued their policy of trying to find new ways to improve internal and external communications. One was to ask foremen at each factory to be responsible for briefing groups of twenty to thirty workers on important issues, which enabled reactions from the shop floor to be passed upwards to management. In the 1984 pay strike at BL, some of the foremen at Cowley, who were reporting for duty in the absence of the manual workers, were given the task of telephoning the homes of the groups of men for whom they were responsible to discuss the likelihood of them returning to work. There had been earlier attempts to telephone workers at home during disputes, but according to the trade unions it was during the 1984 strike that a telephone campaign was for the first time conducted on a co-ordinated basis. The phone calls were followed up on some occasions by foremen visiting, even at night, the homes of men who it was thought would be most likely to return.

It was not until Sir Michael had been chairman for some years that union leaders in the motor industry acknowledged the superiority of management's system of communications within the car factories. This was illustrated in February 1980 when the BL unions decided to follow management's strategy of consultation. The Confederation of Shipbuilding and Engineering Unions organised its own ballot among the BL workers, who rejected the company's 1979 pay offer by 41,422 votes to 28,623. (However, two months later management ignored the result of this ballot and imposed their wage increase on the workforce all the same. An affordable pay settlement was essential, said management, if BL was to survive and secure further government investment.)

One reason for the lack of an effective trade union response to British Leyland's superiority in communications was the rivalry between the separate unions. During the time Sir Michael was chairman, negotiations on behalf of the hourly paid manual workers had to be conducted with ten different unions – although by 1985, after union amalgamations, this had fallen to seven. These competing unions could rarely, if ever, agree on how best to combat management's growing expertise in bypassing the shop stewards. During the 1984 pay strike at British Leyland, for example, the unions issued only one leaflet explaining the trade union case, yet between 17 October and 23 November management prepared a total of nine separate letters and leaflets which were either distributed at work or posted direct to the home of each employee.

One of the few trade union leaders who warned of the consequences of Sir Michael's success in communicationg with the workforce was the Oxford district secretary of the Transport and General Workers' Union, David Buckle, who represented car workers at the Cowley factory. He believed it amounted to intimidation by management for the chairman to threaten to close a factory unless the workers accepted new conditions. In his view, Sir Michael was encouraged to use the car factories as a test bed for trying out industrial relations theories that were backed by the government and by large sections of the news media. Mr Buckle complained frequently about the lack of consultation with the established local union representatives, repeatedly asking BL to allow joint forms of communication, so that management and unions could co-operate in presenting information to the employees. This had long been the established practice at the Ford Motor Company, where the outcome of negotiations on pay and working conditions is reported to the workforce through a jointly agreed bulletin.

Throughout the late 1970s it was generally acknowledged by journalists that Ford had the most efficient public relations department in the car industry. At the time the chairman and managing director of Ford's British operation was Sir Terence Beckett, whose objectives with regard to the news media were sometimes rather different from those of Sir Michael. But Sir Michael did in fact follow the example of Ford in seeking to improve BL's performance in public relations. And whatever argument there may be over the ethics of the techniques used by British Leyland, Sir Michael did show how an employer could derive the maximum possible advantage from publicity.

During the restructuring at British Leyland he went on the offensive in his public relations because of the need to explain the reasons for fundamental changes which management knew would be challenged by the trade unions, with every likelihood of industrial action. Crisis management like this involved different techniques from the day-to-day approach to publicity that was required, for example, by Sir Terence during Ford's annual pay negotiations. On such occasions management was anxious to avoid doing anything that might provoke industrial unrest. If there was a threat of strike action, the view within Ford and much of private industry was that negotiation through the news media could be counter-productive.

Sir Terence based his approach on the belief that industrial disputes were not settled any faster if the chairman went on the hustings. He had learned by hard experience that strikes could sometimes be prolonged if, for no good reason, they were turned into a drama for the news media.

While he was head of Ford's British factories it was the director of employee relations, Paul Roots, who usually did radio and television interviews if management thought them necessary. Sir Terence spoke publicly only as a last resort, preferring instead to stand back and look at the company's options and overall strategy. For much of this time the chief union negotiator for the Ford car workers was Moss Evans, who later became general secretary of the Transport and General Workers' Union. In difficult disputes he shared the management's reluctance to negotiate through the news media; he said that he jointly decided with the company in 1971 that they got nowhere when they tried to conduct negotiations through what he described as the goldfish bowl of the press, radio and television.

When Sir Terence was appointed director-general of the Confederation of British Industry in 1980, he had greater freedom to observe how other chairmen handled the publicity that surrounded major industrial disputes. During one of the several discussions I had with him on the merits of negotiating through the news media, Sir Terence recalled the advice he had given Sir Michael on the day he was appointed chairman of British Leyland in 1977. Sir Terence told him that if he discovered separate or conflicting public relations advisers at BL he should sack them, and instead have just one public relations director whom he could trust. According to Sir Terence, the danger in having too many competing advisers on public affairs was that they tended to take the initiative and often fed information to journalists, which could have the effect of fuelling a disagreement or dispute.

When Sir Michael joined British Leyland on secondment from the Chloride Group, he was accompanied by John McKay, who had served with him at Chloride and who now became BL's communications director. Mr McKay and his staff were responsible for supplying information to the news media as well as for trying to improve BL's internal communications, which involved helping the rest of management to get its message across to the shop-floor workers. Within three months of Mr McKay joining BL, the company reduced its central public relations staff from thirty-seven to three. Mr McKay told me that this was carried out as part of the decentralisation introduced by Sir Michael, and in order to reduce overheads.

At the Ford Motor Company Sir Terence Beckett had proved it was possible to limit confrontation in the news media, sometimes with trade union co-operation. As we have already seen, a particularly close relationship had existed at the National Coal Board under Sir Derek Ezra and Joe Gormley. And there were parallels in other nationalised industries that also illustrated how employers and unions had worked out their own techniques for handling the news media.

The electricity industry went further than most nationalised concerns to reduce the risk of media confrontation, with the Electricity Council refusing all requests for radio and television interviews during the annual pay talks. Roger Farrance, the Electricity Council's board member for industrial relations, was rarely quoted in the news media. When he did talk to journalists he left them in no doubt about his own position: 'I refuse to say anything on the record. You know that is the way I have always seen it and the way I have always played it.' Mr Farrance and his management colleagues believed that this low profile in the news media was one reason why their industry could look back on more than a decade largely free of strikes.

Negotiations during the late 1970s and early 1980s were frequently conducted on behalf of the electricity workers' unions by Frank Chapple, later Lord Chapple, in his role as chairman of the Electricity Employees' National Committee. Mr Chapple was then general secretary of the Electrical, Electronic, Telecommunication and Plumbing Union (EETPU). He was always ready with a headline catchphrase for the popular Sunday newspapers whenever he needed to take on his left-wing and Communist opponents in the EETPU. However, when it came to relations between his union and management, Mr Chapple knew the importance of avoiding unnecessary provocation. He willingly complied with the employers' wish to avoid publicity, even when the Electricity Council went to extraordinary lengths with the news media to play down the percentage value of its wage increases. The management was anxious to avoid having the annual pay rises compared with those in other industries, because, as a result of the consolidation of bonus money, basic rates in electricity were high in relation to those in gas, coal and water, with the result that the Electricity Council's pay rises might have seemed lower than those in other industries when expressed as a percentage.

As the annual pay round progressed each winter there was always considerable sensitivity within the nationalised industries, and no wish to incur criticism from the government. The unwritten convention seemed to be that the miners should stay at the top of the manual workers' pay league. Therefore a public challenge to the miners' supremacy was unlikely, although other essential workers would need similar increases.

Mr Chapple's reluctance to release any more than the barest details of what had been agreed in negotiations was illustrated in March 1983, when the power workers settled for what the news media was encouraged to believe was a pay increase worth around 6.5 per cent. The only official information was that the settlement provided for basic rate increases of between £4.68 and £10.24 a week. Both sides had promised not to divulge the exact percentage value of the increase, as it was feared that this would lead to direct comparison with the miners and other workers, which might be considered provocative. Once the pay negotiations had been completed at the Electricity Council's London headquarters at Millbank, the two sides agreed to hold a short news conference to tell waiting journalists the basis of the settlement. It had been decided that Mr Chapple should conduct the proceedings:

Chapple   We have achieved what we set out to achieve, a settlement that matches the miners' settlement.
Reporter How much is the increase worth?
Chapple   The same as the miners'.
Reporter Well, how much is the miners' increase worth?
Chapple   The same as ours.

Some days later research by Incomes Data Services indicated that the journalists' assessment of 6.5 per cent for the power workers' settlement was too high, which proved only too correct, as the pay rise eventually added 5.7 per cent to average earnings. The news media had apparently been equally over-generous in assessing the value of the miners' settlement at 8.2 per cent. This is just one of the pitfalls of reporting labour and industrial affairs.

British Gas, like the Electricity Council, was another nationalised industry that had adopted a policy of not commenting to the news media during wage negotiations. It too could look back on more than a decade without serious industrial conflict. In both industries the last major disputes had been in the early 1970s. The British Gas chairman Sir Denis Rooke regularly attended pay negotiations with the unions, but, he would go out of his way to avoid speaking to newsmen. During the 1981–2 pay talks he was only seen once by the waiting reporters. As the microphone was thrust forward, Sir Denis quickly wound up the window of his car, tapped on the chauffeur's shoulder and told him to drive on. But, if need be, the British Gas management was quite capable of making effective use of the news media, as happened during the campaign to prevent the government selling off the gas showrooms. This was another occasion when the trade unions worked effectively with management to change a government decision.

Although employers and unions have shown that it is possible to exercise considerable control over the way pay negotiations and industrial disputes are reported by radio, television and the press, each dispute tends to produce its own pressures, of varying impact. In some instances the two sides are eager to use the news media to argue out their case in public, which can have the effect of prolonging negotiations.

In most disputes, trade unions are the first to seek publicity in order to draw attention to a grievance or a decision which affects the livelihoods of their members. Often union leaders adopt an aggressive stance on purpose, hoping to impress the membership and prove their own effectiveness as negotiators, fearing that otherwise they might be criticised for having a cosy relationship with management. Employers frequently have difficulty deciding how best to respond to the publicity generated by the unions, especially during pay disputes or strikes, as any comments they may make could have an adverse effect on the outcome of negotiations. The difficulties that face management can be compounded when trade union leaders within the same industry have opposing political and industrial objectives. This was one complication of the dispute which caused widespread disruption to rail services during 1982, becoming in the process perhaps the prototype of industrial negotiation by way of radio and television.

Rail strikes always command wide coverage in the news media. The main broadcasting organisations have their head offices in London, where industrial action on the railways has a disproportionate effect on the travelling public because of the heavy concentration of commuter lines in the south east of England. During such disputes the daytime news bulletins and programmes devote considerable time and effort to the task of providing the latest information on the availability or cancellation of rail services, in the belief that this is a public service over which the broadcasting organisations have the edge because of their immediacy.

There were intermittent rail stoppages throughout the first six months of 1982, when the train drivers started their industrial action with one- and two-day strikes in protest at British Rail's refusal to pay the annual wage increase. Management argued that the drivers were to blame because their union had not honoured the commitment it had given the previous summer to negotiate the implementation of new shift patterns that involved flexible rostering – that is, shifts a bit longer or shorter than the usual eight-hour day, but which, according to British Rail, would still average out at thirty-nine hours a week over an eight-week period. During the strikes of that year the unions and British Rail began to communicate, and then to negotiate, with each other through radio and television interviews, which tended to result, because of the length of the dispute, in conflict feeding on itself. There was already an air of expectancy in the news media over the outcome of the negotiations, because the broadcasting services realised that the information was of vital interest to the hundreds of thousands of rail commuters.

This awareness of a captive audience waiting for the latest information built up its own momentum, with the broadcasting organisations taking on a wider function as the repeated negotiations ended in failure. Radio and television were assuming a role that occasionally appeared to be more than that of neutral reporter. The continuous round of interviews, lasting for weeks on end, seemed to start influencing the very pace of the dispute.

British Rail had spent months discussing the changes involving flexible rostering with the two main rail unions, arguing the need for greater efficiency. The National Union of Railwaymen, then led by its former general secretary Sidney Weighell, had delivered some of the productivity improvements that management wanted, and he shared to a large degree the enthusiastic approach to the future of the rail network that had been shown by Sir Peter Parker, then chairman of British Rail. The two men had acknowledged that unless there were new working practices, the government would not give approval for new investment in electrification. Mr Weighell had encouraged his union to accept the sacrifices that went with industrial change in the belief that this would be matched by improvements in pay and conditions as well as higher government spending on the rail network.

The train drivers, who were represented by a separate union, the Associated Society of Locomotive Engineers and Firemen, feared they had most to lose from British Rail's drive for increased efficiency. ASLEF had refused to accept flexible rostering, although the new shift patterns were acceptable to the guards, who were members of the NUR. This resulted in the two unions disagreeing on both the nature and the implementation of British Rail's productivity changes. There were other differences too, because in Labour Party politics the train drivers' union executive was well to the left of Mr Weighell, who in turn had little in common with the ASLEF general secretary, Ray Buckton.

Mr Weighell was quite prepared to publicise the disagreements that existed between the NUR and ASLEF, giving the news media every encouragement to contrast the NUR's support for change with the opposition that was coming from Mr Buckton's union. In allowing the flexible rostering dispute to develop into a public confrontation, British Rail had taken on a small but well organised trade union, led by a man who was quite prepared if necessary to stand up against the wrath of a largely hostile news media. When his members' interests needed protecting, Mr Buckton could take the daily punishment of the Fleet Street headline-writers and cartoonists and still fight back. Radio and television found him an attractive interviewee; he responded well to the interviewer who played devil's advocate.

This willingness to take part in radio and television discussion of the train drivers' dispute was more than matched by British Rail, so strong was management's conviction that a productivity agreement had been broken and that ASLEF could be beaten. It was usually possible at a moment's notice to interview Sir Peter Parker or his industrial relations director, Clifford Rose. Even on days when there might be meetings lasting until midnight or later, Mr Rose, as the management's chief negotiator, was prepared to appear on the Today programme on BBC Radio 4 at 7 a.m. and then go direct to the studios of the London Broadcasting Company for another live interview. Within a year, with the arrival of two breakfast television services, there were even greater opportunities for live broadcasting.

The degree of managerial co-operation with the news media that was shown by British Rail was unusual in a major industrial dispute. One consequence of this enthusiasm to negotiate publicly was that it led to a heightened sense of confrontation, which in turn encouraged the news services to attempt to make judgements on which side was winning. The pressure was reflected in the participants themselves, in that ASLEF and British Rail began quoting what the other had said in the latest broadcast as justification for their own actions. Because of the need for accuracy, transcripts of interviews had to be made available as quickly as possible. The practice developed whereby both management and union made cassette recordings of the radio and television interviews given by the opposing side, which were then transcribed by a secretary.

Sometimes during the train drivers' strikes ASLEF and British Rail were not prepared to wait for transcripts, demanding instead an immediate right of reply. The Jimmy Young programme on BBC Radio 2 found, for example, that if it interviewed either Mr Buckton or Sir Peter, then the other side was on the telephone within minutes asking for the same opportunity to appear on the programme. The two sides were so locked in public confrontation that the news media had become one of the few remaining forms of communication that were instantly available, even though the rush to the microphones and cameras sometimes appeared to contribute to further misunderstanding and to frustrate attempts to settle the dispute. By giving their willing co-operation to the publicity build-up, both ASLEF and British Rail had in the process undergone constant questioning by news reporters. This had led union and management to adopt fixed public positions which, they would privately acknowledge, had made them appear more inflexible than they would have liked.

There were three occasions during the dispute when the confrontation that resulted from radio and television interviews influenced the pace of events. The first occurred early in February 1982, when the Advisory, Conciliation and Arbitration Service (ACAS) appointed a committee of inquiry under Lord McCarthy to examine the question of flexible rostering. Although British Rail said it would give evidence, it could give no undertaking that the committee's recommendations would be accepted. In the meantime management would not pay the drivers their disputed 3 per cent pay rise, which had been withheld because of the failure to get flexible rostering. On the day the inquiry was announced, an interview with the industrial relations director, Clifford Rose, was broadcast shortly after 5 p.m. on BBC Radio and LBC. At 5.25 p.m. Mr Buckton emerged from an ASLEF executive meeting to say that his union would not go to the inquiry as there was still no guarantee that the drivers would get their pay increase – quoting as justification what Mr Rose had said in his interview broadcast only twenty minutes earlier.

The second occasion when the content of an interview delayed the proceedings arose two weeks later on the publication of Lord McCarthy's report, which supported ASLEF's original argument that the dispute over flexible rostering should have been considered within the rail industry's own negotiating machinery. On that day it was the turn of British Rail to benefit from the speed of reporting. That afternoon at 4 p.m. Mr Buckton declared that ASLEF would accept Lord McCarthy's report. It was, said Mr Buckton, a total victory for the union, and ASLEF had not had to give a single commitment on flexible rostering. This blunt interpretation was broadcast on the tea-time radio and television news bulletins. When at 7 p.m. on 16 February, at the end of a lengthy BR board meeting, Sir Peter met reporters, he immediately began quoting what Mr Buckton had been saying. In reply to one question by Giles Smith of Independent Television News, Sir Peter said, 'You saw what Mr Buckton said on the 5.45 television news. We must get further clarification before we can pay the 3 per cent.'

An agreement on the question of a timetable for a tribunal to examine flexible rostering would have allowed the drivers to get their money and, hopefully, have persuaded the union to end its strike action. The public argument continued until the moment the two sides were safely inside separate rooms at ACAS, well away from the front door and the waiting microphones. The final round of talks lasted thirteen hours, until just after midnight, with the agreement coming too late to prevent the last of the one-day rail strikes.

The moment the talks were over, Sir Peter, who had not been present at ACAS, was back on the offensive, maintaining that BR was confident it would not be paying something for nothing. In a telephone interview broadcast early next morning on LBC, he predicted that it was no longer a question of whether there might or might not be an agreement on flexible rostering, but rather of deciding how it would be implemented. This was the third interview that influenced the likely course of events, for when Sir Peter spoke to the LBC reporter the ink was hardly dry on the agreement that Mr Buckton had signed just after midnight, and his action had yet to be endorsed by a meeting later that day of the ASLEF executive. During the morning he claimed that Sir Peter's radio interview had incensed drivers at several major locomotive depots, because the men apparently believed that Mr Buckton had given a commitment in advance to the implementation of flexible rostering, when all the union believed it had agreed to was to allow its case to be considered by a tribunal. There were yet more telephone calls between ASLEF and ACAS that morning, before the union executive announced, shortly after noon, that it had approved Lord McCarthy's timetable for talks and had finally called off the one- and two-day strikes.

With the rail strikes, radio and television producers believed they had an opportunity to further the public debate that had started over ASLEF's refusal to accept flexible rostering. The disagreement provided good potential material for a studio discussion, because it was of interest not only to rail passengers, who were facing several days each week without trains, but also to hundreds of thousands of other people who did shift work similar to that being proposed by BR, many of whom could not understand the objections that ASLEF had raised.

The fixed eight-hour day had been guaranteed since 1919. The proposed change would mean up to an hour or more being added to or subtracted from each day's shift, and would also result in a shorter or longer working week. The new work pattern was designed to give management greater flexibility in meeting each day's requirements for passenger and freight trains. ASLEF considered the new system impractical and likely to increase the possibility of rail accidents, as some train drivers would occasionally have to work long hours. The union also feared that if British Rail obtained greater flexibility over the manning of trains, they would require fewer drivers, which was a matter of great concern to the leadership of a small union that represented a group of workers who, though they were declining in numbers because of modernisation and line closures, still regarded themselves as the elite among railwaymen.

Another reason why the programme makers were so determined to get these issues argued out in public was their belief that a studio discussion might help clear the air. At one point during the winter of 1982, several weeks had gone by without any face-to-face meeting between Ray Buckton and Sir Peter Parker. Therefore the first radio or television progamme that could persuade the two men to take part in a live debate would have a major exclusive, which would probably become a news event in itself, as well as enhancing the prestige of the programme. Such live discussions on sensitive issues are usually well promoted in advance, in the confident expectation that the debate may develop into a heated argument, providing viewing or listening that cannot fail to hold the attention of the audience. Also, radio and television producers always like to think there is an outside chance that a studio discussion may result in an unexpected breakthrough, by revealing a point of common ground between the opposing parties that has somehow eluded the negotiators – though in view of what has happened in most television debates on industrial disputes, that prospect seems unlikely.

With live programmes, union leaders and employers usually like to choose what they think is the most suitable moment to put over their case or reply to the other side's publicity or provocation. If there is a realistic chance of making progress in private negotiations, programme invitations are instantly rejected, or cancelled at the last moment. So if a live radio or television debate does take place, those who report industrial affairs assume that a settlement is some way off and that both sides are only interested in scoring points for propaganda purposes.

Few union leaders or chairmen are born radio and television performers, and any lengthy discussion about the background of what has often started off as a minor dispute can easily become repetitive. For some years now senior managers have been undergoing extensive training by specialist companies in how best to respond to radio and television questioning. Few trade union leaders have been prepared to submit themselves to – or could afford – such training, although they often find it particularly difficult to avoid falling back on the slogans that have been used to promote their grievance. During a major strike, when relations are invariably strained and the participants may already be suffering from some degree of over-exposure in the news media, there is always the risk in a live debate that they may become bad-tempered or appear foolish.

During the winter of 1982, Sir Peter and Mr Buckton had their first face-to-face meeting for a month when they agreed to participate in a live debate on Panorama, one of the major current affairs programmes on BBC television, even though earlier, ASLEF had refused an invitation to meet British Rail. The discussion, chaired by Robert Kee, came at a point when there was no real prospect of a negotiated settlement to the flexible rostering dispute, and when the two sides were in the grip of a public disagreement that would in fact continue for some months. The discussion degenerated into futile and angry bickering, as the following exchange illustrates:

Parker For God's sake, Ray, can you look me in the eye over this? Ease down. Just stop for a moment.
Buckton Who's blathering now? You back off.
(BBC TV, Panorama, 8 February 1982)

When the NUR leader Sidney Weighell was interviewed on the same programme, he said that the argument between Mr Buckton and Sir Peter indicated that someone ought to come in and arbitrate. Next day the *Daily Mail* said that the public clash between the two men, which had been seen by millions, had 'dashed hopes of an early end to the five-week-old row'. Any hopes of an early end had in fact been unrealistic – the sterile exchanges between Mr Buckton and Sir Peter had only confirmed it. Indeed, one of Mr Buckton's advisers told me afterwards that ASLEF had realised there was little to be gained by taking part in the programme, but Mr Buckton had been determined to try to show that if the union was being criticised for intransigence then Sir Peter was equally to blame.

After seventeen days of strike action in January and February 1982, there followed a two-month break in the train drivers' dispute while the arguments over flexible rostering were examined by Lord McCarthy's tribunal. It came down decisively in favour of the introduction of the new flexible shifts, subject to a long list of safeguards for the drivers. Even so, the ASLEF executive was bitterly disappointed, and when, some weeks later, British Rail responded to the 1982 pay claim with a 5 per cent wage increase – delayed until September to await agreement on six productivity

Plate 2   Panorama's studio discussion on the ASLEF dispute was a frosty occasion: the stony faces for the official photograph reflected the strained relationships that can develop during controversial industrial action. However, Ray Buckton (far right) was gratified to find that Sidney Weighell (far left) had to sit next to Sir Peter Parker. Robert Kee chaired the discussion.

improvements – there were new threats of industrial action from both the main rail unions.

British Rail had spent the intervening months preparing for the possibility of further disruption, having realised that if there was to be another confrontation with ASLEF then management would have to improve its own communications with the rail workforce and display a more calculated approach to the news media. One weakness in British Rail's position during the winter had resulted from their refusal to pay the earlier 3 per cent pay increase, which had allowed ASLEF to accuse management of breaking an agreement.

Management demonstrated its new-found confidence, inspired by the tribunal's decision, at the first sign of further threats of industrial action, which came first from the National Union of Railwaymen, whose executive had decided on 9 June to call an all-out strike from midnight on the 27th. British Rail immediately began a new publicity offensive which started with the posting of a personal letter from its chairman to the home of every worker, as British Leyland had done three years earlier during the disputes there. This ploy had proved its value at British Leyland, because management found that it could thereby distribute information about the company in a way that could not be disrupted by shop stewards, as had happened when they had tried to distribute letters during working hours. One method that had been used by the shop stewards to thwart the distribution of information inside the factories was to ensure that as soon as the employees were handed copies of the company's announcement, they would be torn up by groups of trade union activists, who would then encourage other workers to join in as a public act of defiance against management.

As soon as managers had seen the advantage of mailing information direct to employees' homes, especially during disputes, specialist advisers had been called in to improve the presentation and wording of the letters, so that if they were read not only by the worker himself but also by his wife, she might be motivated to put pressure on her husband either to refrain from striking or to return to work. Unlike the four-page letter from Sir Michael Edwardes that was sent to the BL workforce in September 1979 to explain the recovery plan, the personal letters from Sir Peter Parker that were posted during the rail disputes were short and to the point, and written in a popular and emotive style. The first, sent six days after the NUR had ordered an all-out strike, was posted to the homes of the 225,000 employees of British Rail and its subsidiaries. It was addressed to 'Dear member of staff' and entitled 'Your job and your future at risk':

> I am taking the unusual step of writing direct to you and to everyone employed by British Railways Board because the industry in which we all work is facing the most dangerous crisis in its history . . . We are in deep trouble. You could say we're broke. This time the threat to jobs will affect you all. I want you to think seriously before you are drawn into industrial action and into a fight which nobody can win.
> (Sir Peter Parker, letter to BR staff, 16 June 1982)

Seven days later, three days before the NUR was due to start its strike, he wrote a second letter (plate 3) announcing that all those railway workers who ignored the strike and reported for work would keep their jobs, even if the rail unions tried to expel them from trade union membership. This letter, dramatic in its presentation – and which effectively marked the end of the closed shop agreement in British Rail – was entitled 'You, your family and your job'. The appeal to a wider audience than the employees themselves marked a new approach. Little research had been done at the time into the effectiveness of communications aimed at the whole family. Active trade unionists would often describe how they had torn up letters from the management, but it was extremely difficult to gauge the reaction across the broad mass of a union's membership. Feedback told management that the letters did have an effect – partly, Sir Peter believed, because of the deep sense of commitment which existed among families who had worked on the railways for several generations.

Although the NUR went ahead with its strike in June 1982, despite Sir Peter's efforts, it was suspended less than forty-eight hours later by the union's annual conference which was meeting in Plymouth. This decision was followed on the same day by an announcement from ASLEF that it was calling an all-out strike of the train drivers, starting on 4 July, because

Dear Member of Staff.

June 1982

YOU, YOUR FAMILY AND YOUR JOB

It is now one minute to midnight. Unless commonsense from ordinary railwaymen takes over, the railways are now due to start the most disastrous strike in their history.

Nobody regrets this head-on clash with responsible union leaders more than I do. But on this occasion, they are wrong, and I am writing again to urge you to ask your union leadership to think again.

Wars are easy to start. Very difficult to end.

So for your sake, the sake of your family and the future of the railway system, help me stop the strike before it starts.

I want you to know these things:

* **If there is a strike, there will be no pay increase.**
* We will not withdraw our productivity conditions.
* I do not believe for a minute the Government will intervene to find the cash we haven't got.
* If the strike does go on, **thousands** of railway jobs, perhaps yours, will disappear forever. That is fact.
* Our business will be crippled. Passenger services will be cut back. I believe we could lose the contract for Post Office letter mail.
* Speedlink and Freightliner traffic will be lost. It will mean less rolling stock and, therefore, fewer maintenance jobs in Regions and in BR Engineering Ltd.
* With less business there will be a substantial reduction in white collar jobs.

Think about it—is it really worth the risk?

I am asking you to follow your own interests. I am asking you not to strike.

If you decide not to strike, the Board will not accept loss of trade union membership as a cause for dismissal.

If the strike goes ahead, this will happen immediately:
For the first week, all staff who report for work will be paid, even if they are unable to do their normal jobs. You must make an effort to get to work, even if no trains are running, and if you don't succeed, you will not be paid.
If the strike lasts beyond one week, the Board will have to decide, after assessing the response to trade union calls for strike action, whether it can continue to pay ANY staff.

We will continue to try to find common cause with your leaders—but I think it is going to be up to the commonsense and intervention of you and other workers this time if we are going to avoid disaster.

Please think very seriously before supporting a strike call. Make no mistake. If there is a strike you may well not have a job to come back to.

Yours sincerely

Peter Parker

it feared that management was about to impose flexible rostering at selected depots. British Rail immediately sent a third letter from Sir Peter, this time addressed 'Dear ASLEF Member':

> Earlier this week the good sense of ordinary railway workers pulled us back from the brink of a real disaster. Now your union has put us back there . . . Let me be blunt. The Board is absolutely determined to introduce flexible rostering . . . For the sake of your own future and that of the railway consider that if this strike goes ahead thousands of jobs will go. Perhaps yours . . . What we are asking is not unreasonable. And it is vital. Give it a chance.
>
> (Sir Peter Parker, letter to ASLEF members, 1 July 1982)

The July strike was unlike ASLEF's one- and two-day stoppages in January and February because some train drivers had now indicated to management that they were prepared to work. On the strength of this, British Rail announced that it would try to operate as many trains as possible, because none of the other railway workers were affected by the dispute and all were reporting for duty. Also the small proportion of drivers represented by the NUR had indicated a willingness to co-operate in management's attempts to maintain services.

From the first day of the strike, the attention of the news media focused on this effort by British Rail to operate trains in defiance of ASLEF. Radio and television regarded the dispute as another opportunity to demonstrate the value of public broadcasting, with the news bulletins giving regular detailed information on the services that were likely to operate each day. As it was only British Rail that knew the number of trains that were running, ASLEF was at a disadvantage when it tried to challenge the management's figures and discourage the media from concentrating on the minority of drivers who were breaking the strike.

British Rail stated that an average of 800 drivers worked each day during the two-week stoppage, with the largest turnout on 15 July, when by midnight 841 men had reported for work, of whom 507 were members of ASLEF and 334 were represented by the NUR. This was less than 5 per cent of the footplate staff, but by giving priority to passenger trains British Rail claimed that it had been possible to operate about 10 per cent of normal services. The management's ability to provide even a small

Plate 3 Sir Peter Parker's letter to BR staff, assuring them that their jobs were secure if they reported for work, even if the rail unions tried to expel them from union membership. Posted on the eve of the NUR strike, this letter, the second of three, effectivley tore up BR's closed shop agreement. Sir Peter wanted the letters, written in a popular and emotive style, to be read not only by BR employees but also by their wives, in the hope that they might put pressure on their husbands either to refrain from striking or to return to work.

proportion of services was unprecedented in a train drivers' strike. In previous disputes the loyalty of the ASLEF membership was so strong that it went almost without question, and union instructions over official strikes were rarely defied by more than a handful of members. Therefore the readiness of several hundred men to break the strike represented a major news story, with radio and television anxious to interview any train driver who was prepared to explain why he had decided to report to work.

The efforts of the management to try to break the traditional solidarity of the ASLEF membership had been reinforced by the findings of an opinion poll which British Rail had commissioned the week before the train drivers started their strike. The survey, carried out at eighty-seven depots, involved more than 600 railway workers, of whom a quarter were train drivers. The poll showed that 53 per cent of the drivers who were questioned were against the ASLEF strike, with 67 per cent of them agreeing that the stoppage would damage the railway industry. These results confirmed the management's own belief that there was a growing sense of frustration among rank and file union members at the tactics which were being adopted by their national leaders.

British Rail made no official statement on its use of opinion surveys, but the findings of the July poll were given during briefings by its public relations staff to those journalists whom the company thought it could trust. After the strike Sir Peter told me that the surveys had been carried out by Opinion Research and Communication, a company established by Tommy Thompson, a leading opinion pollster and former chairman of Opinion Research Centre. (He was among those who had advised Sir Peter on the wording to be used in the letters to the railway workers.) Mr Thompson has adopted a policy of refusing to answer questions from reporters about his clients or his work, although he was a journalist himself on the *Daily Mail* for twenty years, later becoming political editor. He left in 1965 on being appointed special tactical assistant to the chairman of the Conservative Party. In 1979, shortly after he resigned as chairman of Opinion Research Centre, he explained that the reason for establishing his new company, Opinion Research and Communication, was his deep interest in communications between workers and management. He said his work was unconnected with the Conservative Party and that no one who took a look at the surveys he had done could remotely consider him a union-basher. Well before the rail strikes, in reply to some newspaper criticism, he had outlined the objectives of his work:

> About four years ago I came to the conclusion that much of what was wrong with Britain was due to the fact that minorities consistently led the majority in directions they did not wish to travel and that majority opinion was never taken into account. I decided to try to use public opinion where possible as a force for good . . . Towards the end of the year I became convinced that sensible reform of trade

unions and a return of power where it belongs (the Government) was vital to the wellbeing of Britain.

(T.F. Thompson, Letters to the Editor, *Guardian*, 17 April 1979)

The willingness of some train drivers to break the ASLEF strike was perhaps not surprising, in view of the concerted efforts that had been made over several months to weaken the union's position. British Rail had conducted an extensive advertising campaign in the national newspapers explaining the case for flexible rostering. One series of advertisements during the winter, entitled 'Broken Promises', told ASLEF members that they would get the latest pay increase once their union honoured its own promises on productivity. British Rail was prepared to go to the expense of launching an advertising campaign directed largely at the 25,000 members of one small union, because of the continual difficulties it faced in trying to talk directly to the train drivers – their supervisors, also, belonged to ASLEF, which had banned any contact with management on the subject of flexible rostering.

ASLEF responded to the 'Broken Promises' campaign by publishing a point-by-point rebuttal in its union journal (for which it won an award that year from the Trades Union Congress for the best example of trade union publicity). The union's response took the form of a mock advertisement entitled 'Are you still in the dark about flexible rostering?' The small print explained how British Rail had 'dreamt up' flexible shifts as a way of 'getting something for nothing' by ensuring that no two weeks of duty would be the same. The ASLEF journal also analysed the background to the management's advertising strategy in an article entitled 'Whose broken promises?', which accused BR of 'selling confrontation':

> Sir Peter Parker is nothing if not publicity conscious. During his chairmanship, press and publicity at BR have steadily expanded – unlike rail services – and the board now controls the biggest and most professional public relations effort a nationalised industry has ever known . . . BR has spent an estimated £150,000 of public money on newspaper advertisements alone in its campaign against ASLEF . . . Hallmarks of the BR campaign are the highly selective use of facts, the beguiling tone – sweetly reasonable but stern ('We hope you understand why we have to stand firm'), and well-worn rhetoric about modernisation . . . As any advertising agency knows, it ain't what you say that's important, it's what you leave out ... Moral of the tale: an advertiser can be untruthful without telling a lie.
>
> (*Locomotive Journal*, February 1982)

Although the union tried with its limited resources to undermine the effectiveness of British Rail's newspaper advertising, the management's

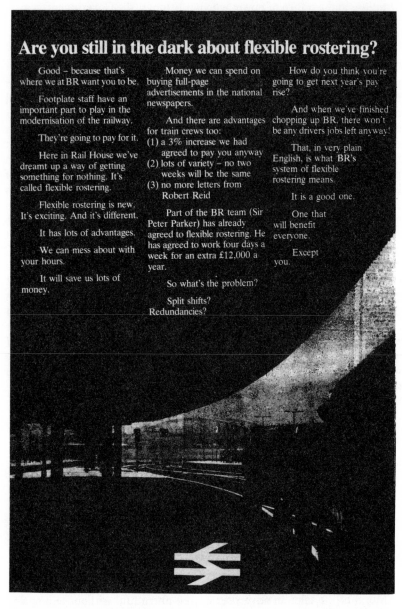

Are you still in the dark about flexible rostering?

Good – because that's where we at BR want you to be.

Footplate staff have an important part to play in the modernisation of the railway.

They're going to pay for it.

Here in Rail House we've dreamt up a way of getting something for nothing. It's called flexible rostering.

Flexible rostering is new. It's exciting. And it's different.

It has lots of advantages.

We can mess about with your hours.

It will save us lots of money.

Money we can spend on buying full-page advertisements in the national newspapers.

And there are advantages for train crews too:
(1) a 3% increase we had agreed to pay you anyway
(2) lots of variety – no two weeks will be the same
(3) no more letters from Robert Reid

Part of the BR team (Sir Peter Parker) has already agreed to flexible rostering. He has agreed to work four days a week for an extra £12,000 a year.

So what's the problem?

Split shifts?
Redundancies?

How do you think you're going to get next year's pay rise?

And when we've finished chopping up BR, there won't be any drivers jobs left anyway!

That, in very plain English, is what BR's system of flexible rostering means.

It is a good one.

One that will benefit everyone.

Except you.

Plate 4   In a sustained advertising campaign in January 1982, to explain its case for flexible rostering, British Rail accused the union of being in breach of previous understandings. ASLEF retaliated the following month with a clever take-off of the BR advertisements in its own publication, Locomotive Journal.

campaign clearly expressed the sentiments of government ministers who had lost patience with what were increasingly regarded as time-consuming and ineffective negotiating procedures. The Secretary of State for Transport, then David Howell, said that the government was not prepared to stand by and allow the train drivers to prolong a 'pointless Luddite dispute'. The Secretary of State for Employment, then Norman Tebbit, was equally explicit in his condemnation of the drivers for thinking that they could 'run off with the cake' while at the same time evading the sacrifices that had been made by the private sector and some other nationalised industries in order to increase productivity.

By the start of the July strike, British Rail was sure that it had the unequivocal government support that Sir Peter felt had been lacking during the stoppages that winter, when management had in the end been forced to pay the 1981 wage increase without a binding commitment on flexible rostering. Sir Peter had blamed his uneasy media performance during the winter partly on the government's unwillingness to back the tough public stand that he was trying to adopt. During the July strike British Rail assumed the same aggressive approach, but this time in the confident knowledge that public warnings by Sir Peter could be translated into immediate action that would be endorsed by ministers. The challenge to the railways' closed shop agreement that had been made in Sir Peter's letters was one of several policy decisions that had full government support.

As soon as the strike began, British Rail warned that it was considering whether to sack those train drivers who refused to report for work and accept flexible rostering. In the second week this threat was followed up by an announcement that all drivers who failed to report for duty by 20 July would indeed be dismissed. The tactic of threatening to carry out a mass sacking of strikers had been used with success two years earlier by the management at British Leyland, which had sent out dismissal notices during a strike over work practices. The letters went to the homes of 100,000 car workers, but the dismissals were not implemented because that strike collapsed within three days.

British Rail's dismissal notices were about to be sent through the post when a fresh initiative towards settling the train driver's dispute was made by the inner cabinet of senior union leaders at the Trades Union Congress. New negotiations now took place between TUC leaders and British Rail that resulted in a formula to end the strike. During the discussions that led up to the TUC's intervention, Mr Buckton had said that ASLEF feared that half the train drivers might report for work the following week rather than face dismissal, indicating that the union's own assessment of support for the strike had been fairly accurately predicted three weeks earlier in the opinion survey which management had commissioned from Opinion Research and Communication.

Because the TUC stepped in to settle the dispute, British Rail was unable to get an accurate indication of the effectiveness of all the measures it introduced to improve direct communications with the workers. But when the strike was called off on 18 July, one new communications technique – which relied on the telephone – had already proved its potential value, even though it had been in operation for only about a week. This new facility, introduced by British Telecom, was Freefone.

During the 1970s there had been a rapid growth in the ownership of telephones, the percentage of homes with a telephone having increased from 45 per cent in 1973 to 76 per cent in 1982. The widespread use of the telephone during an industrial dispute was now worth considering as a possible means of communication, and Freefone fitted the bill. The new service allowed telephone subscribers to dial the operator and to be connected free of charge to any company or organisation that had a message to communicate and that was prepared to pay the cost of the call. Advertisers had been making use of the facility for some years by including Freefone numbers in newspaper and television advertisements as a way of encouraging potential customers to pick up the phone on impulse and thus obtain more information about the product or service being promoted. Calls to Freefone numbers were answered either by the advertiser's own staff, who could deal with immediate inquiries, or by a tape machine which played a recorded message before giving the caller an opportunity to record his or her name and address.

When management decided at the end of the first week of the ASLEF strike to dismiss those train drivers who failed to report for work, newspaper advertisements were published giving a Freefone number that men could contact to hear a recorded voice explaining British Rail's position. The message sought to reassure those drivers who were prepared to break the strike, by emphasising that their jobs would be safe despite the closed shop agreement and the threat of expulsion from the union. There was also information on what would happen to the earnings and pension entitlements of those drivers who might stay out on strike. The message was changed towards the end of the second week of the strike because BR had warned that it would close down the rail system unless the drivers reported for work. This second message advised drivers to make a further transferred-charge call, either to their area manager's office or to one of four telephone numbers in London, where a team from the industrial relations department was ready to give advice to any driver who was finding problems over reporting for work.

This latest technique for encouraging strikers to return was not put to the ultimate test, because of the TUC's intervention to end the strike, but the rail chairman did reveal later the importance that he had attached to the task of finding new forms of communication with the workforce:

> The British Rail Board developed new ways to get through to its
> managers in that six months' struggle, as it did to its employees. You

will remember that by the end we arranged an open-line by free telephone, for any railwaymen on strike. Some 10,000 calls were received in one week from staff wanting to hear a direct statement of our position and what it meant for them.

(Sir Peter Parker, *The Director*, November 1982)

The rail strikes had ended with the ASLEF leadership in retreat, having no alternative but to accept the introduction of flexible rostering under terms negotiated by the TUC. Much of the news coverage was criticised by the union's general secretary Ray Buckton, who said that the media had displayed its thirst for new angles, no matter how ridiculous they might be. This criticism was in part a reflection of developments within the media, the train drivers' dispute having demonstrated the speed with which radio and television could report a fast-moving industrial story, sometimes to the disadvantage of the national newspapers. The late-night negotiating sessions with the rail unions had frequently ended after the Fleet Street printing deadlines, which meant that newspaper reports were often out of date next morning when the early radio bulletins and programmes broadcast news of the latest developments. Because of this competition the newspapers found other ways of developing their coverage of industrial disputes, with the popular dailies devoting more space to human interest stories and the quality papers giving greater analysis of the background of each strike.

One front-page exclusive report published by the *Sun* during the January rail strikes carried the headline, 'Taken for a Ride!', and outlined what the newspaper claimed was an astonishing dossier of 'fiddling, cheating and lying' by ASLEF train drivers. The story continued: 'Drivers who are making life a misery for millions with their guerilla strikes are guilty of drinking and dancing the night away at discos when they should be on the footplate' (*Sun*, 22 January 1982). The report was based on the experiences of two young drivers on Southern Region who were dismissed by British Rail the following month for what management said were the men's own admissions of malpractice, including drinking on duty. The BBC and other radio and television newsrooms tried to follow up the *Sun*'s report by making their own inquiries and by asking to interview Ray Buckton for ASLEF's reaction. However, one allegation, involving large numbers of 'disco-dancing' train drivers, should perhaps have been treated with even greater caution than usual by the rest of the news media, not least because British Rail statistics showed that 53 per cent of train drivers were over fifty.

The tendency of the broadcasting organisations to follow up Fleet Street exclusive stories almost automatically had been examined three years earlier by the TUC Media Working Group; it had taken up this issue because of concern within the trade union movement over the particular way news was projected on radio and television when the source was a newspaper exclusive. The Group reached this conclusion:

> No one studies the media more closely than journalists. Exclusive stories are rare and where they do occur they are often followed up by the rest of the media almost immediately. In this sort of atmosphere it is difficult for the broadcasting organisations to dissociate themselves from the press. At the very least they must consider broadcasting the prominent anti-union stories. And in circumstances where anti-union stories are the norm in the press then this tends to spill over into broadcasting and vice versa. Given the short period of time available for the preparation and presentation of news items it would be surprising if there was not a tendency to fall back on the conventional assumptions about the background to these items. This applies both to newspapers following radio and television stories as well as broadcasters following newspaper stories.
>
> (*A Cause for Concern*, TUC Media Working Group, June 1979)

The Group did not acknowledge that broadcasting companies do provide union leaders and other organisations with an opportunity to expose newspaper 'exclusives' which they believe are inaccurate or nonsensical. On such occasions a follow-up on radio or television can give an aggrieved party an immediate chance publicly to condemn a false report.

Immediately after the publication of the *Sun*'s 'Taken for a Ride!' exclusive, there were protests from some ASLEF members at King's Cross Station in London, who, together with guards and other railway workers, said that they would not take out trains used to distribute the *Sun*, *The Times*, *Sunday Times* or *News of the World*, all owned by News International, of which Rupert Murdoch was chairman and chief executive. When the railway workers did in fact refuse to load the newspapers on overnight trains bound for the north, News International obtained a Sunday hearing at the High Court, intending to seek an injunction against ASLEF. However, two ASLEF branch officials gave an undertaking to ask the ASLEF and NUR members to lift the blacking of the newspapers. The judge, Mr Justice Glidewell, commented that if he had been an engine driver and had read the article in the *Sun* he would have been extremely cross, but no one was entitled to take the law into their own hands. Further stories were published by the *Sun* on subsequent days exposing what it claimed were other fiddles by 'ASLEF drivers who are taking British Rail for an expensive ride'.

On 27 January 1982 the paper published letters from the two ASLEF officials who had appeared in the High Court: they said they were not in the business of censorship, the decision to black the newspapers of News International having been a gut reaction to the report in the *Sun* that had implicated every driver and guard throughout the length and breadth of British Rail.

The railway workers' short boycott of News International newspapers was defended at the time by the Labour Member of Parliament Tony Benn, who told a meeting of journalists that some reporters were guilty of writing what they knew to be lies about the Labour movement. Mr Benn continued:

> Day after day Fleet Street conducts its campaign against working people, ignoring their interests, distorting their arguments and abusing their representatives. Working journalists can no longer evade their moral responsibilities by shielding behind their editors, nor editors by shielding behind their proprietors.
>
> (Tony Benn, 26 January 1982)

Two days later, under the headline 'The paper they can't gag', the *Sun* said that Mr Benn had surpassed himself with these latest 'infamous slurs' against the integrity of the men and women who worked on the newspaper:

> No one employed by the *Sun* is ever ordered, or requested, to write untruths. No one is ever ordered to express opinions that are contrary to his own. No one is forced to work for the *Sun* . . . A journalist is able to follow his conscience and his preference. How long would that happen if comrade Benn were ever to achieve power?
>
> (*Sun*, 28 January 1982)

The train drivers' strikes had tested the resolve of both management and government, having again indicated that disputes over industrial change required not only the determination to see them through but also a new approach to some of the traditional problems of industrial relations. Once the strikes were over, Sir Peter said he believed that management's efforts had been worthwhile, as the final defeat of ASLEF had opened the door to change and new working practices. He described the £170 million that was lost during the thirty-four days of strike action in 1982 as the best investment ever made by British Rail.

The early months of the dispute had graphically illustrated the inherent dangers for unions and employers in communicating with each other through the news media, when the sense of conflict that ensued only added to the pressures on both sides. The following year, during a strike by water workers, Sir Peter's industrial relations director Clifford Rose was to reflect on the impact of news media attention during difficult disputes. He felt sympathy with negotiators from both sides of industry, and during the 1982 rail dispute he had found that the battery of questions, the search for new angles and the sustained efforts of newsmen to make negotiators break confidences had become all too frequent. The whole process had advanced well beyond merely reporting what had taken place: the news media seemed more interested in trying to 'nobble' the negotiators before the meeting, with the result that on countless occasions he had read in the press details of what were supposed to be British Rail's next moves even before they had been considered by himself and his colleagues. Mr Rose recognised that industrial disputes were of interest to the public, who had the right to know what was going on. He had found that the newspapers would print a story anyway, so the negotiators might as well try to ensure that it was as accurate as possible. He wrote briefly of his own experiences shortly before his death in July 1983, leaving these final words of advice to industrial negotiators: 'There is only one place for offers to be made and negotiations to take place, and that is at the negotiating table – not in the press, not on radio or on television, not even in the House of Commons' (Clifford Rose, *Personnel Management*, April 1983).

Within six months of this warning, the mineworkers started a ban on overtime, to be followed by a year-long pit strike in which the degree of participation by the news media would transcend that of all other disputes. Ian MacGregor, the newly named chairman of the National Coal Board, shared none of Mr Rose's inhibitions: he had Arthur Scargill to tackle – a union leader who was to take on the news media single-handed and eventually force government ministers to prescribe via radio and television the preconditions for the reopening of negotiations with the miners' union.

THREE

The Coal Industry:
New Weapons in an Old Battle

The increased parliamentary majority for the Conservative Party that resulted from the general election of June 1983 gave the government a new mandate to continue its policy of seeking greater efficiency in the nationalised industries. By the end of the government's first term in office there had been major manpower reductions in some of the state-owned concerns, with British Leyland and British Steel having achieved by far the greatest shake-out of labour.

When Sir Michael Edwardes left British Leyland in 1982, after five years as chairman, the workforce had been cut by 46.8 per cent, and the rate of productivity had risen from 6.1 to 9.5 cars a year per man. The manpower reduction and productivity increase were even more dramatic in the steel industry. The British Steel Corporation, of which Ian MacGregor had been appointed chairman in 1980, had achieved a 51.9 per cent cut in its labour force over the same five-year period. The National Coal Board, on the other hand, had reduced its manpower in those five years by only 12.4 per cent, and still had one of the largest workforces of any nationalised industry.

Nationalised industry manpower reductions, 1977–82

| | Total employees | | Percentage cut in workforce |
	1977	1982	
British Steel	207,900	100,000	51.9
British Leyland	171,000	91,400	46.8
National Coal Board	242,000	212,000	12.4
British Rail	182,700	166,900	8.6

The coal industry had been identified as the government's next priority even before the 1983 general election, with an announcement in the spring that Ian MacGregor would move from steel to become the new chairman of the coal board. He was appointed to serve a three-year term, starting in

43

September 1983, with instructions to secure for the coal industry the 'earliest practicable return to profitability' through the 'highest possible efficiency and control of costs'.

Mr MacGregor, who was born in Scotland, had spent much of his working life in the United States, where he developed what the British government was later to describe as his 'phenomenally energetic and successful' business career. The Ministry of Supply had sent him to Washington during the Second World War so that he could assist with technical aspects of arms-purchasing for Britain. Once the war was over he stayed in America holding various positions with industrial companies, before taking control of corporate diversification for the American Metal Company (Amax). In 1969 he became chairman of the Amax Corporation, which began investing in coal-mining, becoming the third largest coal producer in the United States. On retiring from the post in 1977, one of the directorships Mr MacGregor took up was in Britain, when in November of that year the Labour government appointed him deputy chairman of British Leyland, to serve under Sir Michael. He returned to Britain on a full-time basis in 1980, when in May, at the age of sixty-seven, he was named chairman of the steel corporation. The appointment involved financial conditions which required performance payments by the government of up to £1.8 million to the New York investment bank Lazard Freres, which had agreed to release Mr MacGregor from his commitments as a senior partner. The announcement was made by Sir Keith Joseph, then Secretary of State for Industry, who said that the government was prepared to compensate Lazard Freres for losing the business services of Mr MacGregor because the financial problems of British Steel needed a man of his calibre, who could restore the industry to profitability as an efficient steel producer. 'For the government to set financial targets is not enough: we must also seek to appoint people capable of achieving those targets,' said Sir Keith in his statement to the House of Commons.

At the time of Mr MacGregor's appointment, the steel corporation was in the process of recovering from a three-month pay strike that had lasted throughout the winter of 1980. It was Mr MacGregor who steered through the main 'rationalisation' process, which required a major reduction in overmanning and the concentration of steel production at the most efficient plants; already the previous year the former chairman Sir Charles Villiers had announced that capacity would have to be cut to 15 million tons, with the loss of 60,000 jobs.

When Mr MacGregor took over in July 1980 the redundancy programme had already started, together with moves to decentralise wage bargaining to the individual steelworks. But it was Mr MacGregor who steered through the main streamlining process. During his three-year chairmanship of the corporation British Steel cut its manpower by 70,000, at a cost to the country of nearly £600 million in redundancy payments, which had averaged out at around £8,000 for each steelworker. Mr MacGregor was proud of his achievement. At the height of the speculation about the possibility of his switch to the coal board, he appeared before a House of Commons select committee to defend his record at the steel corporation, claiming that he had reduced the payroll in line with 'the realities and the opportunities' for gainful employment. Later, in a newspaper interview, he expanded on the task that he had faced:

> If you have a plant that has become overgrown and begun to look seedy and seems to be dying away, you may have to take action, no matter how much it hurts. You have to prune hard to get growth. British Steel was in that category. It was overgrown, non-competitive and was clearly on its way out of business. Today it is in better shape and will provide a better future for those still working in it.
>
> (*Daily Mail*, 14 March 1983)

Ian MacGregor left British Steel convinced that the industry was on target to break even once demand improved. His enthusiasm had rubbed off on the rest of the management, with productivity having improved so dramatically that some works had reported a level of efficiency that equalled the best in Europe and was not far behind that of Japan. The Llanwern steelworks in South Wales became the showpiece for the corporation's slim-down policy: by 1982 it was able to produce the same two million tons of steel a year with less than half the previous labour force. Anxious to demonstrate its success to the news media, management invited industrial and labour correspondents to visit Llanwern, where the workers spoke of their pride and pleasure in the new working arrangements.

The rationalisation of the steel corporation was achieved without the degree of confrontation in the news media seen in some other nationalised industries. The circumstances were different because most of the redundancies took place in the aftermath of the three-month strike, which had left the steel unions in no position to launch further industrial action. Since there seemed no risk of fresh conflict, the management began supplying details of the plans for the rationalisation of the corporation direct to the workforce, rather than relying on the steel industry's trade unions to pass on the information. According to the chairman, the intention was not to bypass or ignore the unions but to develop a separate communications route to the steelworkers.

In tune with Mrs Thatcher and her ministers, Mr MacGregor believed it was the responsibility of management, not the unions, to inform the workforce of the need for industrial change. As deputy chairman of British Leyland for three years under Sir Michael Edwardes, he had participated in the development of the communication techniques that were used

45

during the major BL strikes. He had his own ideas on how to communicate with the steelworkers, which he started to introduce after spending the summer months of 1980 assessing the likely markets for British Steel in the aftermath of the three-month strike.

The new chairman's first task was to produce a survival plan for the steel industry which would involve seeking new finance from the government. As the main steelworkers' union had instructed its members not to co-operate with his proposals for futher redundancies and a capacity cut of 600,000 tons, Mr MacGregor realised he would have to make a direct appeal to the workforce for support, because he was not prepared to ask for more government money unless he had the men's backing. The method of communication that he decided to adopt was video, which other employers had turned to since it had become possible to record a message on video tape and then show it on a television set through a video cassette machine. By the mid-1970s many firms were using video to communicate internal information, to help retrain workers or to promote new products and services. In some firms a member of the management appeared on the video, while other companies brought in specialist producers to prepare short programmes, with actors or radio and television personalities presenting the information on behalf of the employer.

The American computer company IBM was one of the first to use video as part of a direct appeal to the workforce, in an attempt to diminish trade union influence. IBM had been non-union since it opened in Britain in 1951, but in 1976 the Association of Scientific, Technical and Managerial Staffs applied for union recognition on behalf of workers at IBM's manufacturing plant at Greenock near Glasgow, a claim that was later supported by three other trade unions. Two videos were produced by IBM as part of the management's campaign to persuade the workforce to support their policy against the recognition of trade unions. The opportunity to obtain trade union representation was later rejected overwhelmingly in a ballot held by ACAS, when 90.2 per cent of the Greenock workers voted against union recognition.

By the time that Mr MacGregor was to make his first use of video in 1980, there had been further advances in video production techniques. Within six months of taking office as BSC's chairman, he had recorded two personal messages in the form of fifteen-minute programmes. The corporation made sixty-five copies of each video cassette, as it was important that the chairman's message should be seen at the same time at all the steelworks throughout the country. On the appropriate day, workers were taken off shift in order to watch the programmes on television sets in the works canteens.

The second programme that featured Mr MacGregor was made to coincide with the announcement of the BSC 'survival plan', which was published in the middle of December 1980. Steel-making capacity had to be reduced from 15 to 14.4 million tons a year, said the corporation, with a

STEEL NEWS

15 DECEMBER 1980

Mr. I. MacGregor

Chairman Ian MacGregor announces his plan to save BSC. It is urgent. Each time the clock ticks we lose £30. Even Governments can't afford that. He tells every employee: Make no mistake. What we are talking about is

SURVIVAL

THE PLAN which will decide the fate of British Steel within seven months, is an urgent mix of closures, manpower cuts mainly through more efficient working, aggressive selling and cost-cutting which will affect every works, department and office in BSC.

It is an all-out attack on our own failings and failures . . . and on outside pressures like high energy costs which make us less competitive than the opposition.

But it cannot succeed without YOUR total co-operation — the backing and understanding of everyone who works for BSC. If it fails, there is no doubt that there will be more closures and redundancies on a far larger scale.

Chairman Ian MacGregor is confident the Plan CAN succeed, unless the market collapses or other unpredictable disasters blow us off course. He says: "I'm convinced after six months with British Steel that you have the talents in people at all levels of the business . . . you have the skills and knowledge to achieve the objectives and ensure the future."

Background

The timing of the Plan is vital. The measures it describes must be implemented immediately, without obstruction. No later than July, 1981, the results of the Plan will be reviewed. If it has not produced the essential improvements, then other, harsher measures will have to be used at once.

The Survival Plan is being discussed with the unions and Government against the background of BSC's losses in the first half of the financial year which ended on September 27, 1980.

Our total trading loss, after depreciation and in-

terest, was £279 million. And it is certain that the losses in the second six months will be even worse, because of the state of the market.

The Plan was discussed by BSC senior management at meetings with the TUC Steel Committee and the Steel Industry Management Association last Friday. It calls for:

- A cut in the Corporation's manned liquid steel-making capacity from 15 million tonnes to 14.4 million tonnes a year.
- A further reduction in personnel of at least 20,000.

The Plan makes it clear that most manpower reductions will be achieved by improved efficiencies rather than closures, but it states that further reductions in capacity are necessary because demand is not sufficient to fill existing capacity.

Continued on back page

Plate 5   Within six months of becoming chairman of British Steel in July 1980, Ian MacGregor had prepared his 'survival plan', announced to the corporation's workforce in a special issue of Steel News. *He was determined to communicate directly with his employees, to explain the need for an 'urgent mix' of closures and manpower cuts which would affect 'every works, department and office in BSC'.*

further cut in personnel of at least 20,000. The full details were published in a special issue of the corporation's staff newspaper *Steel News*, which reprinted the text of Mr MacGregor's recorded statement under this announcement: 'The video age came to BSC with Ian MacGregor . . . the reaction from all levels has been good. Now he intends to make video a regular form of communication in his leadership of British Steel' (*Steel News*, 15 December 1980). The showing of the fifteen-minute programme on the survival plan was accompanied by a personal letter from the chairman, which was posted to the home of every BSC employee. The special issue of *Steel News* carried a reminder urging workers to read the letter and 'discuss it with your workmates and your family as its message is vitally important to your future.'

Within a month of sending the letters, the Electoral Reform Society conducted a postal ballot on behalf of the steel corporation in which 78 per cent of the steelworkers voted to support Mr MacGregor's plan. The percentage of those in favour was not as high, though, as that obtained in October 1979 in the secret ballot organised at British Leyland over the Edwardes recovery plan (87 per cent). And 65 per cent of the steelworkers returned their ballot papers – again down on the 80 per cent participation achieved at BL. The lower response by the BSC workforce was undoubtedly a reflection of the opposition there had been from the main steel union, the Iron and Steel Trades Confederation (ISTC), which had organised a rival ballot reporting a two-to-one vote among its members against the corporation's closures and redundancy proposals.

There had been an earlier disagreement over secret ballots in the steel industry during the three-month strike in the winter of 1980, when the corporation held what became known as 'the ballot about a ballot'. Of those employees who participated, 68 per cent voted in favour of management holding a second postal ballot which would have allowed the workforce an opportunity to vote on BSC's 14.4 per cent pay offer. The voting went no further as the strike was called off at the end of March 1980, after a committee of inquiry recommended that another 1.5 per cent should be added to the pay increase. The postal ballot over the survival plan that Mr MacGregor ordered for the steelworkers nearly a year later in January 1981 was the third organised by a state employer within the space of fourteen months, all three having produced majorities for management proposals, despite attempts by the trade unions to persuade their members not to vote.

The steelworkers' union had asked its members to ignore 'the ballot about a ballot', believing it had more to gain by branding the management's intervention as unnecessary interference, which it thought would help reinforce the leadership's appeal for solidarity during the strike. However, when it came to the second ballot in 1981 the union had decided to counter any possible propaganda advantage to Mr MacGregor by organising its own ballot as part of its campaign against further closures and redundancies. The ISTC had placed advertisements in local newspapers in areas around the steelworks, to remind members to attend branch meetings so that they could vote.

Most trade unions had faced severe difficulty in trying to come to terms with the success that managements had achieved in bypassing the leadership through the use of the postal services to deliver personal letters and voting papers for secret ballots. A severe handicap was that few of the major unions representing manual workers even had the home addresses of their own members. This information was not usually required, since union subscriptions were either paid at work or collected automatically on the union's behalf by the employer, who deducted it from an employee's wage or salary under the system known as 'check-off'. Since it was customary for an employee to give his address and telephone number to the employer when he was taken on, management frequently possessed more personal information about an individual union member than the union itself.

The failure of the wider union movement to keep abreast of the advances that employers had made in improving direct communications with employees had not been lost on management. Because manual unions relied on the workplace distribution of information – their only point of contact with the membership was at work or at branch meetings – many had no other means of making immediate direct contact with the membership, especially during a strike when no one was at work. The specialist advisers who had assisted British Leyland, British Rail and British Steel had realised that the manual unions were vulnerable on this point, and that if contact could be made with a striker inside his own home there was every likelihood that both he and his wife might be open to persuasion.

The cost of conducting postal ballots can be considerable. British Leyland estimated that it spent £150,000 on the ballots that were held while Sir Michael Edwardes was chairman. British Rail's bill for postage during one fortnight of the rail dispute in July 1982 was £73,500 – the cost of sending two letters to 225,000 BR employees and a third letter to 25,000 ASLEF members. Union finances were invariably under pressure during strike action, with few unions having the resources to compete with management, even if the home addresses of the members had been available.

The communications strategy that Ian MacGregor developed while he was chairman of British Steel included another of the techniques that had been used at British Leyland. In the summer of 1982 he commissioned an opinion survey to see if the corporation's workforce still supported his survival plan. The existence of the survey was made public after one of the workers questioned by Opinion Research Centre revealed that he was a lay union official with the main steel union, the ISTC, upon which the

49

interviewer terminated the conversation, tore up the unfinished question-naire and threw it in a bin. The sheets of paper were retrieved, stuck together and then published by the ISTC, which declared that the poll had been divisive because the workers had been asked to say which of five remaining steelworks they thought was most at risk and under threat of closure. Later British Steel said the survey, which was carried out among 3,000 steel workers, showed that a clear majority of the workforce still supported Mr MacGregor's leadership and the need for further closures and redundancies.

The ORC survey revealed the importance that Mr MacGregor attached to communications with his workforce. Each of the workers interviewed had been asked to say whether it was or was not helpful to receive letters at home from Ian MacGregor; to see television films of the chairman; to read about British Steel in newspaper advertisements, or to have information about the corporation passed on at work by a foreman. The answers to these questions were not made public, but his public relations advisers had suggested to Mr MacGregor that he should be sparing in his use of personal letters because some workers might regard them as an invasion of privacy. However, there was general agreement within the corporation that during critical moments a letter from the chairman was an effective means of communication, because the employee could read what management had to say in the privacy of his home without being under any pressure from his workmates or local union officials.

While Mr MacGregor was chairman, the steel corporation virtually withdrew from national trade union negotiations on pay claims and major operational issues. Instead, authority was devolved to local management at the individual steelworks, where the emphasis was placed on providing extra pay only in return for improvements in productivity. After BSC had refused for the third year running to make a national wage increase, Bill Sirs, then general secretary of the ISTC, complained of blatant discrimi-nation against the steelworkers. At the time there seemed no point in asking for a radio interview with Mr MacGregor: his policy was apparently to ignore not only the national union leaders but also the news media, except on those occasions when he was prepared to give private briefings to selected groups of journalists. If there was fresh speculation about the future of another steelworks or a protest by the steel unions, most reporters knew they would be lucky to get even a one-line comment from the steel corporation. The message from the chairman was a clear one: he was not prepared to enter a 'table tennis match' with the unions by using the newspapers, radio or television. If there were no press statements or interviews, there was less chance of media confrontation.

Mr MacGregor's reluctance to enter into a public debate over the future of the steel industry reduced Bill Sirs to a lonely voice, a union leader without a contest. The chairman seemed safe in the knowledge that whatever Mr Sirs might say, union opposition had effectively collapsed after the 1980 strike. That dispute had put the media spotlight firmly on Mr Sirs, yet throughout the strike he was always at pains to be courteous and appear reasonable when interviewed on radio and television. Unlike many previous disputes, the steel strike ended with a union leader declaring that he found himself on better terms with the media than when the industrial action had started. Indeed, in later years, Mr Sirs said he was always surprised by the public recognition and popularity that he believed he had achieved during that strike, through the way he had presented the steelworkers' case.

Mr MacGregor approached his chairmanship of the National Coal Board with the same conviction that he had shown at British Steel, expressing the same passionate belief in the government's drive to make British industry more competitive. He wanted Britain to take full advantage of its coal reserves so that the rest of British industry could be supplied with the cheaper energy that he thought it deserved. That could only be achieved through reducing surplus capacity by closing some of the older high-cost pits.

When Mr MacGregor was appointed in March 1983 the coal board employed 197,000 mineworkers – still the largest labour force in a state-owned enterprise engaged in heavy industry. The coal mines were the first industry to have been nationalised after the Second World War, and both management and union leaders often gave the impression in later years that they regarded themselves as part of what was virtually a public service, which deserved the subsidies it was receiving. Within the government there was a widespread view that the NCB had become a profligate drain on the national exchequer, with a management that had failed to tackle the need for greater productivity, largely because it had become an inbread, closed community, made up mainly of mining engineers and men who had come up through the pits. In the Prime Minister's view, it seemed, it was the management that needed the attention of Mr MacGregor almost as badly as the uneconomic pits.

The appointment of the new chairman coincided almost to the day with the completion of Arthur Scargill's first twelve months as president of the National Union of Mineworkers. It had been a year during which the miners had twice voted against strike action, despite frequent warnings from Mr Scargill that the coal board probably had a 'hit list' for pit closures. The prospect of confrontation between Mr MacGregor and Mr Scargill had begun to excite the news media early in 1983, when speculation had started over Mr MacGregor's possible switch from the steel corporation to the coal board. Fleet Street headline-writers were full of eager anticipation, and determined to personalise any likely conflict: 'Mac the Knife is set to take on Scargill' (*Sun*, 7 February 1983). Mr MacGregor acknowledged from the start that as the new head of the coal industry he would face opposition and criticism, with the attendant risk of at least some public unpopularity. On the day his appointment was announced he held a joint news conference with the outgoing coal board chairman Sir Norman Siddall. Why, Mr MacGregor was asked, when he was already seventy and would soon have completed three years at British Steel, was he prepared to sign another three-year contract and become the new chairman of the National Coal Board? His reply indicated that he knew the risks that went with the job:

> There are probably not too many people around who want to get into the unsatisfactory position of having their every move criticised and analysed by everyone in the country. This job is an exposed position which you find not many people are keen on. It falls to some of us older, more relaxed and somewhat more philosophical citizens to be prepared to take the stick which goes with these situations.
> (Ian MacGregor, BSC–NCB news conference, 28 March 1983)

Mr MacGregor made an unspectacular arrival at Hobart House, the London headquarters of the NCB, agreeing to a photo-call but declining all interviews on the grounds that he wanted to postpone any public statements until he had become more familiar with the problems of the coal industry. This seemed in keeping with the low profile that the chairman had adopted at British Steel, where the head of the information services, Ronald Melvin, had also frequently refused to make any comment on the many news stories that were printed or broadcast about the future of the steel industry, preferring instead to give briefings to selected journalists.

Mr MacGregor's predecessor Sir Norman Siddall had spent fourteen months quietly and patiently encouraging local management to close uneconomic pits wherever possible. As a result, under Sir Norman's chairmanship the rate of closures had nearly doubled. There had been opposition from the miners' union, but two pit-head ballots within four months had failed to produce the necessary majority for strike action. The industry was also looking ahead to the future, as by then some coal was turning at the new computer-controlled pits that made up the Selby coalfield in Yorkshire. And the next new coalfield was already being planned to come on stream at Asfordby in Leicestershire. Against this background of change, management believed that it was making progress towards meeting the government's objectives. The coal board's North Yorkshire director, then Michael Eaton, pointed to the success there had been in his area, where older pits were being successfully closed, and the men were accepting transfers to the new mines at Selby.

Now, the impending arrival of a new chairman was creating a noticeable concern within management. The unease of Mr Eaton and his fellow directors arose through a fear that Mr MacGregor might make a blunder that would somehow play into the hands of Arthur Scargill – even though in their view he had begun to destroy his own credibility through the increasingly political tone of his statements, coupled with the union's failure to win the most recent pit-head ballots. Throughout the spring and summer of 1983 Mr Scargill had warned that the appointment of Mr MacGregor, whom he described as the 'American butcher of British industry', was the first step towards the closure of seventy pits and the loss of 70,000 jobs. While waiting to take over as chairman, Mr MacGregor had refrained from replying to any of Mr Scargill's jibes, limiting himself to the odd comment about liking miners, to which the NUM president had retorted that the suggestion that miners would welcome Mr MacGregor was 'as bizarre as a blood bank opening its doors to Dracula'.

Within a fortnight of taking over, Ian MacGregor had his first meeting with leaders of the miners' union, describing it later as a 'very civilised' occasion. Afterwards, for the benefit of the photographers and television cameramen, he shook hands with Arthur Scargill, who said he was encouraged that his union's first meeting with Mr MacGregor had not produced the inevitable conflict that the news media had so confidently predicted. That remark was characteristic of Mr Scargill's approach to journalists: he liked to surprise, tease and even intimidate them. It was by the attitude that he displayed towards Mr MacGregor that he had encouraged the interest of the news media. Given the level of expectation that he had aroused, it was hardly surprising that the entrance hall of Hobart House was packed with reporters, photographers and cameramen anxious to record the first meeting between the two men. Instead of walking away or refusing to be seen speaking to the new chairman, Mr Scargill stayed smiling and chatting with him, knowing full well that he had guaranteed himself time on the evening television news bulletins, and that the photographs of himself and Mr MacGregor shaking hands were likely to be printed next day in every national newspaper – thus confounding his Fleet Street critics.

Mr Scargill's rise to power had been helped by his ability to increase his own newsworthiness by exciting the news media. He knew how to project himself on radio and television; he was not alarmed by the brightness of the lights or the confusion of the studio surroundings, as he had quickly learned to intimidate interviewers and take advantage of television and radio presenters. Some of his opponents in Fleet Street blamed the BBC and ITV for allowing a union leader to exploit the broadcasting services. Mr Scargill's runaway victory in the 1981 pit-head ballot for NUM president had caused consternation in the popular national dailies, with newspaper columnists offering an assortment of explanations for the fact that he had secured 70.3 per cent of the total vote. Paul Johnson wrote frequently about the reasons behind Mr Scargill's rise to power:

How did a man like Scargill, whose judgment is so weak, whose sense of what his members want is so flagrantly and repeatedly in error, ever become president of a great union? The answer is simple: the media. It was the media, and above all the BBC and ITV, by their massive exposure for this glib exponent of political showbiz, who put Scargill where he is. Media distortion of the relative weights of personalities within the union allowed Scargill, for a brief instant, to blind many miners to their true interests and so win himself the life presidency.

(*Daily Mail*, 10 March 1983)

The suggestion that the NUM president was simply a 'glib exponent of political showbiz' overlooked Mr Scargill's skill as a communicator on behalf of his union. The interviews that he gave on radio and television were unlike those of almost any other union leader, because of the strength of his resolution in defending himself in the face of hostile interrogation, avoiding a direct answer to any question that he thought might put the union or himself at a disadvantage.

When an interviewer began to get impatient, Mr Scargill had his own defensive mechanisms. His tactic was to unsettle the questioner by the very tricks of the trade that are used almost subconsciously by many interviewers. A tough question could be reinforced by beginning, 'Mr Scargill, what about . . . ?' where use of the surname, although it might appear no more than a courtesy, could add a menacing dimension to the question, depending on the emphasis and tone of voice. If Mr Scargill knew the name of his radio or television interviewer he frequently used the same device in reply – if need be, with equal menace – realising that this could heighten the sense of confrontation already created by the questions. By reversing the process, by seizing every opportunity to challenge the interviewer, Mr Scargill believed there was every chance that he would lose the thread of his questioning and perhaps fall back on an irrational or muddled statement which could then be pounced on as a blatant example of BBC or ITN bias.

The conventional view of industrial as well as political interviews is that they are more likely to be lively and effective if the radio or television journalist plays the role of devil's advocate. By taking the opposite point of view to that of the person being interviewed, the reporter hopes to maintain a sense of balance within the interview, while at the same time asking provocative questions which he or she thinks will be of interest to the listener or viewer. This adversarial approach suited Mr Scargill, who had served a long apprenticeship in the art of cross-examination. During one of his appearances on the BBC Radio 4 programme Any Questions? in October 1983, he said that if he had not become a union leader he would have liked to be a barrister, having developed a close interest in legal work.

After starting in the pits as a teenager he rose through the union ranks to become a pit delegate, which led in 1972 to his first full-time position as compensation agent for the Yorkshire area making claims on behalf of sick and injured miners, which often involved briefing solicitors and barristers. The year after becoming president of the Yorkshire branch, he represented the union at the public inquiry which followed the Lofthouse pit disaster, cross-examining each of the witnesses, a role he repeated in 1975 after the Houghton Main accident. Then as national president he put the miners' case at the Sizewell nuclear inquiry, and during the early months of the 1984 strike he was to spend a fortnight representing the union at the High Court in London, during which he cross-examined NCB trustees in an unsuccessful challenge by the NUM over the investment policy relating to the mineworkers' pension fund. The president's skill in cross-examination drew praise from one legal correspondent: 'Mr Scargill gave a performance of which many barristers would not have been ashamed. He was well briefed and had a sound grasp of his material. His questions were, for the most part, clear and to the point. His supplementary questions in response to the witnesses' answers demonstrated his ability to think on his feet' (Raymond Hughes, Law Courts correspondent, *Financial Times*, 6 April 1984).

Mr Scargill was still a branch delegate when he gained national prominence through his part in organising a mass picket at the Saltley coke depot in Birmingham during the 1972 miners' srike. Within a year he had been elected Yorkshire president. Five years after Saltley he was arrested on the Grunwick picket line in London. He had grown accustomed to the sense of power that went with his reputation as a militant trade union leader. He had realised that even by hinting at his particiaption in an industrial dispute, he could command the immediate presence of radio, television and the press.

The tactics that he adopted during his nine years as Yorkshire president regularly led him into conflict with the miners' national president Joe Gormley, later Lord Gormley. After the monthly meetings of the miners' national executive, of which Mr Scargill was a member, it was the tradition that the national president briefed the news media on what the executive had decided, in order to ensure some consistency in the news-reporting of the union's affairs. This established practice was challenged by Mr Scargill when, at the start of his campaign for the presidency, he began pre-empting the offical briefing by giving his own version of what the executive had agreed. He would try to ensure that he spoke first to the newsmen as they waited on the steps of the union's headquarters in Euston Road. This was a regular and friendly doorstep assignment for the industrial journalists, but as Mr Scargill began campaigning for national office the reporters and crews working for radio and television faced a difficult balancing act as they jostled together on the steps. The sight of the Yorkshire president coming down from the executive's first-floor meeting-room was the signal for the electronic news media men to spring into action, because there might be only a few minutes in which to try to record an immediate reaction from Mr Scargill before joining the rest of the reporters who would by then be crowding into the council chamber for the official press conference.

Mr Gormley had noticed what was happening; occasionally he would peep over the balcony to identify those reporters who were taking part in this unofficial briefing. He was then ready to chide the latecomers to the formal press conference and warn that he would throw out any journalist who he discovered was going elsewhere for information. It was a neat way of bringing the younger and pushier reporters into line. However, after a time one could see that it was a half-hearted threat, often delivered with a knowing wink or grin. Mr Gormley had too many friends among the labour and industrial correspondents to want to erect any serious obstacles for the news media.

In the run-up to Mr Gormley's retirement and the presidential election, the push and shove of the doorstep interviews in the Euston Road made it difficult to establish any more than a fleeting contact with Mr Scargill during his visits to London for national executive meetings. Although my interest in reporting industrial news had begun in the late 1970s, I had to wait some time for an occasion to talk to him at length.

One opportunity occurred in 1980, when the miners held their annual conference at Eastbourne. Over the weekend that preceded the official Monday opening, Mr Scargill was only too willing to talk to journalists. After recording a lengthy radio interview, he stayed to chat, and what struck me immediately was the charming manner he adopted; he appeared to enjoy talking to a reporter, engaging in friendly discussion which seemed so much at odds with his public criticism of the news media. Some of the other union leaders who attack the press so dislike the company of journalists that they do everything they can to avoid their presence, except on official occasions. Yet here was Mr Scargill revealing his knowledge of and obvious fascination with the news media.

The Yorkshire president had been prepared to challenge the established union conventions over the briefing of the news media because Mr Gormley was on the point of retiring, thus giving him an opportunity to run for national office. When nominations closed in October 1981 for the pit-head ballot to elect Mr Gormley's successor, there were four candidates. Mr Scargill was unchallenged on the left, but the coalfields that had consistently supported Mr Gormley were divided, nominating three separate candidates: Trevor Bell, leader of the union's colliery staff section, COSA; the Nottinghamshire miners' president, Ray Chadburn; and Bernard Donaghy from Lancashire. Mr Scargill spent much of that autumn on the campaign trail, rounding off a series of speeches with a final rally in the City Hall, Sheffield, where row upon row of his supporters could be seen wearing yellow badges saying 'Scargill for President'. On 8 December 1981, during a break in the annual pay talks at the NCB, Mr Gormley announced the ballot result: Mr Scargill had secured an overwhelming victory, obtaining 70.3 per cent of the total vote.

Next day in a signed column in the *Daily Express*, Mr Gormley advised Mr Scargill to adopt a 'slowly-slowly' approach, saying that the new president had been elected to look after the interests of the miners, not to alienate the people of Britain. Mr Gormley then paid him this tribute:

> One of the good things about Arthur is that he knows how to get publicity. He has done it while repeatedly saying how appalled he is at the media's behaviour. He realised ten years ago, I am sure, that no publicity is bad publicity, and decided to get his face in front of the public. As a result he has created an image for himself. He is now as much a household word, so far as the miners are concerned, as I am. The problem he now faces is that the same household word is not used for both of us.
>
> (Joe Gormley, *Daily Express*, 9 December 1981)

After the handshake and smiles of the ballot result, while the union waited for the final hand-over, came three difficult months which ended in open hostility between the retiring president and Mr Scargill. At this point the mineworkers were having to decide whether to follow the advice of the national executive in rejecting the 9.3 per cent pay offer, which had been made in response to the union's 1981 wage claim. The union had demanded a £100-a-week minimum wage, equal to a 24 per cent pay increase, which Mr Scargill had campaigned for during his election campaign for presidency. When the board refused to increase the offer, the union held a delegate conference which agreed to recommend strike action.

An attack of bronchitis had forced Mr Gormley to miss the conference, but this did not deter him from writing another full-page article for the *Daily Express* on 13 January 1982, on the eve of the pit-head ballot, entitled 'My message to the miners'. Mr Gormley told the men that he was against the recommendation for strike action because he believed the union should have accepted the board's 9.3 per cent offer. The retiring president urged the miners to think before they destroyed what the union had built up, stressing that they should not allow themselves to be used as political shock troops to bring down the government.

Mr Gormley's *Daily Express* article was one of the last outspoken attacks from within the executive on the rising power of the president-elect. Later Mr Scargill accused Mr Gormley of an 'unparalleled and shameful act of betrayal', for, he said, the president had gone against a decision of his own executive. During a censure debate at the next NUM executive meeting Mr Gormley survived by only thirteen votes to twelve. Nevertheless the outgoing president had proved a shrewd judge of the membership, because the ballot showed a 55–45 per cent vote in favour of accepting the pay offer and against strike action.

Mr Gormley's departure was followed almost immediately by the retirement of the National Coal Board chairman, Sir Derek Ezra. The new NCB chairman, Sir Norman Siddall, met the newly installed NUM president and the full executive two days after his own appointment had been confirmed. The meeting ended abruptly, with Mr Scargill and the rest of the union leadership departing after three and a half minutes, saying that the coal board had failed to produce, as promised, evidence of what Mr Scargill said was a 'hit list' for pit closures. A fortnight later Mr Scargill was in Inverness for his first annual conference as president. Sir Norman, who had been invited to speak, warned of the need to reduce the uneconomic tail of the coal industry, which, he said, comprised the 12 per cent of capacity that was losing £250 million a year. Sir Norman made only a fleeting visit: there was none of the reciprocal hospitality between union and coal board that had been such a feature of annual conferences during the years that Mr Gormley and Sir Derek held office.

In the autumn of 1982 the union held another pit-head ballot recommending strike action, for the second time in a year, having rejected the coal board's offer of an 8.2 per cent pay rise. The 1982 pay negotiations were the first that Mr Scargill had conducted on behalf of the union. The executive's recommendation in the ballot linked the wage claim with concern over the future of the coal industry, by calling for industrial action to secure a satisfactory pay settlement and, if necessary, to prevent the closure of any pit. Despite some hard campaigning by Mr Scargill, the miners again ignored the advice of the leadership, voting by 61 to 39 per cent to accept the NCB's pay offer. The majority against strike action was even higher than in the previous ballot, when Mr Gormley had advised the membership against industrial action.

Once it was clear which way the vote had gone, Fleet Street spent several days preparing for what it described as the humiliation of 'King Arthur' – a monarch, said the *Daily Express*, 'without a throne, a leader without followers, uttering blood-curdling threats to make up for the grim reality of being deserted'.

The official announcement of the ballot defeat was made at a press conference that well illustrated Mr Scargill's sense of timing. He showed a flair for knowing in advance how journalists would react and, given satisfactory circumstances and the right material, he could turn adversity on its head. He was always careful to prepare in advance what he intended to say to journalists, having taken personal control over all press statements issued by the union from the moment he was installed as national president. As this was the first strike ballot that had been conducted under his presidency, there was considerable media interest. Once the executive meeting that preceded the press conference had finished, the reporters, photographers, television cameramen and technicians rushed towards the first-floor council chamber, struggling with each other to get the best positions. Mr Scargill sat there smiling.

When the hubbub had subsided all eyes were on the president. How would he handle the humiliation of this ballot defeat after only seven months in office? Mr Scargill, the communicator, was ready to give a display of sheer professionalism. The journalists did not know that the pile of papers in front of him included what he was to claim was a confidential coal board document providing the first official proof of the secret 'hit list' that he had spoken of so often.

Mr Scargill's sense of timing can best be appreciated from a tape-recording of the news conference, in which he is first heard announcing that he has a copy of a secret document. In front of him are the outstretched microphones of the radio and television reporters, the newspaper cameramen and the journalists with their notebooks. At the precise moment that he announces he has some secret information, he holds up the document in his right hand, just beside his face, ready for the instant pictures for television and the press. On the tape the clicking of the flashlights can be heard coming precisely on cue. Next day Fleet Street gave its account of the news conference:

> Scargill had pulled out a white rabbit, a coal board briefing on pit closures. It was his only shot. He kept the rabbit bouncing on the table. Scargill slapped the 14 pages of the coal board document. 'It's sensational. I'm shocked. I'm stunned.' He made the white rabbit bounce again so everybody could see it.
>
> (*Daily Mail*, 3 November 1982)

Although Fleet Street had tried to ridicule Mr Scargill, he had succeeded to a large degree in diverting attention away from the ballot defeat, redirecting the news media towards a re-examination of his claim that the coal board was planning extensive pit closures, which in turn had the effect of putting management on the defensive. The incident demonstrates to the full Mr Scargill's resilience and ingenuity. He never seemed daunted on entering a room packed with journalists, baying like hounds, waiting for the moment when Arthur Scargill would have to admit he was beaten. Like the conductor of an orchestra, he rarely showed any sign of first-night nerves. When challenged by a sea of staring faces, he knew precisely how to bring on and interest each section of the media.

There was considerable admiration within other unions for the adept way he handled journalists; some leaders said that the miners' new president had become the best communicator within the movement. However, there were drawbacks to the confident, overbearing manner that Mr Scargill frequently adopted, especially when refusing to give a straight answer to a journalist's question. This prevarication often appeared unproductive, and tended to build up hostility against him.

Reporters who specialise in covering industrial affairs have to acknowledge that there are two versions to almost every story they write or broadcast, as trade unions and employers rarely agree even on the basic facts that surround a dispute. These conflicting details have to be summarised in a way that will interest the reader, listener or viewer. Newspapers are in a strong position when it comes to reporting detailed information – like the full figures for wage claims or pay offers – as this can be given in lists and tables that the reader can then study. And on television, statistical information can be illustrated through the use of pictures or captions. But there is a limit on the number of facts and figures that can be delivered in a radio report, as complex information can be difficult to take in on one quick hearing. To help overcome this difficulty, radio reports include live or pre-recorded interviews, in the hope that those involved in confusing or controversial industrial disputes will be able to express themselves in a straightforward way that will be readily understood by the listener.

In any dispute, the radio reporter has to ask questions that will not only elicit information but also probe the underlying issues. Occasionally he needs to be provocative, in order to retain the attention of the listener and to force the employer or union leader to address himself directly to the point. Care has to be taken, though, both in the phrasing and the delivery of the question, so as not to appear objectionable either to the interviewee or to the unknown listener. It is important not to cause unnecessary offence, because the interviewer's aim is to represent the public, whose support he wishes to retain. The union leader or employer being interviewed may regard the questions as unhelpful or provocative, but if the interviewer's conduct is above reproach then the interviewee can sometimes lose the sympathy of the listener simply by prevaricating rather than answering the question, or by becoming unreasonable or obstructive.

Mr Scargill's line of defence when faced with questions he did not like was to challenge the interviewer by attempting to undermine the validity of the question or, if necessary, by attacking the integrity of the journalist or the organisation for which he worked. He prided himself on his ability to avoid getting trapped by awkward questions, and sometimes, when in friendly conversation with journalists, he liked to recall those occasions when he had escaped unscathed from some particularly difficult encounter on radio or television.

One occasion when Mr Scargill might have regretted what he said took place after the union decided to relocate its headquarters in the central coalfields. A site was chosen in Sheffield, so that most of the staff in London had realised by the end of 1982 that they would be redundant unless they were prepared to move north. The relationship between Mr Scargill and the London staff had been uneasy from the moment he was installed as president, and within a few weeks there were complaints from the clerical and secretarial workers. As the union's area leaders arrived for an executive meeting on 10 June 1982, they were greeted by this notice on the front door: 'NUM women want more consultation, less dictation.' Six months later when the move to Sheffield had finally been agreed, those grievances sparked off a strike. About twenty of the staff, led by Paul Noble, head of the union's industrial relations department, stopped work and formed a picket line on the steps of the Euston Road office. Mr Noble had never thought he would live to see the day, he said, when he would lead a strike of trade unionists against his own union. He described the relationship between the staff and Mr Scargill as akin to that with nineteenth-century pit-owner. Later, at a hurried news conference, Mr Scargill said his staff had better wages than most miners, plus full fares to and from work, and he thought the only explanation for the breakdown in relations was resentment caused by the decision to move to Sheffield. But why had an experienced trade union leader allowed the grievances of his staff to build up in this way and spark off a strike?

Scargill   The issues to which you have referred I suspect you can't even identify, because the representatives of the staff themselves can't identify them either.

Jones   I was here in June and there was a big notice on the front door of the union office which said the NUM members were fed up with dictation and wanted consultation. That was six months ago.

Scargill   What do you mean by that?

Jones   I don't know. I didn't write the notice. I don't work here.

Scargill   But you did quote the notice. If you quote something you should substantiate it and if you can't you should withdraw it.

Jones   But what do you think about these comments in the staff's statement today and their earlier comments?

Scargill   There have been a number of little trivial issues which have been raised. I will give you one example. The press, those defenders of freedom in Fleet Street, have said Mr Scargill and his colleagues have stopped the staff getting coffee and tea. Well, that's both true and it's not true. What we have done is to recognise that the people who supply the money to this union are the miners who work in this industry underground, and it's their money that we are looking after. As far as I am concerned the staff in this organisation will have to recognise that as well, and when we purchase tea or coffee or anything else we have got to bear that in mind, that it's our members' money we're spending. All we have said is that we need some control and we are not prepared to have anyone in this office going out and buying tins and jars of coffee at will.

(BBC Radio 4, PM programme, 7 January 1983)

When that interview was broadcast there were telephone calls of congratulation to the BBC. Some of the callers said they were usually critical of Mr Scargill, but were now delighted to have heard him give such a clear explanation as to the reasons why an employer had to keep firm control over the petty cash.

Despite unfavourable newspaper reports over his relations with some of the London staff, Mr Scargill once again demonstrated his flair for publicity when it came to the actual move to Sheffield: he invited the news media to witness the union's departure, on 15 April 1983. Inside his private office were rows of packing cases, rapidly being filled with his collection of newspaper cuttings, which he kept in large leather-bound volumes, with 'A. Scargill' inscribed in gold on the binding. While Mr Scargill turned the pages of one of the volumes for the benefit of the photographers, the removal men downstairs were having difficulty inching out into the Euston Road the eight-ton black marble statue which had taken pride of place in the entrance hall. The statue depicted two miners, wearing only shorts, hacking out coal in a narrow seam with a pick and shovel. After a lengthy struggle it was finally clear of the foyer, and a crane began lifting it up on to a removal truck. At this point in stepped the Fleet Street photographers asking Mr Scargill to take on the role of Atlas, only instead of holding up the heavens to appear to take the weight of the statue. Although the president was not wearing a safety helmet, he duly obliged, much to the consternation of the removal men who protested that it was against health and safety regulations to stand under a heavy load.

Shortly before the move to Sheffield, Mr Scargill had to announce the second ballot defeat for the union within the space of four months. The executive had recommended strike action following local stoppages that began in South Wales over the closure of the Tymawr-Lewis Merthyr pit near Pontypridd. The result of the pit-head ballot, declared on 10 March 1983, again showed a 61–39 per cent vote against strike action – exactly the same majority that had been recorded the previous November. Later Mr Scargill complained that the South Wales miners had jumped the gun in calling for a national strike so soon after the previous defeat.

The general election of June 1983, which had returned the Conservatives with an enlarged majority, led some union leaders to question the blanket opposition offered by the union movement towards government policy on employment law. The then TUC general secretary Len Murray, later Lord Murray, warned that the TUC would have to think again about the need to reopen contacts with the government. He criticised Mr Scargill for continuing to call for extra-parliamentary action, because it was plain daft, he said, for a union leader to try to put up two fingers to the general election result.

Mr Murray's rebuke came on the eve of the miners' annual conference in Perth, where Mr Scargill faced criticism from within the union. One delegate claimed the president had threatened to call more strikes than there were numbers in a game of bingo. Another said that presidential roadshows of the kind Mr Scargill had favoured during his election campaign were not going to impress the membership; perhaps it was time he went back down a pit. These comments were an indication of the unease that was developing among some active members of the union at what they perceived to be Mr Scargill's growing interest in trying to impress the media rather than to communicate with the miners. At times of internal pressure and criticism many union leaders retreat from publicity, but when Mr Scargill was being questioned or challenged he remained preoccupied with the need to project himself, appearing dissatisfied if the affairs of the union and his own activities were not commanding the constant attention of radio, television and the press.

Arthur Scargill took every opportunity to read and monitor what was said about him. He regularly listened to the morning news bulletins on the radio; when being driven to work he would look through the national morning newspapers; once in the office he kept the television set tuned to the teletext news services of Ceefax or Oracle, and whenever possible watched the lunchtime, tea-time and evening news bulletins. At union conferences he often preferred to sit in his room, working or looking at the news programmes, rather than spend his time in late-night socialising.

The close attention that the president paid to the news media was partly a reflection of his fascination at seeing how journalists reported what he had said and whether his use of some provocative or catchy phrase had been picked up by newspaper headline-writers or cartoonists. Once he had established a friendly relationship with a journalist, he liked to hear what he thought of the way he had made a possibly controversial announcement or handled a potentially embarrassing incident. In view of this, I mentioned to Mr Scargill at the start of the Perth conference that some of the newspaper industrial correspondents had decided to give the miners a miss that year and go instead to the Isle of Man, where the Transport and General Workers' Union was holding its biennial conference the same week. Later I discovered that Mr Scargill had clearly given some thought to my suggestion that the media might be losing interest in the miners, because on the final day of the miners' conference, after recording an interview in the BBC radio caravan, he said with a smile, 'Well, I didn't let you down, did I? The miners were top of the news bulletins all week.'

This preoccupation with what the press, television and radio were saying about him was viewed with increasing concern by some area union leaders, who were beginning to wonder whether his high news profile might be counter-productive. This became clear to me during a discussion with Peter Heathfield, who was then general secretary of the NUM's North Derbyshire area. My note of the conversation shows that he was outspoken in his assessment, fearing that Mr Scargill was in danger of making a fool of himself. He also thought that the miners did not like to see their president on television two or three times a week, particularly when it appeared to them that Mr Scargill was dictating to them what he wanted to happen.

Mr Heathfield had a straightforward approach to the news media, and was well liked by journalists. Unlike Mr Scargill, he was willing to allow reporters to telephone him at home, which meant he was much in demand during pit-head ballots, as the North Derbyshire area had for long been regarded as an accurate barometer of opinion within the coalfields. He had a take-it-or-leave-it attitude, and although he was quite prepared to be interviewed by radio reporters, he did not share Mr Scargill's zeal for publicity.

Two months after that conversation in Perth, on the eve of the TUC's 1983 conference in Blackpool, it appeared that Mr Heathfield's worries were justified, for Mr Scargill had become embroiled in a media saga that tested his credibility and provided a field day for his opponents in the rest of the trade union movement.

Mr Scargill had been in Moscow the previous weekend at a peace conference of mining unions. In a speech that warned of warlike moves by the United States and by other sections of the capitalist world, Mr Scargill declared: 'The most dangerous duo, President Ray-gun and the Plutonium blonde, Margaret Thatcher, jointly present a threat to world peace.' On arrival back at Heathrow he defended his remarks, maintaining that they were consistent with the NUM's policy in favour of peace rather than nuclear annihilation. Five days later, a Russian jet fighter shot down a South Korean 747 with the loss of 269 lives. Mr Scargill was immediately reminded by the news media of what he had said in Moscow. Fleet Street criticised him for not joining other union leaders in an instant condemnation of the shooting down of a civil airliner.

On the third day of the TUC conference there was further criticism of the NUM president, which on this occasion came not from the right wing of the trade union movement but, rather unexpectedly, from a section of what Mr Scargill described as Britain's 'ultra left'. Earlier in the year he had received a letter from the Workers' Revolutionary Party, seeking his views on Solidarity in Poland. Most union leaders refrain from entering into correspondence of this nature, but Mr Scargill wrote back. The WRP's daily newspaper *News Line* decided to publish his reply at a moment when it knew it could cause him maximum embarrassment.

In his letter to the WRP Mr Scargill had said that he wanted to clear up any ambiguity about his position: 'I am opposed to Solidarity because I believe it is an anti-socialist organisation who desire the overthrow of the socialist state.' The publication of these words led to further protests within the TUC, especially from the many delegates who were wearing the red and white badges of Solidarność. But, far from retreating from the criticism, Mr Scargill was ready to take on all comers in the media, giving

64

a masterly performance the following evening during a live television interview on Newsnight.

Mr Scargill preferred being interviewed live on such programmes not only because what he said could not be edited, but also because the presenters rarely had as much detailed knowledge of the miners' union as the specialist correspondents that he would encounter at press conferences and the like. But even in these situations, as we have seen, he had become expert at side-stepping difficult questions whether during a formal news conference or on the doorstep after meetings with management. With a group of reporters all asking questions together, it is quite easy to ignore certain questions and choose which ones to answer. If an industrial correspondent persisted, Mr Scargill could draw on a full repertoire of techniques for intimidating him.

Most studio guests admit to feeling at least some nervousness just before the transmission of a live broadcast, often because they are confused by their surroundings, dazzled by the lights, and do not know which microphone or camera will be used. The presenter, accustomed to working in a studio, has the added benefit of hearing in his or her earpiece the instructions that are being given by the programme director. In such circumstances, once the broadcast starts the guest is often quite willing to allow the interviewer to take control of the discussion.

As a seasoned radio and television performer, Mr Scargill gave every indication that he could follow the sequence of the studio directions even though he could not hear what was being said. His knowledge of the techniques of broadcasting allowed him to pay close attention to the questions. He had realised over the years that presenters are often at a disadvantage themselves, as they have to prepare each day for interviews on several widely different subjects. They are also tied to the studios for long periods, often having to rehearse or pre-record, and so there is always the risk that they may not have had sufficient time to do all the research necessary for an important interview. Even if all the relevant information has been prepared in advance by the programme's own research staff, which is often the case, the presenter still faces the task of assimilating the important details in a short time, while keeping pace with other developing news stories.

Any slight omission in the research is not usually important, as the studio guests are frequently on edge, which gives a competent presenter with a commanding presence every opportunity to skirt round any lack of knowledge or mistake that he may have made. When interviewing Mr Scargill, however, there was no room for any such complacency, for he was always ready to seize on any opportunity to undermine a hostile question that he thought might be ill prepared or mistaken.

The interview on Newsnight which followed the publication of Mr Scargill's letter to the Workers' Revolutionary Party and his visit to Moscow was conducted by Peter Snow, a broadcaster of considerable experience, well versed in international affairs. The NUM president was in a particularly aggressive mood that evening, seemingly determined to deflect the criticism he had faced all week – as Mr Snow quickly discovered when he began the interview by asking why in the speech he had given to the Russians he had not attacked anything President Andropov was saying or doing:

Scargill	Have you read my full speech in Moscow?
Snow	Yes, I have.
Scargill	Have you? I don't believe you. I'm sorry. Have you seen the full text, honestly?
Snow	I have not seen any reference in that text to an attack on what President Andropov's troops are doing in Afghanistan or the military government in Poland.
Scargill	Have you seen the full text, because other broadcasters have told me they have not? Have you seen it, truthfully?
Snow	I have not seen any reference . . .
Scargill	I did not ask that. Have you seen the full text?
Snow	Would you answer my question? [Interruption] Well, I am asking the questions if I may say so.
Scargill	Oh no, not this time, you're not. I am asking you if you have seen the full text.
Snow	Well, to be quite honest, I have not seen the full text.
Scargill	Right, now I will answer your question, now you have admitted you have not seen the full text.

(BBC TV, Newsnight, 8 September 1983)

Here for all to see were Mr Scargill's undoubted skills in presentation and verbal dexterity, demonstrating so well that attack is often the best form of defence at an embarrassing moment. But while he may have been impressed by his own performance on Newsnight, the audience at home may not necessarily have agreed with him. Viewers and listeners build up a warm affection for the presenters they see and hear regularly. They often admire their ability to ask questions on a wide variety of subjects, and they get annoyed when a visitor on a programme is rude, evades the question or tries to make the interviewer look foolish.

Mr Scargill had spent almost the whole week of the TUC conference defending himself on issues that had little immediate relevance to the miners or to the coal industry. When his own reputation was at stake he seemed unable to refuse any request for an interview. The inherent danger in trying to be an expert on too many subjects at once was that it often led to further over-exposure in the news media, which was liable to reduce his credibility when he had to address himself to the central task of representing the miners.

The week that ended with Mr Scargill's appearance on Newsnight had been one of considerable significance for British industry for on 1 September 1983 new chairmen had taken over in three nationalised industries – coal, steel and shipbuilding. The arrival of Ian MacGregor had received most attention, with extensive speculation as to how the new coal board chairman would tackle Mr Scargill. But the first, cordial, meeting between the two men in the second week of September, described in some newspapers as an unexpected honeymoon, was not to be reflected in subsequent encounters. Within seven weeks the miners had banned overtime at the start of what eventually became not only the longest strike in British industrial history, but also one which saw unparalleled participation by radio and television.

FOUR

The Miners' Dispute and the Struggle for Media Supremacy

Once the Conservatives were re-elected in 1983, it was clear that there would come a point when the NUM would have to decide whether to stand and fight over pit closures. Trade union activists saw the miners as the only group that had a chance of taking on the government and halting the loss in industrial capacity, with its continuing haemorrhage caused by redundancies. It was a challenge Mr Scargill could not ignore, yet by the tone and content of his pronouncements to the newspapers, radio and television he had almost invited the media to portray any fight by the miners in personal terms, as an issue that might make or break his authority as president of the miners' union.

The industrial disputes that had taken place in the first four years of the Conservative government had shown that trade union leaders could no longer rely simply on the solidarity of their membership. The fear of redundancy had eroded traditional loyalties. There had been no sustained or successful industrial action in defence of jobs, for organised resistance had been weakened by the growing proficiency of management in communicating directly with the labour force. There was no guarantee that any union would succeed with a mass appeal for support: the two ballots against pit closures that had been held in the first year of Mr Scargill's presidency had both ended in defeat for the union.

The miners were to a degree paying the price for their own success, because in the decade since the 1974 strike and the introduction by the then Labour government of the Plan for Coal, over £4,000 million had been invested in the industry. As the new and improved capacity came on stream, production increased and the miners broke their own productivity records. In February 1983 output reached 10.8 tons per man per shift at the coalface and 2.65 tons per man per shift throughout the industry. The increase had coincided with the peak of the recession, coal production during 1983 having exceeded demand by nine million tons. And that surplus had to be added to what was already a record stockpile of 52 million tons.

An attempt in 1981 to push ahead with a closure programme for the older, uneconomic pits had been abandoned after Mrs Thatcher and the cabinet had decided against a possible confrontation with the miners' union, preferring instead to provide another £300 million on the coal industry's cash limit. But two years later there had been an acceleration in the rate of pit closures, which had doubled under the chairmanship of Sir Norman Siddall. By September 1983 twenty pits had been closed within a year, the most in any twelve-month period for a decade, and after the Conservatives' election victory the government was determined to make a significant reduction in the subsidies that were being paid to the coal industry.

The NCB ended the 1982–3 financial year with a £111 million loss, despite the new productivity records and the receipt of £500 million in government grants. Over half the money was going towards keeping open the thirty most uneconomic pits, with the total subsidy for the whole industry working out at £6 for every ton of coal mined. Events moved quickly in autumn of 1983, with the union realising that it was at a tactical disadvantage because of the record stockpiles of coal at power stations and pit heads. In the fourth week of September, when Mr MacGregor had served less than a month as chairman, the miners' executive decided to call a special delegate conference in October that would decide how best to oppose future pit closures.

Three days after that announcement the annual pay negotiations opened, at which the coal board made what it described as its 'first and final' offer of a 5.2 per cent pay increase. The special conference on 21 October unanimously rejected the NCB's offer, with the delegates voting in favour of an overtime ban that would start at the end of the month as part of a combined campaign to stop pit closures and achieve a higher wage increase. That conference established the link between pit closures and pay, in effect laying the foundation for the strike action that was to follow five months later.

As we have noted, during his three years at British Steel Mr MacGregor had shunned the public spotlight, avoiding a debate in the news media over his plans for the steel industry. And throughout the spring and summer of 1983, while waiting to take over the coal industry, 'the American butcher' had refrained from responding to the many insults that Mr Scargill had heaped on his head. In keeping with this low profile he had played little public part in the initial discussions with the union; instead, he had made a series of visits to the coalfields, often spending several hours underground at individual pits. At the pay talks, the deputy chairman James Cowan had presented the management's case and spoken to the reporters.

Then, after the special conference had voted in favour of the overtime ban there was a second meeting with the miners' leadership at which Mr MacGregor insisted that although the pay offer was final it was a separate issue and not conditional on the union accepting more pit closures. Afterwards, he held a news conference outlining the firm stand that the board had taken: 'When we made our proposal of a 5.2 per cent increase, we emphasised that it was our final offer as well as our first. And we meant what we said. We believe in straight speaking. We are not playing games with our people. There is no more money.' It was to be the first of many blunt statements from Mr MacGregor.

When the overtime ban began on 31 October, Mr MacGregor appeared unconcerned. He had arranged a working breakfast next morning for labour and industrial correspondents, who were told that they must be at the coal board's London headquarters by 8 a.m. as the chairman would begin promptly. He was as good as his word, standing with a glass of orange juice in his hand as the journalists were ushered into the dining-room.

As the breakfast was being served, Mr MacGregor began by showing a series of slides that illustrated world coal prices and the problem that management faced in trying to reduce its costs. The priority for the NCB, he said, was to close eight million tons of uneconomic capacity where the coal was costing anything from £70 to £100 a ton to mine, which was at least twice the selling price. Despite the need to close the loss-making pits, Mr MacGregor was ready to offer a new working relationship with the miners' union, so that they could make a joint approach on the future of the coal industry, as had happened with the Plan for Coal in 1974.

Most of the journalists looked impressed by his presentation. Mr MacGregor had been enthusiastic; he had made out what seemed to be a convincing case for his proposition of a joint management–union approach to the government. As the journalists' breakfast took place on the second day of the miners' overtime ban, the question was immediately raised as to why this same friendly presentation had not been made to the miners' national executive committee. Though they might have disagreed with all Mr MacGregor's conclusions, they could not but have been impressed by his commitment to what he saw as the future for the coal industry and his wish for management and union to tackle the government together. But presumably Mr MacGregor had called in the industrial correspondents at this point in the belief that they could help put his message across to the union. A dynamic hard sell to a group of selected journalists must have seemed potentially more productive than the prospect of having to go through the long grind of negotiations with the miners' union, with all the rituals that this entailed. Mr MacGregor saw the coal industry as a business; he was saying through the journalists that he was ready to do a deal if the miners' union was interested.

As chairman of British Steel Mr MacGregor had grown accustomed to briefing reporters on his own terms, with few of the restrictions that faced other managements fearful that a casual or thoughtless remark from the chairman might provoke industrial conflict. During his three-year chairmanship, the steel unions had been recovering from the 1980 strike, unable to mount any sustained opposition to British Steel's redundancy programme. Therefore Mr MacGregor had not had to negotiate under the threat of industrial action, nor had he been locked into delicate or time-consuming negotiations, and this had given him the freedom to communicate those news stories about British Steel's activities that he and his advisers thought fit.

There was little to suggest that he should change his style or show any concern during the first few weeks of the overtime ban, as management was reporting an actual increase in the rate of productivity, with coal output on most weekdays higher than when the disruption started. As overtime largely involves maintenance work, which is carried out at the weekend in order to prepare the pits for the main Monday-to-Friday shifts, the ban meant that essential maintenance had to be completed first thing on Monday morning. This inevitably delayed the start to that week's production, but as there was normal working throughout the rest of the week, the men had a chance to increase output on the remaining days so as to minimise any loss in earnings or incentive payments.

The determination of the men to protect their own earnings was one consequence of the change in working practices and attitudes that had followed the introduction in 1978 of incentive payments, which had encouraged the miners to work together in small teams, in the knowledge that their joint effort could have a marked impact on what they earned. This greater degree of self-interest had made it harder for the union to mobilise the membership towards industrial action. The two ballot defeats in Mr Scargill's first year as president indicated that the union would have to build up its case before it could expect to succeed by a mass appeal for support. Mr Scargill had introduced measures to improve communications with the membership, turning the union's monthly publication *The Miner* into a campaigning newspaper that gave a more forceful presentation of union policy. He worked closely with his editor Maurice Jones, who had been with him when he was president in Yorkshire, and had edited the *Yorkshire Miner*.

From the start of the overtime ban the union began printing a special weekly edition of *The Miner*, drawing attention to what it described as the 'American-style union-busting techniques' which were being considered by the coal board. Mr MacGregor was reported to be in the process of 'weighing up the possibility of going over the heads of the NUM and trying to influence directly the workforce'. Alongside this report was a personal statement from Mr Scargill in which he gave this warning of the consequences of Mr MacGregor's policies:

His imported American poison has already crippled the workforce at British Leyland and massacred half the jobs at British Steel. But there is perhaps one point above all others, which Mr MacGregor has not fully grasped: this time he is dealing with the National Union of Mineworkers, the oldest and proudest effective industrial union on this planet.

(Arthur Scargill, *The Miner*, special issue, November 1983)

Fleet Street was another frequent target for the NUM's newspaper, with Mr Scargill and his editor rarely losing an opportunity to criticise or ridicule the national press. Maurice Jones recognised that there was no way that the union or *The Miner* could ever match the scale of anti-union publicity that was contained in some of the popular tabloid newspapers, but he believed it was possible to go some way towards reducing the effectiveness of Fleet Street's propaganda. He tried to achieve this by questioning the accuracy, and hence the credibility, of the nationals. *The Miner* highlighted whenever possible any mistakes that were made, in the hope that the NUM membership would then question the reliability of all national newspaper reports.

If there was a misleading item in a national newspaper, the union did everything it could to get a correction. If it was successful, *The Miner* then reproduced both the original report and any reply that was published, in order to draw attention to Fleet Street's inaccuracies. For example, after the *Sun* had suggested in its leader column on 2 November 1983 that Arthur Scargill had forbidden NUM branches to have a ballot on the overtime ban, the union obtained a correction which said that NUM national headquarters had not issued any such instructions. After explaining that the *Sun*'s correction of 4 November had 'cunningly' failed to make any mention of the original mistake, *The Miner* said that such misleading press reports would only increase as the union escalated its campaign for pits and jobs. There was a follow-up in the next issue, with another warning over Fleet Street's behaviour: 'The oldest trick in the journalistic book is already getting into its stride. Totally false stories are now being written about imaginary thousands of miners being at loggerheads with the NUM. Already the distortions and lies are so serious that legal action is being considered against a number of newspapers' (*The Miner*, special issue, November 1983).

When Mr Scargill read the national newspapers each morning he was always on the look-out for any inaccuracy that he thought might give grounds to a claim for damages. Indeed, most journalists who reported on the affairs of the miners' union soon discovered that Mr Scargill would not hesitate to take legal action. In the run-up to the 1981 election campaign for the presidency he had threatened to sue any journalist who repeated the allegations made by another leading contender in the election, Trevor Bell, that there was no satisfactory explanation as to why the Yorkshire NUM, of which Mr Scargill was then president, had declared 4,000 more members than there were miners on the books of the NCB. In January

1983 *The Miner* reported that as a result of a series of libel actions he had been awarded £6,000 in damages, of which, the paper said, every penny had been donated to the union.

Towards the end of December 1983 there was some sign of open opposition to the miners' overtime ban, when winding engine men in North Staffordshire said that they intended to start working normally. The colliery winders, who are responsible for the operation of the pit cages, regularly work overtime and were now losing money; some men had forfeited £70 a week and more, although the average loss in wages was about £30 to £40 a week for the 40 per cent or so of miners who did overtime. The total loss of earnings was added up each week and published in the coal board's own monthly newspaper *Coal News*, which reported in the same month that the coal industry was 'learning to live' with the ban because it was not directly affecting customers. The power stations were reporting that they had 32 million tons of coal in stock, plus the ability to call on the NCB's own pit-head stocks of another 24 million tons.

The management believed that once the Christmas holiday was over there would be increased pressure on the union's leadership to call off the overtime ban, which, it said, had led to a cumulative loss in overtime and incentive earnings of around £30 million. Further disruption had arisen in the North Staffordshire coalfield, where the winders had staged a retaliatory one-day strike in protest at the fact that miners had prevented them from working the previous weekend. This disagreement had prompted the *Sun* to publish its own ballot form on 10 January 1984, asking miners to vote on whether they wanted the ban to continue. The poll was described as 'the ballot that Arthur Scargill won't give you'. There was an immediate response in the next issue of *The Miner*, which accused the *Sun*'s proprietor Rupert Murdoch of conductiong an 'infantile piece of propaganda' against the union.

The colliery winders' protest had little impact at the January meeting of the union's national executive, which unanimously reaffirmed support for the overtime ban in what was then the run-up to the final week's campaigning in the election to appoint a successor to Lawrence Daly, who was retiring as general secretary. The favourite to succeed him was the North Derbyshire general secretary Peter Heathfield, who had campaigned with the endorsement of Arthur Scargill and the rest of the leadership. The two other candidates, John Walsh and Les Kelly, had both campaigned against the overtime ban by urging the union to allow the miners a pit-head ballot on the pay offer. As the ballot to elect a new general secretary took place in the twelfth week of the overtime ban, it was viewed in the news media as a test of rank and file support for the union's policy over the pay dispute and pit closures.

Mr Heathfield was elected by a narrow majority, securing 51.2 per cent

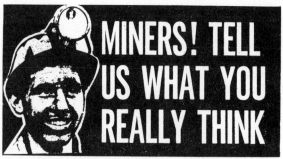

MINERS! TELL US WHAT YOU REALLY THINK

☀ Sun Ballot form

Do you wish to continue with the Mineworkers Union ban on overtime?

YES ☐

NO ☐

COLLIERY WHERE I WORK _ _ _ _ _ _

Send this form to Miners' Ballot, The Sun, Freepost, London EC4B 4NP

● *The address above can ONLY be used in connection with the miners' ballot*

★ CALLING Britain's miners! This is the ballot that Arthur Scargill won't give you.

The Sun today presents its own ballot on the 10-week-old overtime ban which is costing miners and their families an average £50 a week in lost wages.

★ We are asking all of the country's 190,000 miners to vote in this special Sun poll.

It is confidential and it is free. It won't cost you a penny to send back the form. Just tick Yes or No.

We will publish the results as soon as possible.

The NGA and The Sun

The members of the National Graphical Association employed on this paper object to the above ballot paper on the grounds that it interferes with the democracy of the National Union of Mineworkers.

Plate 6 'The ballot that Arthur Scargill won't give you.' Two months before the start of the miners' strike, in response to protests at some pits over the NUM's overtime ban, the Sun *published its own ballot form on 10 January 1984. Two days later, members of the National Graphical Association employed by the* Sun *obtained space for a right of reply for Mr Scargill. The Miner responded to the* Sun's *initiative with its own ballot form asking readers whether they were 'in favour' of Rupert Murdoch owning the* Sun *and the* News of the World, The Times *and the* Sunday Times.

of the total vote, but only on the second count after one of his two opponents had been eliminated. In announcing the ballot result on 23 January, Mr Scargill rebuked the news media for suggesting that the election had in effect become an unofficial referendum on the union's rejection of the NCB's 5.2 per cent pay offer.

Mr Scargill was critical of the way journalists had linked the overtime ban with Mr Heathfield's election campaign, declaring that it was another example of the news media's insistence on personalising industrial disputes. In a signed article in the January 1984 issue of *The Miner*, he accused the press of focusing its attention on that tiny section of the union's membership which had complained most vociferously about losing overtime pay, while totally ignoring major policy statements issued by the union. These statements had been published during the first two months of the overtime ban, in the form of a series of seven well presented and well argued campaign booklets explaining the NUM's policy on a wide range of issues affecting the coal industry, including nuclear power and the possible privatisation of the pits. There was some justification in Mr Scargill's complaint that the statements had not received wide coverage in the newspapers or on radio and television. But the union had failed to make any allowance for established practices within the news media.

When organisations issue major statements in the hope of gaining publicity, it is customary to hold a news conference, or to at least give a date for publication, thus allowing journalists working on rival newspapers and news bulletins an opportunity to publish their reports at the same time, without fear of being beaten by a competitor. Sometimes documents are sent out in advance under the strict condition that there shall be no publication before the specified date. If press releases are sent out without any suggested publication time, as happened with the NUM's policy statements, they can often be ignored because in the day-to-day rush of newsroom life the staff may assume that they are either out of date or have already been published or broadcast elsewhere. To add to the confusion, the documents had been published out of sequence. The NUM was at a further disadvantage during late 1983 because it chose to launch its policy statements at a time when most labour and industrial correspondents were concentrating on a major printing dispute involving the National Graphical Association and the free newspaper proprietor, Mr Eddie Shah.

The most surprising omission was the NUM's failure to hold a news conference to publicise its statements, especially in view of its constant criticism of journalists for personalising news stories about the union by linking them with references to Mr Scargill. The publication of the booklets could have provided the union with an opportunity to organise news briefings without the confrontation that invariably followed negotiations with the coal board or meetings of the national executive. This would have given reporters a chance to question those members of the NUM's staff who had prepared the statements, which in turn would have proved that Mr Scargill was not the only official spokesman for the union, thus lessening the likelihood of personalised reports.

The lack of formal press conferences on policy issues was not an isolated example of the union's failure to take constructive steps towards improving its relations with the media. Another was Mr Scargill's insistence on being the only official spokesman for the national union.

Arthur Scargill was responsible for issuing press statements on behalf of the union, writing almost all of them himself, and then presiding at every news conference. As the official spokesman, his word was final when it came to the presentation of NUM policy. He was assisted by Nell Myers, the NUM's press officer and also the president's personal assistant. She took telephone calls from journalists, read out official statements and arranged interviews for Mr Scargill, but she insisted on seeking instructions from the president before answering or even giving guidance on questions that related to union policy. All other NUM staff employed at the union's headquarters in Sheffield were told not to answer questions from reporters and to refer inquiries to the press officer. Nell Myers lived in London, frequently working at home, and telephone callers would be told to ring her London number if she was not in the office.

Soon after the union moved to Sheffield Mr Scargill instructed the NUM telephone operator to log the time every call was received and the name of the union official asked for by each caller. Mr Scargill introduced this procedure partly in order to keep a record of all calls from the news media, so that if a newspaper or radio or television programme published or broadcast a report in which it said it had been unable to contact him, Mr Scargill was then in a postition to challenge the report if necessary.

His role as official spokesman for the NUM also gave him control over *The Miner*, edited by Maurice Jones. Mr Jones worked separately from Nell Myers, having no responsibility or jurisdiction over the NUM's day-by-day press relations. Neither was he allowed to answer journalists' questions, nor had he any authority to act independently. Each issue of *The Miner* was prepared under Mr Scargill's close supervision, and Mr Jones had to make any changes that the president thought appropriate, right up to the printing deadline. He lacked the independence that exists in those trade unions where the journal editor holds an elected position, as in the case of the National Union of Journalists, which conducts a postal ballot to choose the editor of *The Journalist*. In some other unions that do not hold such elections, the journal editor is still guaranteed a considerable degree of independence. This has become the established practice, for example, in the biggest civil service union, the Civil and Public Services Association, whose annual conference has insisted on the editor of *Red Tape* being allowed the freedom to make editorial judgements.

Many unions insist on editoral independence for their newspapers and journals because it encourages scrutiny of official policy and acts as a check on the leadership. An editor with an independent status can build up his own reputation with journalists, by giving a balanced account of the union's affairs. His knowledge of the media can be used to assist the union internally by providing a frank assessment, without fear or favour, of the way it has been presenting policy issues, especially if the president or general secretary are thought to have mishandled union publicity or needlessly antagonised reporters.

Mr Scargill enjoyed relying on his own judgement when making statements to the press. His skill as a communicator seemed entirely self-taught, acquired through observation; he was held in awe by his staff, many of whom he had selected or recommended for appointment following the union's move to Sheffield.

The one tactical advantage in not holding news conferences on pre-arranged subjects was that when the union held its regular briefings after meetings of the national executive, Mr Scargill could create an element of surprise. This tended to increase journalistic interest, which guaranteed the attendance of a large number of reporters as the newspapers, radio stations and television companies knew that they could not afford to be absent.

Before the journalists crowded in to hear Mr Scargill, some members of his staff would try to reserve seats for themselves, later looking on with obvious admiration at the way the president handled those reporters who asked difficult questions. Midway through the overtime ban the union started making its own video recordings of news conferences, with one member of the NUM staff filming Mr Scargill while another filmed the questioner. When the cameras first appeared after the executive meeting of 12 January 1984 Mr Scargill said in answer to one inquiry that the journalists should examine their own conduct rather than take offence at the union's decision to film and record what he had said.

While the overtime ban continued through the early weeks of 1984, Ian MacGregor made more of the pit visits that he had started soon after taking over as coal board chairman. There was extensive local news coverage of his movements, especially on those occasions when his presence provoked demonstrations. But there was little national interest except for the day late in February when he lay dazed on the ground outside the Ellington colliery in Northumberland, after falling backwards through a fence that had collapsed behind him when he was grabbed by the lapels by a miner protesting at his visit. The previous day he had announced new financial targets for his area directors in an attempt to reduce the size of the NCB's loss – then estimated at nearly £700 million for the 1983–4 financial year.

The following week at an area review meeting miners' leaders in Yorkshire were told of the management's decision to accelerate the closure of the Cortonwood pit near Barnsley. Within days of that announcement, which had led to a call for strike action by Yorkshire's 56,000 miners,

Arthur Scargill and the rest of the union's leadership were told in London by Ian MacGregor of the board's proposal to make another four-million-ton cut in the coal industry's total capacity. In the previous twelve months the rate of pit closures had doubled, twenty-one collieries having closed or merged, with the loss of around 20,000 jobs. Explaining its plans for 1984–5, the coal board again expressed its confidence that the reduction in jobs could be achieved through voluntary redundancies or the transfer of miners to other pits.

Two days after the meeting with Mr MacGregor, the union's national executive decided to give official support to area strikes, which by then had been called in both Yorkshire and Scotland. By the following Monday nearly half the country's miners had stopped work.

The dispute was extended by the 'domino effect', as miners in coalfields like Durham, South Wales and Kent joined men in Yorkshire and Scotland who were already on strike. However, there were immediate demands in other areas, particularly in the East Midlands, for a national pit-head ballot, which led the union's vice-president and Scottish leader, Mick McGahey, to say that the miners most threatened by pit closures were not going to be 'constitutionalised' out of taking industrial action. When the Yorkshire area began sending its members south to picket pits in Nottinghamshire, the coal board moved swiftly to the High Court, securing an injunction on the third day of the strike to stop Yorkshire miners from picketing other collieries. The following day, after a young miner from Yorkshire had collapsed and died on the picket line at Ollerton, near Mansfield, the Nottinghamshire area called on its members to join the strike, only to reverse the decision at the end of the week when an area ballot showed that the Nottinghamshire miners had voted by a 73 per cent majority against strike action. Other coalfields in the East and West Midlands reported equally large majorities against the strike, which reinforced the coal board's decision to keep as many pits as possible open for work, with the backing of the largest number of police that had ever been mobilised for an industrial dispute.

As a trial of strength developed between pickets and police, both union leadership and management seemed surprised by the determination of the working miners to defy the strike. Ian MacGregor and his fellow directors believed the pressure that was building up within the union would force the executive to call a national pit-head ballot. Eight area leaders from coalfields which had voted locally against the strike met near Leicester to organise a direct challenge to Mr Scargill and his supporters on the executive. They called on their members to work normally, believing they could command thirteen votes on the executive – just enough to force a national ballot.

When the executive committee met on 12 April 1984, Mr Scargill ruled that it could not discuss a ballot as a similar motion had been rejected at the executive meeting the previous month. The committee agreed instead to hold a special delegate conference the following week, which Mr Scargill said could order a ballot vote and would be asked to change NUM rules by reducing the majority required for strike action from 55 per cent to a simple majority. The leaders of the working coalfields continued to seek a national ballot, but their efforts were not successful: delegates at the special conference on 19 April approved by 69 votes to 54 a resolution from the Kent area reaffirming the national executive's original decision of 8 March to give official support to area strikes. The campaign to prevent pit closures had united the leaders of the big coalfields of Yorkshire, Scotland and South Wales. The proposed rule change was also agreed, thus reducing the majoirty needed in any future pit-head vote. Mr Scargill had demonstrated his organising ability, successfully outmanoeuvring those coalfields that were against the strike.

In the six weeks that led up to the special conference, the coal board had been doing all it could to encourage moves by the working coalfields to force a national pit-head vote. The April issue of *Coal News* expressed the wish of management in a banner headline: 'National ballot wanted'. But at this point management held back from a major publicity offensive against the union, for fear of jeopardising the position of those area leaders who were campaigning for a ballot.

When, however, the special conference had rejected a pit-head vote, the coal board had no alternative but to dig in for what Ian MacGregor acknowledged was a strike that looked like continuing for 'many, many weeks'. Until then the NCB had done little to explain the need for pit closures, but although the chairman remained implacable, saying he was ready to sit it out, there now seemed a slow realisation among the other directors of the awesome task they faced, in terms of public relations, in having to present and then sustain the case for the four-million ton cut in capacity. The board gave every indication at the time of being caught in the middle of a serious dispute without having given any thought as to how it should communicate with the miners or convince them of the need for change. In the months leading up to the strike that he had spent campaigning against pit closures, Arthur Scargill had rarely met any sustained challenge or opposition from Ian MacGregor.

The two men had a totally different approach when interviewed on radio and television. Mr Scargill, as we have seen ignored most questions in order to get across his own point of view, repeating the same key phrases in every answer, while Mr MacGregor, unlike many public figures, usually gave a straight answer to a reporter's question, whatever the consequences. His public relations advisers prepared statements for him, copies of which were always available for the journalists who attended his news conferences. However, when the chairman was interviewed afterwards, he often seemed quite content to think on his feet, despensing with much of the guidance he had been given beforehand. His conduct infuriated his advisers, and caused consternation amongst the rest of the management, as it soon became evident that once Mr MacGregor started answering questions from journalists he was willing to go along with almost any hypothetical proposition that Fleet Street might suggest as a way of breaking the strike.

Both men were prepared to speak their mind, but while Mr Scargill could if he wished remain tactfully obscure, Mr MacGregor had no time for the diplomatic niceties that were occasionally required to smooth the path of industrial relations. His preference was for short, sharp answers that created the impression that as chairman he was firmly in control, although the abruptness of some of his replies suggested impatience and a lack of tolerance. His one overriding limitation as a communicator was that he seemed to assume, almost certainly unintentionally, that the viewer or listener knew as much about the coal industry as he did. His answers invariably failed either to reflect his own commitment to the mining industry, or to convey any vision of the future that lay ahead for the coal board once it could build on such new technological developments as the Selby coalfield.

Mr Scargill did all he could to exploit the chairman's two other handicaps: his age and the fact that he was a naturalised American. When the strike began Mr MacGregor was seventy-one to Mr Scargill's forty-six, which encouraged the union to make much of the inconsistency of a coal board chairman in his seventies suggesting that miners in their late forties and fifties should accept voluntary redundancy and make way for younger men. And Mr Scargill rarely mentioned the chairman's name without some reference to the need to stop an American old-age pensioner from 'butchering' British industry, and in particular, their industry. While the union tried to build on the hostility the miners might feel towards him Mr MacGregor did not seem unduly concerned, although he did his best to make a virtue of his age and experience, emphasising that he was born in Scotland and wanted to help the recovery of British industry.

Public relations advisers throughout government and industry were in general agreement that it was usually best for ministers and chairmen to avoid a public argument with a union leader, because the level of debate was rarely improved. And while it might be acceptable for a workers' representative to use the everyday language of the street, such freedom of expression was hardly likely to win wider public sympathy or encourage the process of negotiation. Therefore as the strike progressed many industrialists expressed surprise at the enthusiasm that Mr MacGregor showed for the verbal confrontation that was developing between himself and Mr Scargill.

After his low-profile success at British Steel, Mr MacGregor knew there were advantages in remaining silent, yet as the strike wore on he seemed unable to refrain from responding to Mr Scargill's taunts, which only encouraged the news media to personalise its reporting of the dispute. While he remained more or less calm during interviews, when asked to respond to the more insulting comments that had been made about him his expression sometimes revealed that he was irritated and even wounded. At British Steel his policies had been bitterly attacked by the steelworkers' leader Bill Sirs, but there he had not been subjected to personal abuse. He was soon responding to Mr Scargill, taunt for taunt, so that journalists quickly realised that they could rely on the chairman for a good quote, if necessary by provoking one themselves through their questions.

When challenged at a press conference or in an interview, Mr MacGregor tended to fall back on American expressions that were often out of place, providing yet further ammunition for Mr Scargill – as happened in the aftermath of the coal board's decision to withdraw from the legal action it had started in the first week of the strike, when in response to a comment by a BBC interviewer that he was not showing his usual resolute approach, he retorted: 'Don't worry about that, sir. If you want to get into a shoot-out at noon, just let me know.' On another occasion early in the dispute, he referred to the strike as 'a little temporary problem the other side of town'. Mr Scargill joined in: 'Big Mac sounds like an American hamburger and looks like one as well.' Mr MacGregor was ready with his response in the next interview: 'The miners are a damn sight smarter than union leaders who stand and shout at the top of their heads in front of screaming mobs.' This was not the only time that the dialogue was to reach a low ebb.

The chairman's readiness to compete with Mr Scargill in a public confrontation distressed the board's director general of industrial relations, Ned Smith, who believed that the problem of the loss-making pits should have been left for discussion with local management rather than become a national issue. Mr Smith, who began work at the age of fourteen at the former Chislet colliery in Kent, had risen through administration and then management to become head of industrial relations in March 1983. He spent the early weeks of the strike maintaining close contact with leaders of the working coalfields, doing all he could to help them in their efforts to persuade the national executive to call a pit-head ballot. In the sixth week of the strike Mr Smith agreed unexpectedly to give his views on the war of words that had developed between Mr MacGregor and Mr Scargill:

Smith   For myself and many thousands of other people in this industry, who have been in it all their lives, it is very, very unfortunate that we now have a situation developing in which to the world at large this appears to be a head-to-head confrontation between the president of the National Union of Mineworkers and the chairman of the National Coal Board. That is a pity for this industry.

Jones   But they are two people who are on different political courses, aren't they? Mr MacGregor is following the decisions which seem to have been taken by the government, and Mr Scargill is going against them. On that basis isn't there going to be an open confrontation between two people?

Smith   The government don't manage the National Coal Board. The NCB manages the mining industry. We have also always consulted deeply with the NUM and other unions on the management of this industry, and it is a fact if we get a situation in which the politics of either of those individuals confuses the issues in our industry we are going to damage the industry, and that is not what the people in it deserve.

(BBC Radio 4, PM programme, 17 April 1984)

Mr Smith's criticism of the chairman's conduct was the first public expression of the disquiet that was developing among senior management at the coal board. Once the request of the working coalfields for a pit-head ballot was defeated at the special conference later that same week, and as Mr MacGregor and his deputy chairman James Cowan began isolating themselves from the rest of management, Mr Smith and those of his colleagues who had built up a close relationship with the miners' union saw their influence diminish. The chairman's office was assuming total control over every decision affecting the strike and over the negotiations with the union.

Much of the news coverage in the early weeks of the strike concentrated on the demand for a ballot and the efforts of the police to prevent picketing at pits in Nottinghamshire and the other working coalfields. Reporters were constantly asking Mr Scargill why the union would not allow a vote, and whether he was prepared to condemn the violence that was being reported each day. But he was determined not to criticise either those areas which backed the strike or the union's most active supporters who were going regularly on picket-line duty. Each time he was asked to condemn picket-line violence, he turned his reply into an attack on the police or the news media, by suggesting that the reporter should redirect his inquiry to the police. He repeatedly said that it was time Fleet Street and the rest of the media reported the violence being used against the miners.

Long interviews were recorded for radio and television in which Mr Scargill steadfastly evaded questions about a ballot or about the violence. It was the same at news conferences after the national executive and on the doorstep after other meetings. Little was gained by challenging Mr Scargill or by accusing him of not answering the question, as he had a ready supply of responses designed to cause the questioner maximum discomfort. His favourite reply was that he would be quite prepared to give journalists the answers they wanted once Fleet Street started printing the truth.

Mr Scargill's conduct presented the greatest dilemma for the radio and television services, which have a clearly defined responsibility, laid down in the BBC's licence and in the Independent Broadcasting Authority Act, to remain impartial and to broadcast balanced reports on issues of political or industrial controversy. News editors and programme producers were particularly anxious to allow the NUM leadership plenty of opportunity to reply to the working miners who were criticising the areas of the union that were sending flying pickets into those coalfields that had voted against the strike. But Mr Scargill's radio and television interviews were becoming repetitive and unproductive because of his refusal to answer the working miners' complaints. If an interview had been pre-recorded, the broadcasters had the option of cutting the unsatisfactory bits, but on many occasions Mr Scargill was the only senior official – including the area leaders – to have spoken on behalf of the miners that day, and his replies were used to maintain balanced reports.

Within the broadcasting services there is no clearly defined procedure for conducting an interview with a public figure who consistently tries to avoid the issue. The customary response of the interviewer is to try again, perhaps by rephrasing the question, especially if the issue is central to the discussion. If after several attempts a direct answer has still not been given, there is often no alternative but to change the subject. In these circumstances the interviewer can only hope that the listener or viewer will draw his own conclusions. A reporter or presenter has to exercise care if he chooses to go further in challenging the interviewee.

Programme producers are anxious to prevent presenters and reporters from indulging in messy confrontations or sterile arguments which do nothing to help further a general understanding of the subject. When an argument does occur during a live broadcast, the interviewer is well aware that he could be held responsible, which may result in criticism from his editor and possibly from listeners or viewers. If the interviewer is to retain the support of his employer as well as of his audience, he has to refrain from being discourteous or from abusing his position. There will be little support for an interviewer who attempts to ridicule a person who may be refusing to answer the question on a point of principle or because of a deeply held conviction. The restraint that broadcasters exercise in trying to avoid an unseemly argument is largely self-imposed, particularly in the case of political and industrial journalists who have to keep going back to interview the same person.

Arthur Scargill was quite prepared to take advantage of the long-cherished tradition of self-restraint that has evolved in public broadcasting. He had learned by long experience that his persistent refusal to answer questions was unlikely to produce a sustained challenge. One consequence of the attitude he adopted was to encourage radio and television reporters to try their hand at some tough questions, well aware that any hint of aggression on the part of the interviewer could be interpreted by the NUM's supporters as another example of the hostile questioning to which the miners' leader was being subjected.

During the early stages of the strike there were many reporters who would have relished the opportunity to take on Mr Scargill in a live interview, if only they could have been confident that, should an argument develop, they would not be in danger of falling foul of the generally acknowledged standards for public broadcasting. The conventional practice was broken in the sixth week of the strike in an interview broadcast live by Independent Radio News from the studios of Radio Hallam in Sheffield. Each time Mr Scargill evaded a question, he was challenged by the interviewer Chris Mann. An argument developed quite quickly, which continued until the closing moments of the programme:

> *Mann*   Are you afraid of losing a pit-head ballot?
> *Scargill* Are you going to shut up? If IRN or any other independent organisation that you term as independent had the same democratic structures you would have no problems.
> *Mann*   It seems you are incapable of answering any question, Mr Scargill.
> *Scargill* It seems you are the most ignorant person that I have discussed with on radio. Now you are either going to listen to the answers, even if you don't like them, or you are not. It's entirely up to you.
> *Mann*   Mr Scargill, thank you for joining us and, I am afraid, not answering any of our questions here in Sheffield this afternoon. This live interview with the miners' leader Arthur Scargill . . .
> *Scargill* This live interview has been absolutely appalling . . .
> *Mann*   . . . My name is Chris Mann. This is Independent Radio News. It's 1.30.
>
> (IRN, 18 April 1984)

The broadcast provoked an immediate reaction from listeners to the independent radio stations that had transmitted the interview. Some of those who telephoned or wrote letters to IRN complained about the way the discussion had been conducted; other listeners congratulated Chris Mann on standing up to Mr Scargill, saying it was about time that a reporter had challenged the NUM president and exposed his evasiveness. Among the telephone calls received by Radio Hallam and IRN were a number of anonymous threats from callers who said that they were miners and who warned they would be on the look-out for Chris Mann if he tried to report the union's special conference being held in Sheffield the following day. Because of the threats IRN decided Mr Mann should leave Sheffield that evening and return to London.

Mr Scargill was so annoyed by what happened during the discussion that he declared he would not allow himself to be interviewed again by IRN. The IRN editors were divided, some saying the discussion had been effective, others agreeing with IRN's managing director, then George Ffitch, who felt the Mr Mann's conduct had been unprofessional and discourteous. Mr Ffitch believed no interviewer had any excuse for being ill-mannered. On his return to London Chris Mann was taken off the miners' story, and he told me that his newsdesk had informed him that he would not be allowed to do another interview with Arthur Scargill.

IRN's interview was one of the most forthright broadcasts during the dispute. It was mentioned next day by some of the national newspapers, but did not receive anything like the publicity that would have been forthcoming if the same argument had been broadcast at peak time on television, or had involved a well known interviewer. Chris Mann has defended the way he kept on challenging Mr Scargill: he believes that during the strike the radio and television services consistently retreated from their responsibility to those listeners and viewers who wanted to hear Mr Scargill cross-examined as firmly as possible, and who could not understand why he was allowed in effect to dictate his own terms to the news media. But by his interruptions and challenges during the interview, Mr Scargill had demonstrated – if not as effectively as usual – that he would not be forced by the news media to modify his answers. He was still determined to exercise as much control as possible over what he said in the live programmes in which he had agreed to appear.

However, his manner had become increasingly aggressive, as if to use the opportunities afforded by radio and television interviews to hit back at the mounting vilification that he was being subjected to by the Fleet Street newspapers. The personal attacks on Mr Scargill plumbed new depths on 9 May, when the *Daily Express* devoted its front page and centre spread to what it described as the speech the NUM president would be making if he 'cared less about toppling a democratic government and more about the truth'. Mr Scargill's mock speech began with an 'honest' admission:

> We have made no progress at all. Let me tell you frankly that this is the century's most senseless dispute . . . I want to say only this: I have lied. I have lied about coal stocks at the power stations . . . and I have lied when I have told you, over and over, that we are winning. . . . You see, comrades, the fact is, and I'll be perfectly

Plate 7 *The front page and centre spread of the 9 May 1984 issue of the* Daily Express *were devoted to a mock speech – the speech Arthur Scargill would have made, according to the* Express, *if he 'cared less about toppling a democratic government and more about the truth'. When Lord Matthews, the* Express *chairman, refused the following evening to print in full a reply from Mr Scargill, the paper lost all its London editions.*

honest with you, all the struggle, all the pain has been in vain. We won't win. It's all been for nowt.

(Daily Express, 9 May 1984)

The following day the general secretary of the Society of Graphical and Allied Trades, Bill Keys, who represented some of the *Daily Express* printworkers, demanded a right of reply on behalf of Mr Scargill, declaring that he had never seen a more politically biased article in his forty-seven years as a trade union official. Lord Matthews, the *Daily Express* chairman, agreed to print a reply, but when Mr Keys insisted it should appear on the front page the paper's editor Sir Larry Lamb felt that his position had been compromised and offered to resign. However, when Mr Scargill's reply arrived it contained what Lord Matthews described as an introductory page of 'rhetorical abuse' which, he said, was totally unacceptable. Mr Scargill had compared the news coverage of the miners' strike in the *Daily Express* with the techniques of news management practised by Hitler's principal propagandist, Joseph Goebbels.

When Lord Matthews refused to print Mr Scargill's reply in full, Mr Keys responded by threating to stop production of the paper through withdrawing the printworkers, which in turn resulted in the journalists voting not to process Mr Scargill's reply unless Mr Keys withdrew his threat to shut the paper. In the confusion the *Daily Express* lost all the editions that should have been printed in London that night. The following day an agreement was reached with the unions over the content of Mr Scargill's reply, which would no longer have a front-page introduction, and Sir Larry withdrew his resignation. Three days later the centre spread was given over to a 2,000-word article by Mr Scargill which, the *Daily Express* said, was his reply to the mock speech printed the previous week. But on the front page the paper carried a picture of Mr Scargill at a miners' rally in Mansfield, showing him with his arm outstretched. The same picture, headlined 'Mine Fuhrer', was prepared for publication on the front page of the *Sun*, beside a news story which reported that Mr Scargill had given his supporters a 'Hitler-style salute'. When the printworkers saw the front page they refused to allow production to continue, and the *Sun* eventually appeared without either the picture or the headline, the blank space filled with the following explanation: 'Members of all the *Sun* production chapels refused to handle the Arthur Scargill picture and major headline on our lead story. The *Sun* has decided, reluctantly, to print the paper without either' (*Sun*, 15 May 1984).

The retaliatory action taken by the *Sun*'s printworkers was hailed by the Campaign for Press and Broadcasting Freedom as another example of the pressure that was building up over media bias against the miners. There had been regular contact between the miners' union and representatives of the Campaign, which, since its founding in 1979, had attracted affiliation

Sun picture special

MINE FUHRER

Sam . . . and her vital assets

Sam's assets insured for £¼m

SUN EXCLUSIVE

By JOHN KAY

PAGE Three stunner Samantha Fox is insuring her biggest assets . . . for a whopping £250,000.

She fears an accident to her breasts could leave her flat broke.

So Samantha's agent asked insurance giant Lloyds to come up with some suitable cover.

Under the five-year policy Samantha's boobs will be insured against sagging, shrinking, health risks or accidents.

Stunned

Agent Yvonne Paul said: " When we asked Li. yds there was a stunned silence.

" But they're now working .ut a premium."

The amazed insurance men till had a few worries to get

Continued on Page 3

By CHARLES RAE and BRIAN DIXON

MINERS' leader Arthur Scargill gives a Hitler-style salute as he addresses his supporters at a mass rally yesterday.

The gesture was made by Mr Scargill as thousands of striking pitmen poured into Mansfield, Notts.

The big demo passed off peacefully — but after the miners' president left for his Sheffield headquarters, a bloody flare-up left 20 hurt.

CLASHED

Miners spilled out of pubs at closing time and clashed violently with police.

Several officers were felled by stones and bottles. Strikers were dragged to the ground.

And police staged mounted cavalry charges in

Continued on Page Four

£40,000 BINGO! *Today's lucky numbers on Page 16*

Plate 8   This lay-out of the Sun's front page, describing Arthur Scargill as giving 'a Hitler-style salute', was prepared for publication on 15 May. Members of the National Graphical Association, objecting to both the headline and the picture, refused to allow production to continue.

THE Sun

Tuesday, May 15, 1984   16p   TODAY'S TV: PAGE 12

Sam . . . and her vital assets

Sam's assets insured for £¼m

By JOHN KAY

P A G E Three stunner Samantha Fox is insuring her biggest assets . . . for a whopping £250,000.

She fears an accident to her breasts could leave her flat broke.

So Samantha's agent asked insurance giant Lloyds to come up with some suitable cover.

Under the five-year policy Samantha's boobs will be insured against sagging, shrinking, health risks or accidents.

Stunned

Agent Yvonne Paul said: " When we asked £¼.yds there was a stunned silence.

" But they're now working out a premium."

The amazed insurance men till had a few worries to get
Continued on Page 3

Members of all The Sun production chapels refused to handle the Arthur Scargill picture and major headline on our lead story. The Sun has decided, reluctantly, to print the paper without either.

By CHARLES RAE and BRIAN DIXON

M I N E R S ' leader Arthur Scargill gives a Hitler-style salute as he addresses his supporters at a mass rally yesterday.

The gesture was made by Mr Scargill as thousands of striking pitmen poured into Mansfield, Notts.

The big demo passed off peacefully — but after the miners' president left for his Sheffield headquarters, a bloody flare-up left 20 hurt.

CLASHED

Miners spilled out of pubs at closing time and clashed violently with police.

Several officers were felled by stones and bottles. Strikers were dragged to the ground.

And police staged mounted cavalry charges in
Continued on Page Four

£40,000 BINGO! *Today's lucky numbers on Page 16*

Plate 9   The 15 May edition of the Sun *as finally published.*

from the major trade unions representing journalists, printworkers, broadcasters and radio and television technicians. The Campaign was soon extending its work on behalf of the miners, from Fleet Street to the whole of the country, issuing a checklist of advice for each NUM area. Local solidarity committees were urged to appoint someone to monitor media coverage and watch for any examples of bias that deserved a right of reply. The areas were advised to establish contact with local branches of the unions representing media workers, so that the branch officials working for local newspapers, radio stations and television companies could then exert whatever pressure they could on the relevant editor or programme producer.

In the space of a few months the printworkers successfully challenged the editors and proprietors on several other occasions. In January 1984 the National Graphical Association had obtained both a disclaimer and the right of reply for Mr Scargill, after the *Sun* had published its own 'ballot form' for miners. In February NGA members at the *Sunday Times* secured equal space for Arthur Scargill in which to reply to an article by Ian MacGregor and a similar right of reply was obtained for the NUM president in the *News of the World* and the *Observer*.

By the end of June the print unions were ready to launch a co-ordinated demand for the right of reply. Each national newspaper was asked to publish a printworkers' statement of solidarity with the NUM, as part of a day of action in support of the miners organised by the south-east region of the TUC. Some papers printed the statement as a news item or as a letter to the editor; others insisted on it being published as an advertisement; but three papers, the *Sun*, *Daily Mirror* and *Financial Times*, failed to appear after their managements refused to print the message, which declared that 'the men and women who make your daily newspapers are resolute in their support of the miners.'

The action of the print unions prompted indignant comments from members of the Conservative Party. The Minister of State for Industry, Kenneth Baker, accused the Fleet Street unions of dressing up their anti-libertarian action as a democratic demand for a right of reply, when in fact the miners' case had been presented forcefully and eloquently in the media, with Mr Scargill having had much greater television exposure than Mr MacGregor.

The first three months of the dispute saw a rapid deterioration in relations between the strikers and those who worked for the news media. Some television crews had been threatened and attacked when filming picket-line violence. The pickets' distrust of the reporters and cameramen was a reflection of the anger felt both by rank and file and by leadership over the way much of the television news coverage of the strike had concentrated on the violent incidents. Television crews were vulnerable when filming picketing because they were instantly recognisable through the equipment they carried, and journalists from the popular newspapers were careful, whenever possible, not to reveal their identity, as strikers outside many pits had made it clear that all newsmen were unwelcome.

Reporters felt particularly uneasy when covering rallies or meetings addressed by Mr Scargill, for he began almost every speech with an attack on the news media, criticising not only the Fleet Street editors, the BBC and ITN, but every working journalist. One member of the TUC general council who shared a platform with Mr Scargill in the third month of the strike afterwards expressed his alarm to me on seeing young miners in the audience start threatening journalists and photographers when the president criticised the media. The reporters usually did little to attract attention, although at one rally in London, which formed part of a mass lobby of the House of Commons, the stewards moved the journalists and photographers away from the platform and tried to marshall them together in one indentifiable group. As the welcoming cheers subsided Mr Scargill directed his opening words to the reporters, explaining why he was careful not to make any gesture which Fleet Street might have taken for a salute:

I wanted to wave to all the union members here, had it not been for the fact that one of these vermin here might have taken a photograph of me waving my arm in the air and then written something underneath it. [Cheers.] Throughout this dispute, day after day, television, radio and the press have consistently put over the view of the coal board and government and even when the board and government have been exposed as being guilty of duplicity and guilty of telling lies, not only to the House of Commons but also to the British public, this bunch of piranha fish will go on supporting Mrs Thatcher. [More cheers.]

(Arthur Scargill, miners' rally, Jubilee Gardens, London, 7 June 1984)

The suggestion that all journalists were guilty of biased reporting and of supporting Mrs Thatcher was typical of the insults that the reporters had come to expect from the NUM president. He had attacked all sections of the media, while doing nothing to improve the channels of communication between the union and those specialist newspaper, radio and television reporters who had been covering the strike full-time, and who were members of the Labour and Industrial Correspondents' Group. The television correspondents were most concerned about the violent threats being made against cameramen and sound recordists. They thought Mr Scargill was being somewhat hypocritical in complaining about the omission from news bulletins of reports on his speeches, when young miners were threatening television crews in response to the president's own attacks on the media. At one rally in Mansfield there was so much abuse that the cameramen were unable to film all of Mr Scargill's address.

The greatest operational difficulty for all correspondents was the lack of official spokesmen who could give information on behalf of the NUM. The only point of contact, as mentioned earlier, was the union's press officer Nell Myers; and as she was also Mr Scargill's personal assistant and sometimes accompanied him on major engagements, there were inevitably long periods when she was inaccessible and when there was no one else in the union who was willing or had the authority to speak to the media. Although journalists could leave messages and their telephone numbers on the answering machine at Nell Myers' London home, there was no guarantee that they would get a call back, as Mr Scargill had instructed her not to answer questions from certain journalists: he believed the union had little to gain in making contact with the representatives of those newspapers which had been most critical of the miners.

There was no reliable system for making immediate contact with the union at area level, either. Although many of the local presidents and general secretaries had been willing, initially, to speak to reporters (and some were also prepared to supply their home telephone numbers), as the picketing intensified, so did the animosity towards journalists. The distrust was so great that some local strike headquarters would not accept calls from the media, and reporters who went in person were refused admission. From the start of the dispute journalists found the utmost difficulty in obtaining daily figures from the union on the number of miners on strike or at work. And the need for up-to-date statistics became greater as the strike progressed.

Press officers employed by trade unions usually find they are heavily outnumbered by the large staff of public relations advisers that most big companies and nationalised industries employ. In previous disputes some unions have drafted in extra help to cope with telephone calls and to prepare news releases, and in some involving healthworkers and civil servants the individual unions have co-operated and even pooled their resources, so as to provide a constant flow of information about the impact of their action and the likely consequences for the public. But no such contingency plans appeared to have been considered by the miners' union.

In total contrast to the NUM, the coal board employed twenty-three public relations officers who were authorised to speak to reporters. Five were based at NCB headquarters in London, and the rest divided up between six regional offices. All twenty-three took telephone calls at home and a rota system ensured that there was a press officer on call in London and most of the areas each evening and at weekends. In addition, there were another fifteen members of staff in the NCB's public relations department in London who worked either on *Coal News* or on the preparation of films and exhibitions.

The difficulties that journalists were encountering with the miners' union had been the subject of discussion for some weeks within the Labour and Industrial Correspondents' Group. In an attempt to repair the deterioration in relations, the Group asked for a meeting with the new general secretary, Peter Heathfield. Although he had been in office for less than four months, the correspondents thought it was an opportune moment for a meeting, especially as most of the reporters had experienced an easy-going and constructive relationship with Mr Heathfield when he had been an area general secretary in North Derbyshire. The delegation from the group committee which saw Mr Heathfield on 11 June 1984 armed itself with a list of what it hoped would be regarded as helpful suggestions for improving media relations with the NUM.

Although acknowledging that the Group was genuinely concerned and had some constructive ideas, Mr Heathfield said he could see no immediate likelihood of the NUM seeking the assistance of temporary press officers from the National Union of Journalists, or from any other union that might be sympathetic to the miners. Mr Scargill was responsible for issuing press statements on behalf of the NUM, he said, and even if the union brought in extra press officers he thought it doubtful if they would be authorised to speak at either a national or local level. When a member of the delegation suggested that the union might get more publicity if information flowed more freely, Mr Heathfield said that the president had no difficulty in securing press coverage – it had become one person's almost full-time job to cut out and paste up Mr Scargill's collection of newspaper cuttings. It was clear that while Mr Heathfield was prepared to speak to the news media, he had every intention of abiding by Mr Scargill's wish that the president should be the NUM's main spokesman.

The other major issue discussed with Mr Heathfield was the violence being experienced by some journalists. While accepting that the union could not predict what might happen on an individual picket line, the correspondents inquired whether the NUM could appeal to its member-ship to refrain from threatening reporters and television crews. At least, they said, members might assist the news media at major rallies and marches by nominating an NUM marshal or steward to be an official point of contact to whom the newsmen could report, who could intervene if any incident developed, and who would at the same time have an opportunity to monitor the behaviour of the journalists and photographers. Mr Heathfield promised that this suggestion would be examined: he could see no justification for journalists being manhandled at miners' rallies, and if this had occurred, he said, it was a reflection of the hostility engendered by the Fleet Street tabloids. According to him, Mr Scargill's family felt equally vulnerable when reporters and photographers waited day and night outside his house and followed Mrs Scargill to work.

Later, in an exchange of correspondence, the Group listed a total of fifteen proposals for improving the balance of news media coverage. When Mr Heathfield replied on 25 June he emphasised the NUM's wish to 'establish better relations' with industrial correspondents. He repeated that there was some merit in the possibility of appointing one or two media marshals, but he made it clear that the NUM was unable to respond to the other fourteen suggestions. The experience of the public relations department attached to Mr Scargill's office was that many NUM statements had either not been published or had been 'so severely mutilated' that the ensuing publicity was of little value. Daily statistics on the state of the strike were not readily available, as the NUM had no facility for logging accurately that kind of information.

A fortnight after the group had met Mr Heathfield, I had a long discussion with Mr Scargill over his motives behind the public hostility that he had been displaying towards reporters. I had suggested in several of my reports that he was often abusive to journalists on purpose because he knew it struck a responsive chord among his most active supporters. If the news media could be represented, almost like the police, as another symbol of authority and of the repression of the capitalist system, then this would help the NUM president portray the miners' struggle as a fight between the working class and the full forces of the British establishment. Mr Scargill was quick to dispute my analysis, but agreed with a number of my observations. He explained how some years earlier he had taken a calculated decision to include in his speeches an attack on the news media, believing the applause this provoked proved there was widespread concern among union members and the public over the news values and judgements of Fleet Street, the BBC and ITV. He had no alternative but to criticise all reporters in the same breath, for he remained convinced that journalists were like piranha fish: if need be they would eat each other to get to the juiciest story.

Of all his explanations, perhaps the most revealing was his justification for questioning the integrity of individual reporters and the organisations for which they worked. The president had found over the years that his policy of accusing them of bias had not only increased his own newsworthiness but also created an air of self-doubt among the journalists themselves, which he hoped might lead eventually to a reduction in biased reporting.

Arthur Scargill's knowledge of the workings of the media was not limited to Fleet Street; only the week before, on 18 June, he had presented his own filmed report for ITN's Channel 4 News. Both he and Ian MacGregor had been supplied with a television crew and offered the opportunity to prepare their own reports on pit closures, thus presenting the respective arguments of the NCB and the NUM. Part of Mr Scargill's report was filmed during early June outside the derelict colliery beside the coking plant at Orgreave, near Sheffield, where there had been violent picketing over a period of some days as miners tried to prevent the British Steel Corporation from using lorry convoys to move out supplies of coke. The programme was welcomed by those who had argued for a right of reply for the miners. The Campaign for Press and Broadcasting Freedom congratulated Channel 4 on showing the way for a new type of broadcast journalism, which, it said, could replace the usual 'impartial' and 'balanced' reporting – the alleged 'consensus' – with programmes that might include several understandings of an issue.

Mr MacGregor's report illustrated the changes that had taken place in the coal industry, showing the modern mining complex the board was developing at Selby in Yorkshire. This was compared with earlier working conditions by the use of old film of men working with horses underground and of women washing coal. Mr MacGregor explained that too much coal was still being produced from costly, time-expired pits, which should have been closed under the agreement reached in the Plan for Coal. New investment was going ahead but, he said, the uneconomic capacity had to be reduced. Surplus production of eight million tons in the 1982–3 financial year had been cut back to four million tons in 1983–4; around 20,000 jobs had been eliminated that year through natural wastage, and the board's proposals for 1984–5 were a continuation of that policy.

When the two television films were ready, Mr Scargill was informed by Channel 4 that they would be transmitted the following Monday, 18 June – which turned out to be the day of the 'Battle of Orgreave', when, according to South Yorkshire police, ten thousand pickets were to face four thousand policemen in the biggest demonstration of the strike, as the miners again tried to stop the lorry convoys leaving the coking plant. Among those injured that day was the NUM president, who had been seen earlier on in the demonstration giving instructions to picket marshals over a walkie-talkie set. The newspapers descibed it as 'Bloody Monday' when, according to the *Daily Express*, a 'trembling, rubber-legged Arthur Scargill' had to be helped to his feet by ambulancemen. That evening ITN's film of a policeman using his baton at the Orgreave picket was just one of the images that dominated the opening sequence of the Channel 4 News. There followed film of a bedside interview with Mr Scargill, recorded late that afternoon while he recovered in Rotherham hospital, where he spent the night under observation.

The hospital interview was the perfect cue for the next item in the programme – Mr MacGregor's, then Mr Scargill's, filmed report. At the time of transmission Mr Scargill was sitting up in bed in his orange pyjamas. As an avid viewer of television news, he must have afforded himself a smile as the credits rolled. The presenter Peter Sissons gave the NUM president the ultimate accolade: 'That report by Arthur Scargill'.

A week after the Orgreave picket I had a conversation with Mr Scargill during which the one subject he wanted to discuss was his television broadcast. He told me that when he had been advised that his film would be transmitted on 18 June, he had told the Channel 4 editors that they had chosen a particularly appropriate day, although at the time he refused to say why this should be so. He had enjoyed working with the television crew, and was well satisfied with his report. He was, however, like any

Plate 10 Arthur Scargill with headphones and a hand-held lip microphone. He frequently displayed his mastery of the technicalities of broadcasting, and sometimes would spend much of the day going from one studio to another for live radio and television interviews.

television performer, anxious for some feedback. 'What did you think of that first miner I interviewed?' he asked me. 'It wasn't planned like that. It just clicked into place.' I asked him if he had found it difficult to memorise what he wanted to say: 'You mean my walk-in shot to camera? Oh, that was easy.' It had taken him longer than he had expected to write and time his script for the voice-over that was recorded in the studio to fit the pictures, but he had soon got used to the technique.

Mr Scargill had mastered the jargon of television news production – 'walk-in shot', 'voice-over' – faster than some union leaders memorise their own rule book. He had obviously been an enthusiastic reporter, yet his interest in the workings of television news seemed somehow out of place for the man who was leading the miners in what was then the sixteenth week of a national strike.

The Channel 4 report had been filmed during a busy period for Arthur Scargill, when he was involved both in organising the Orgreave picket and in presenting the union's case at series of informal discussions with the National Coal Board. The opening weeks of the strike had gone by without any meeting between union leadership and management. Ian MacGregor would not accept the NUM's precondition that the board must first withdraw the proposals of 6 March for the four-million-ton reduction in output and the loss of 20,000 jobs. Leaders of the other mining unions and senior figures in the Labour Party worked behind the scenes in an attempt to conciliate, but it was the eleventh week of the strike before the board and the union finally reached agreement on a basis for talks.

The full national executive met management on 23 May, only to leave the the board's headquarters after just over an hour, blaming the breakdown on Mr MacGregor, who was said to have replied 'no comment' when asked by Mr Scargill to withdraw the closure proposals. Although the NUM president accused Mr MacGregor of treating the miners with contempt, the union accepted an invitation for a further informal meeting between management and the NUM's three national leaders.

The second round of talks took place well away from the usual glare of publicity, in Yorkshire on 31 May, the day after Mr Scargill was arrested at Orgreave for obstruction, in the build-up to the mass picket the following month. The meeting was significant because here, for the first time, the management team started discussing with the union those areas that might form the basis for a possible settlement: it was the first indication by the coal board of a willingness to give ground.

That evening at a miners' rally in Islington, Mr Scargill gave a speech that reflected the confidence he felt following his discussions with management earlier in the day. He reiterated the determination of the union to resist closures and redundancies, and claimed that the government was scared stiff by the escalating cost of the strike, as the bill for extra oil for the power stations was already twice that for the Falklands War. There had been a record trade deficit the month before which, said Mr Scargill, explained why the City of London was worried by the prospect of a prolonged strike. It was the speech of a union leader who thought he was winning a dispute.

Next morning news bulletins on BBC Radio 4 carried a report of his speech. When the coal board directors heard a tape-recording of the same news summary later in the day, they were concerned at the speed with which Mr Scargill had taken advantage of the concessions outlined by management only hours earlier at the talks in Yorkshire. Correspondents speculated as to exactly what the board was conceding; my own inquiries indicated that the NCB did have new proposals, which it wanted to discuss with the union at a meeting tentatively arranged for the following week. When I was asked on the World at One what the new proposals might contain I said:

It is a question of degree. At the moment the union seems confident that the National Coal Board has almost admitted it won't now go ahead with the closure of the Cortonwood colliery in Yorkshire, which was at the start of the dispute, or the Snowdown pit in Kent, which is another one which is threatened, or Polmaise in Scotland.

97

> Now that's not enough for Arthur Scargill. He wants more.
> (Nicholas Jones, BBC Radio 4, World at One, 1 June 1984)

The close attention that the NCB paid to news broadcasts was illustrated immediately after the programme, when there was a telephone call to BBC radio from the coal board's director of public relations, Geoffrey Kirk, to say that one statement in the interview was inaccurate. He had been advised by those directors who had met the miners' leaders the day before that there had been no discussion at all on the future of individual collieries. Nor did the board's area directors in Yorkshire, Scotland or Kent know of any such plan to safeguard the future of the pits mentioned in the programme. Mr Kirk stressed that he had been told to contact me immediately, and hoped the information I had given on the World at One would not be repeated. There was no way of checking back instantly with the original source of the information, and in the face of Mr Kirk's adamant denial I decided there was no alternative but to amend my later broadcasts by deleting all reference to the likelihood of the coal board offering to safeguard the future of the three pits. My decision was a personal one, based largely on the respect which the labour and industrial correspondents had for Mr Kirk. He had served as director of public relations under three previous NCB chairmen, having been with the board since nationalisation in 1947.

Within days of my broadcast there was speculation by other journalists about the possibility of the board going some way to guarantee the future of collieries such as Cortonwood and Polmaise. The following month the NCB confirmed in full the original news item on the World at One, when during a break in negotiations it published details of four specific proposals made to the union. The second proposal stated: 'The following collieries referred to specifically by the NUM – namely (a) Polmaise, (b) Herrington, (c) Cortonwood, (d) Bullcliffe Wood, (e) Snowdown – will be the subject of further consideration' (NCB draft agreement, 9 July 1984).

Mr Kirk's intervention over the World at One broadcast showed the lengths to which the coal board was prepared to go to prevent the premature disclosure of sensitive information about its negotiating position.

The board's ability to mount an immediate challenge over the accuracy of a broadcast is facilitated by the speed with which transcripts of radio and television programmes can be obtained. Recordings or transcripts are usually essential, because few people can memorise with complete accuracy the whole of a statement or interview that they have probably heard only once. In order to meet the demand for transcripts, several firms have established a regular business copying and transcribing radio and television programmes. The main customers for this expensive service tend to be government departments, nationalised industries, big companies and certain pressure groups. The firm that works for the coal board uses facsimile equipment which enables a copy of a typed transcript to be transmitted by telephone direct to NCB headquarters within about an hour of the original broadcast.

As the strike progressed the NCB began to publicise only those facts and figures which would benefit the management's case, such as the number of miners who had decided to ignore the strike and work. Under Geoffrey Kirk's leadership, the board's public relations department had taken great pride in the reputation it had established for accurate and unambiguous public statements. As the first of the nationalised industries, the NCB had from its earliest days operated an open style of management which had ensured over the years that the employees were provided with an unparalleled degree of access to information about the board's perform-ance and work practices. No other state-owned concern could boast such an extensive network of consultative machinery in which the trade unions participated. These traditions had benefited the news media, which rarely had cause to doubt the reliability of the board's public statements.

The NCB began to build up its publicity against the strike soon after the delegate conference had voted in April 1984 to reject a pit-head ballot. Ian MacGregor decided to bring in experts from outside, and the new offensive was planned and co-ordinated from his office. In May, two months after the start of the strike, he appointed a private consultant to advise on public relations, advertising and communications. This was Tim Bell, international chairman of the advertising agency Saatchi and Saatchi, who had been advising Mr MacGregor since 1977, the year he was appointed deputy chairman of British Leyland. Mr Bell was a founder member of Saatchi and Saatchi and had been responsible for the Conservative Party's advertising account, having produced their 1978 campaign entitled 'Labour isn't working.'

Even before the strike began, Mr MacGregor had tried to improve communications with the miners, and in February had recorded a message on video tape which explained the need for the closure of uneconomic pits. When he used video at British Steel, the corporation had arranged for steelworkers to be taken off shift in order to see the chairman's message. The NUM, however, asked miners not to attend the showings of the NCB video. In the face of the union's refusal to co-operate, management eventually withdrew the cassettes, especially since in some coalfields there had been threats to smash cassette machines or television sets found showing the video.

After the initial failure with video, the board began to introduce other communication techniques used by employers in previous disputes. They achieved an immediate success when they advertised a Freefone number of the kind used by British Rail during the train drivers' strike in 1982. The NCB wanted to make contact with those miners who might be prepared to volunteer for redundancy, as both they and the government were confident that the required 20,000 reduction in the labour force could be obtained entirely through natural wastage. On 8 March, two days after Mr MacGregor had announced the NCB target of a four-million-ton cut in capacity, the board published details of a major improvement in its redundancy payments in an attempt to persuade more men under fifty to leave the pits. Details of the new redundancy payments were recorded on telephone tape machines which were installed from April onwards in each of the board's six regional headquarters. Miners who wished to hear more about the redundancy terms were invited to make a free call to the board. After hearing the message the caller was asked either to ring another local office in his own area or to give his name and address so that the information could be recorded and his inquiry followed up at a later date.

Redundancy payments in the coal industry are paid for by the government – at a cost to the taxpayer of £189 million in the 1983–4 financial year. The board estimated that well over £200 million would be needed in 1984–5, as management had decided to lower the qualifying age, which had been 50, in order to attract younger men. Miners aged 21 to 49 were now told that they would be entitled to lump-sum payments of £1,000 for each year's service from the age of 16, on top of the redundancy payment already guaranteed by the state. The severance terms for miners aged 50 to 64 were already the best available for any industrial worker in Britain, allowing a miner aged 54, for example, to qualify for a cash payment of £24,128, plus an additional payment of up to £78.75 a week until the age of 65. By widening the scheme to include younger men miners aged 21 to 49 could qualify for total lump-sum payments ranging from £5,217 to £36,480, depending on their age.

Staff at NCB regional offices were overwhelmed by the number of calls received through the Freefone system. Many miners used the normal telephone numbers, as they found the special lines were constantly engaged. Management acknowledged that some of the inquiries might be from strikers trying to block the lines in order to disrupt the board's work, but nuisance calls were far outweighted by the number of miners asking for information. In Yorkshire 1,000 calls were received in the first twenty-four hours; in Northumberland and Durham 2,110 miners left their names and addresses in the first three days. Within a week 12,000 inquiries had been received from miners throughout the country, and after six weeks the total reached 21,000 – more than the NCB's original requirement for a 20,000 reduction in manpower.

Although some members of management wanted the redundancies to begin at once, the NCB was prevented from taking immediate steps to pay off all those strikers who had volunteered to leave, since employees have to have been at work for up to three months before redundancy payments can be made. However, this did not detract from the breakthrough the board had achieved, because once it had received over 20,000 inquiries it could proclaim publicly, with some degree of confidence, that the required reduction in manpower could be obtained voluntarily without any need for compulsory redundancies. The list of men who wanted to leave the industry was to prove of considerable value to the board, once it started encouraging miners to give up the strike. Pit managers had the names and addresses of 21,000 men who might be tempted to return to the pits, because they could not qualify for redundancy payment unless they were back at work.

The response achieved by the NCB had proved the value of Freefone as a system for contacting workers during a controversial or violent strike: the employee was able to establish contact with his employer in the privacy and safety of this own home. There was no need to ask the striker to put anything in writing, and no fear of immediate indentification by neighbours or fellow workers. Towards the end of the strike, once the return to work had gathered pace, the NCB put up notices at the pits giving another Freefone number, on which miners could telephone management if they felt they were being intimidated at work or had worries about the safety of their families.

The scale of the response to the redundancy Freefone was a reflection of the care that had gone into the board's efforts to persuade miners to inquire about early retirement. The campaign had started off with the publication of a centre-page spread in the April issue of the NCB's *Coal News*, which listed examples of the redundancy payments that could be obtained by any miner aged between twenty-one and sixty-four. *Coal News*, established over twenty years earlier, had become an important means of communication within the industry, with thirteen area editions giving local coverage of the individual coalfields. It had built up a reputation for balanced reporting through the space it devoted to union affairs and by providing a forum for discussion on controversial issues, often allowing the mining unions an opportunity to state their case side-by-side with management. Unlike most staff newspapers, *Coal News* had to be purchased, and the income from the cover charge of eight pence was shared between the cost of production and various pit charities.

Once the strike started, the NCB decided to follow the example of other major employers and post *Coal News* free of charge direct to the homes of the men on strike, instead of continuing to sell it at the pit head or by subscription. The newspaper was one of the few means of direct communication that was instantly available to manangement, and as soon as the April issue had been mailed to miners in the areas on strike, the board followed it up with local newspaper advertisements which gave details of the Freefone numbers. The coal board's advertising agency, CM Partnership, realised that by the time the miners had been on strike for over a month many of them would be so short of money that they would probably have cancelled their newspaper orders with the local newsagent – might, indeed, have stopped buying daily or weekly newspapers altogether. In fact, Mick Carter, the NUM pit delegate at Cortonwood in

Yorkshire, told me later that most miners at his colliery had cancelled their orders within the first fortnight. So in an attempt to reach all strikers' homes, the agency made every effort to place as many advertisements as possible in the free local newspapers which were being distributed in the mining communities.

In the late 1970s and 1980s there had been a marked increase in the spread of free newspapers. The number of separate titles had risen from 194 to 730 in the space of a decade. By 1984, the Association of Free Newspapers estimated, 80 per cent of British homes were receiving one or more free papers, compared with less than 50 per cent in 1979. Their widespread distribution often made them more cost-effective for advertising than the established weekly newspapers, which had to be purchased and which might have a lower circulation. The year of the miners' dispute was an important one in the development of free newspapers: not only were they used for the first time to carry an employer's advertisements during a national strike, but their total advertising revenue reached £224 million, finally overtaking the advertising income of the paid-for local weekly papers.

By the mid-1980s publishers of free weekly newspapers claimed saturation coverage in most urban areas, guaranteeing that a copy of each issue was distributed without charge to every household in the localities they served. The CM Partnership regarded this new advertising medium as an effective means of communication for the NCB during the strike, because there seemed every chance that an advertisement in a free local paper would be seen by most strikers and their families. By the end of the campaign, CM Partnership estimated that about a quarter of the NCB's local advertising budget was going to such newspapers.

Advertising was to become one of the principal forms of communication for the NCB during the strike, much of the emphasis going on campaigns in the national newspapers. Tim Bell of Saatchi and Saatchi – who was employed, as we have seen, as Ian MacGregor's private consultant – considered large newspaper advertisements gave the board an opportunity to outline its position in a clear and straightforward manner. In the management's experience radio and television news bulletins and newspaper reports rarely gave a complete or entirely accurate presentation of what the board was proposing, especially on those occasions when negotiations finished late at night, well after the transmission time for the main news programmes and the deadlines for the printing of the national newspapers.

In the fourth month of the strike the NCB placed a series of full-page advertisements in the national newspapers, all under the same banner headline, 'How the miners on strike have been misled', and claiming that the miners had been 'deliberately misled by their leaders'. There was no mention of the NUM itself or any attempt to question the men's loyalty to it; the NCB's intention was to persuade the miners to re-examine what they had been told by their own leadership. Arthur Scargill was not referred to, but the same sentence, printed at the end of each advertisement, constituted in effect a reply to one of his favourite taunts – that the NCB was out to 'butcher' the industry. It read: 'It is the strike – not the Coal Board – that could butcher the industry.' The six separate advertisements appeared over a seven-day period at an estimated cost of £1 million.

The first advertisement followed up the board's success in obtaining inquiries for voluntary redundancy, by confidently proclaiming that it was incorrect for miners' leaders to suggest that men were about to be thrown on the scrap-heap:

Not one single compulsory redundancy has been asked for in the past three years, or this year. About 20,000 jobs went last year – all of them on the basis of voluntary redundancy and all with very generous redundancy pay. We are sure that we will be able to do this again. No one who wants to stay in the industry will be asked to leave.

(NCB advertisement, 4 July 1984)

Advertisements issued during strikes are closely analysed, not only by the protagonists but also by any other organisations that are named, for fear that their reputations may be harmed if they are shown to be taking sides. The first NCB advertisement, which asked whether the striking miners were killing future growth, quoted Imperial Chemical Industries as saying that the miners' strike had led the company to have 'second thoughts' about converting its Wilton plant to coal. ICI promptly retorted that the pit dispute was only one of several reasons for the delay in converting Wilton, and the NCB did not repeat this claim. Another advertisement in the series stated that miners were angry, and then asked if they had been 'told the truth' about the Plan for Coal. It went on to explain that the government and coal board considered the plan had been honoured in full, with the provision of £6.5 billion for investment in the industry between 1974 and the start of the strike.

The campaign was directed at three separate groups: the strikers, the working miners and the general public. As well as trying to undermine support for the strike by explaining how the men had been misled, the board was anxious to reassure the working miners that they had made the right decision in ignoring the strike. In the early months of the dispute, communication with the public had not been regarded as being of crucial importance, since the NCB thought that public opinion was largely on their side – because of the prominence that the news reports had given to picket-line violence, which in turn had helped create a favourable climate for the NCB's policy of keeping the pits open for work.

The Campaign for Press and Broadcasting Freedom objected to the advertisements. Mr Scargill wrote to national newspaper editors asking for a right of reply, but although the Campaign organisers were ready to take action on behalf of the NUM, there was no further disruption by the printworkers as the miners' leaders were by then involved in another round of informal talks with management.

In the run-up to the national advertising campaign, Ian MacGregor had considered whether the NCB should hold a postal ballot of the full NUM membership, as had been done at British Leyland and British Steel, to see if there was a majority among the miners in favour of a return to work. However, he was advised against this by other senior members of management, who feared a ballot organised by the board might be interpreted as unnecessarily provocative, in view of the NUM's well established tradition of holding pit-head votes. Ned Smith warned the chairman that, in the highly charged atmosphere of the strike, a ballot organised by the NCB would almost certainly go against management and give the dispute the very legitimacy which Mr Scargill had been unable to provide. Instead, the envelopes prepared for a possible ballot were used to send out Mr MacGregor's first personal letter to the miners. The letter was addressed 'Dear Colleague', and the theme was the same as the newspaper advertisements, explaining why the NUM members had been 'deliberately misled' by their leaders:

> I am taking the unusual step of writing to you at home because I want every man and woman who has a stake in the coal industry to realise clearly the damage which will be done if this disastrous strike goes on a long time . . . Your president talks continually of keeping the strike going indefinitely until he achieves 'victory'. I would like to tell you, not provocatively or as a threat, why that will not happen, however long the strike lasts.
>
> (Ian MacGregor, NCB letter, 22 June 1984)

The letter and the advertisements had been used by the NCB to present its case in some detail, because the negotiations which were then under way with the miners' union were about to produce what Mr MacGregor was to describe as some 'major concessions' by the management. By outlining its position in advance, the board hoped that the forthcoming proposals would be welcomed by the NUM membership, which would then put pressure on the leadership to settle the strike. Three meetings were held within four days, and by 14 July Mr MacGregor was ready to write again to the miners to tell them what the board was proposing.

Those areas on which there was agreement with the union were outlined in this second letter, which repeated the assurance given in the advertisements that there would be no compulsory redundancies. Mr MacGregor then explained the management's new definition of uneconomic pits: when a pit could not be 'beneficially developed', then the NCB should stop wasting human resources, money and equipment on its continued operation. But the NUM could not accept the new definition – which explained, said Mr MacGregor, why the board could not withdraw its original closure proposals.

The chairman's second letter was posted on 9 July, five days after negotiations had been adjourned, when each side had published draft agreements referring to the possibility of safeguarding the five pits threatened with closure. The adjournment coincided with the declaration of a national dock strike, called by the Transport and General Workers' Union in protest at the use of non-registered labour at Immingham to unload iron ore, which the dockers were refusing to move in accordance with union instructions to support the miners' attempt to limit steel production. The announcement of the dock strike was welcomed by the miners' delegates, who had begun arriving in Sheffield for an extraordinary annual conference convened to consider a High Court challenge to the union's proposal for a new disciplinary committee to handle miners who were defying the strike, by suspending or expelling them for detrimental conduct.

When, in defiance of the High Court, the conference approved the new disciplinary procedures, the NCB issued a statement designed to reassure working miners who feared they might lose their jobs if they were expelled from the union, promising them that their employment with the NCB would not be at risk. Unlike the railways and other nationalised industries, the pits had no closed shop agreement, as the NUM had previously experienced no difficulty in maintaining full union membership. The board's guarantee of future employment was comparable with that offered by British Rail to those railwaymen who were prepared to ignore the 1982 rail strikes.

Events moved quickly during what was now the eighteenth week of the dispute. The declaration of a national dock strike, coupled with an increase in the bank rate, had added to concern over the pound, which gave further encouragement to the NUM leaders as they prepared for another round of negotiations with the NCB on 18 July, which might well turn out to be the last negotiating session before the summer holidays. There was little optimism within the coal board or cabinet, and in a speech that weekend the Prime Minister promised that her government would do everything necessary to keep the country working.

There had been no attempt to keep secret the location of the 18 July meeting, as there had over the previous informal discussions. Well before union leaders and management had arrived, reporters, photographers and television crews were filling the lounge of the Rubens Hotel in London, waiting impatiently for any information on the progress of the talks. After spending a fruitless morning and afternoon, these newsmen were more

Plate 11 The 'snatch' photograph of Arthur Scargill, Ian MacGregor and their negotiating teams, taken for the London Standard *by freelance photographer Paul Massey during talks at the Rubens Hotel, London, on 18 June. When the door was pushed open, Mr Scargill 'leapt from his chair' and Mr MacGregor 'threw up his hands'. Clockwise from Mr Scargill: Peter Heathfield, NUM general secretary; Mick Clapham, NUM industrial relations adviser; Roger Windsor, NUM chief executive; James Cowan, NCB deputy chairman; Mr MacGregor; Merrik Spanton, NCB personnel director; Ned Smith, NCB director general of industrial relations; Kevan Hunt, NCB deputy director of industrial relations; and Mick McGahey, NUM vice-president.*

than a little surprised to see that day's issue of the London evening paper the *Standard* showing a 'snatch' picture of management and union leaders sitting round the negotiating table. Unknown to the rest of the newspaper cameramen, Paul Massey, a freelance photographer who worked for the *Standard*, had walked up to the Rembrandt suite, pushed open the door and photographed the two negotiating teams as they sat facing each other across the table. The picture was reproduced next day in several of the national newspapers. The *Daily Mail* described in its caption how, when the photographer entered the room, Mr Scargill 'leapt from his chair and glared', and Mr MacGregor 'threw up his hands and hid his face'.

Many organisations are quite happy to allow photographers and televisions cameramen to take pictures before the start of important meetings, so long as they restrict it to a photo-call and there is no attempt to report or record what might be said, even in casual conversation, by those taking part. But such facilities are rarely, if ever, granted during industrial disputes. Representatives of the news media usually have to stand outside in the street, only occasionally having the good fortune to be allowed to wait inside, as happened at the Rubens Hotel. The rest of the press corps admired Paul Massey's enterprise in going uninvited into the negotiating room, but the labour and industrial correspondents knew the incident would do little to improve the already strained relations between the news media and the NUM leadership.

As the journalists waited, the conversation turned, as usual, to the question of when the talks might finish. They had started at 10 a.m., and the lunchtime and early evening news deadlines had all passed without any firm indication of what was happening. As the evening wore on, the deadlines passed for the first editions of the next day's national newspapers, and neither the Nine O'clock News on BBC TV nor ITN's News at Ten were able to report the outcome. The final breakdown occurred well after 11 p.m., thirteen hours after the talks had started. The two sides blamed each other for the breakdown. Mr MacGregor said he hoped the NUM would consult its members on the NCB's latest proposals, even though the leadership had refused to accept the board's decision to close pits which could not be 'beneficially developed'. The union believed the definition still meant the closure of collieries on economic grounds, which Mr Scargill described as a death sentence for many mining communities.

Even though the reporters had been given no information all day, they had sensed the tension that surrounded the meeting. Speculation about the outcome had been heightened by the arrival in mid-evening of a senior government information officer, George Munro, who was employed at the Department of Energy. There appeared to be considerable nervousness within the government over what Mr MacGregor might say when the talks finished, and Mr Munro had instructions to take back an up-to-the-minute report to his minister, the Secretary of State for Energy, Peter Walker, who stood by all evening in case he had to give television interviews and respond to whatever the NCB and NUM might have decided.

Government information officers had not been present at previous talks, although it was accepted practice for a reporter from *Coal News* to attend news conferences given by the NUM. If the miners' leaders were the first to speak to the reporters, the *Coal News* representative would either telephone or report in person to a member of the management, informing him of what the NUM had said, so that the chairman or the NCB spokesman could then take full account of it in his own statement. Maurice Jones, the editor of *The Miner*, performed the same function for the union, although as he worked on his own he did not have time to monitor every press conference given by the board.

The presence of a government information officer at the Rubens Hotel was one small indication of a major turning-point in the dispute. Throughout the opening weeks of the strike the Prime Minister and her cabinet colleagues had stressed that negotiations to find a settlement were the responsibility not of the government but of the coal board and the miners' union. But by mid-July there was too much at stake to maintain this stance. Dissatisfaction within the Conservative Party over the handling

107

of the negotiations had forced ministers into the open: the government's involvement could be concealed no longer.

Many backbench conservative MPs believed the coal board had already gone too far in offering the 'major concessions' which Mr MacGregor had proposed. They feared Mr Scargill was on the point of being able to claim a significant victory, as the NCB had agreed to 're-examine' and 'revise' the original closure proposals, giving an undertaking that the five pits would 'continue in operation'. Once the terms were published, many other union leaders shared the view of some Tory MPs that the concessions were such that Mr Scargill should have settled immediately and hailed the agreement as a victory for the NUM. And as the news of the breakdown reached a group of Conservative MPs (including the party's deputy chairman Michael Spicer), gathered that evening on the terrace of the House of Commons, there was an audible sigh of relief that Mr Scargill had rejected a package of concessions which the party managers believed they would have had difficulty in selling to some of their own supporters.

The collapse of the July talks was a watershed in the strike. Mr Scargill declared that each day that passed took the union closer to the autumn, when 'General Winter' would be marching with the miners. The NUM was already preparing the ground for the TUC and Labour Party conferences, where the president would launch an appeal for the united support of the Labour and trade union movement. Mr MacGregor would soon be on holiday, temporarily relieved of the burden of trying to compete with Mr Scargill's propaganda.

The government saw this as the moment to change gear and stiffen the party's resolve. Mrs Thatcher led the way the night after the talks broke down, when she spoke to members of the Conservative 1922 Committee about the threat to the country posed by the miners' strike and the stoppage in the docks: 'In the Falklands we had to fight the enemy without. Here the enemy is within, and it's much more difficult to fight but just as dangerous to liberty.' Although the dock strike was settled three days later, the Prime Minister's rallying cry was echoed by a chorus of speeches from cabinet ministers, as the government launched the full weight of its publicity machine against Mr Scargill and the NUM. The miners' strike had moved into the political arena.

FIVE

The Political Dimension

After the collapse of the July talks, the efforts that had gone into finding a negotiated settlement were dissipated within days; it was as though the union, the coal board and the government had all half-expected the negotiations to fail. There seemed general agreement that little, if anything, could be done to stop the dispute continuing through the summer. Much of the Whitehall machine was already on the point of winding down for the parliamentary recess, and no new initiatives were planned by the government or the coal board. The general secretary of the National Union of Railwaymen, Jimmy Knapp, summed up the prevailing view within the trade unions when he compared the imminent summer lull in the pit dispute to half-time at a football match.

Arthur Scargill had one important propaganda advantage: he could hold out the prospect of power cuts once the cold weather approached. As no coal had been delivered for several months to the big power stations in Yorkshire, the miners were convinced that the NCB would soon be forced to negotiate a settlement on terms favourable to the union. However firmly government ministers tried to counter Mr Scargill's predictions, by stressing the confidence of the electricity industry that coal stocks would last through the winter, their argument lacked conviction, coming as it did in the middle of summer and at a time when the NUM was preparing its case for united trade union action which, it was hoped, would stop winter deliveries of coal and oil to the power stations.

The coal board had entered the summer without any clearly defined public strategy, and appeared to have placed total reliance on the belief that the dispute would end through a drift back to work. Ian MacGregor was frequently quoted in the early months as saying that management was thinking of holding its own secret ballot to see if the NUM membership wanted to give up the strike. It was one of several recurring possibilities about which the chairman was regularly asked to comment by the news media, and over which he always seemed willing to speculate.

But Mr MacGregor's public indecision worked against him, as did his rather abrasive style in answering questions, because it tended to arouse the latent resentment felt by many miners and some members of the public over the fact that a British industry was being run by an elderly American. All too often he appeared to be on the defensive or gave the impression that he was thinking aloud, which only confused the Fleet Street newspapers and lacked impact on radio and television. His inadequacy as a public spokesman dismayed some of his fellow directors, who thought the strike could well have collapsed had it not been for Mr Scargill's ability to create new diversions which kept it in the headlines and encouraged the strikers to wait for the victory that he had promised.

It was the Secretary of State for Energy, Peter Walker, as minister responsible for the coal industry, who found it hardest of all to restrain his impatience. He had served in Edward Heath's government during the 1974 miners' strike, which had ended with a general election and a defeat for the Conservatives. Mrs Thatcher and her cabinet had made extensive preparations in case of another miners' strike. Mr Walker's own department had taken the precaution of building up record coal stocks at the power stations. A national reporting centre had been operational within days to co-ordinate the response of the police to the mass pickets organised by the miners. The one contingency for which there had been no forward planning was the need to counter Mr Scargill's proficiency as a propagandist. The first few months of the strike had exposed the failure of Mr MacGregor and his management team to agree on a strategy for handling the news media and then to follow it through. It was an omission that Mr Walker was determined to correct.

The coal board's inability to match Mr Scargill's flair for publicity was all the more galling for the government, since the violence seen on the picket lines had reduced public support for the strike to a minimum. The news coverage in most of the national newspapers had been largely sympathetic towards both the working miners and the NCB's efforts to maintain coal production, yet the vast majority of the NUM's membership remained loyally on strike. If the coal board and the government were going to succeed in turning the trickle of returning strikers into a flood, there would have to be the sustained propaganda offensive that Mr MacGregor had proved incapable of providing.

Peter Walker had worked for weeks behind the scenes, ready for the moment when the government would want to step up its publicity against Arthur Scargill. Two days before the latest unsuccessful negotiations in July, Mr Walker had made two private predictions: the negotiations would get nowhere, and there would then be a marked change in the presentation of the case against the NUM president. The Secretary of State had prophesied correctly. The negotiations did collapse; and early on the following morning the Department of Energy had issued a statement on behalf of Mr Walker. It was not the usual government press-release fare, but a strongly worded personal attack which accused Mr Scargill of using 'mobs' to spread the 'misery' of the miners' strike. It was a theme Mr Walker developed later that day in a round of radio and television interviews.

Mr Walker's approach to the news media was similar to Mr Scargill's in several respects. The Secretary of State, like the NUM president, rarely gave a direct answer to an interviewer's question. As a politician he had learned how to skirt round difficult questions rather more diplomatically than Mr Scargill, but once the pleasantries were over he would hammer home his message, reiterating each time all the points that Mr MacGregor had failed to convey. Although he varied his presentation, he became as repetitive in content as Mr Scargill: not one miner had a 'genuine' grievance; there was a job for all men who wanted to work, and a generous redundancy payment for those who wished to leave the pits; Mr Scargill had delivered 'nothing', as he had not stopped a single power station or steelworks, or closed a single pit where the miners had stayed at work.

He shared with Mr Scargill an interest in the workings of the news media, but while the NUM president was fascinated by the technicalities of newspapers, radio and television, and preoccupied with his own performance, the Secretary of State was more concerned about the practicalities of news management and the presentation of the government's case. He knew that he would gain substantial political credit if sufficient miners could be persuaded to vote with their feet and return to work. It was an objective that could only be achieved by a sustained campaign, a campaign that would require regular priming, as each striker had first to make the decision to go back, then be encouraged to brave the picket line, and finally be reassured that in returning to work he had made the right decision. Coal production stops at the weekend to allow for maintenance work, and the miners start again each Monday on either the morning or afternoon shift, so Monday was always the crucial day. If the publicity was to be effective it had to have most impact at the weekend, when a striker was likely to be under the greatest pressure from his family, and thinking hard about what to do. The NCB and the government had to convince each striker that there was no point in staying out any longer and then, if possible, provide an incentive which might tip the balance in favour of returning to work.

Any organisation seeking regular publicity has to start by identifying those sections of the news media which it thinks are likely to prove most effective for its particular purpose. The next priority is to establish the individual requirements of the editors, journalists or programme producers. If newspapers are to be involved, the information they need will have to be supplied in a suitable form at the right time. Radio and television programmes require not only facilities for recording and filming, but also ready access to a variety of official spokesmen who are prepared to be interviewed – a facility hitherto all too frequently absent during the miners' strike.

In the case of an industrial dispute, there are often particular objectives that determine the strategy to be adopted. As we have seen, Sir Michael Edwardes had shown at British Leyland how management could help project its own case by meeting the requirements of the news media. When there was strike action at the car factories, the BL public relations department concentrated its efforts each morning on trying to provide a new story or angle on the dispute for local newspapers and radio stations, in the hope that management could set the agenda and put the unions on the defensive. If there was a major announcement for which BL wanted national publicity, the company went to great lengths to make sure radio and television interviews could be conducted with Sir Michael in sufficient time to meet the deadlines of the late afternoon or early evening news bulletins.

After his many years at Westminster as a Conservative MP and government minister, Mr Walker was well aware of the importance of the national Sunday newspapers in setting the agenda for other sections of the news media, especially at weekends when the NCB wanted to gain maximum coverage. Sunday newspaper journalists are always looking for new material that is different from what has been published or broadcast all week. They are willing to co-operate, either individually or as a group, with organisations prepared to provide information that has not been given to journalists working on national daily newspapers, radio or television. Most Sunday papers have far more room for editorial matter than the national dailies, which can result in an exclusive report by a Sunday journalist receiving more space than it might expect or deserve in the daily press. Politicians regularly use Sunday newspapers to 'float' proposals that might be controversial. They do this by holding private lobby briefings with one or more political journalists who can be relied upon to report what they have been told without any direct attribution. Once the story is published, the politician can safely deny all knowledge of it, while at the same time having the opportunity to assess likely reaction before making a final policy decision.

Because of their large readership, Sunday newspapers are of great value to any person or organisation seeking publicity. During 1984 the average total weekly sale of popular and quality Sunday newspapers was eighteen million copies, compared with a combined weekday sale of just over fifteen million for all the national dailies. The publishers also claim a wider readership for the Sunday newspapers, because, they say, they are more likely to be shared between members of the same household and looked at again later in the week.

There are other tactical advantages in co-operating with the Sunday newspapers, particularly if the aim is to influence the way a specific item is reported by other sections of the news media. If it is a quiet weekend for news stories, Sunday exclusives can have an influence that lasts for several days. By about 8 p.m. on Saturday, copies of all the first editions have usually been obtained by radio and television newsrooms, which first check to see if any new stories are being published. If a newspaper has a major exclusive, or if all the Sundays have the same angle on a running news story, it may be followed up on the late evening radio and television news bulletins. If the story is of national significance it will almost certainly be reflected in the Sunday morning bulletins, especially if few other fresh news stories have broken. By Sunday lunchtime, radio and television programmes may be reporting reaction to the item, a process which can often continue into Monday morning as well. And it will almost certainly be taken up by journalists on the national dailies, who by then will be writing their stories for Monday's newspapers. If the timing has gone to plan, publicity can spread over three days for a story that might well have been swamped by daily news if it had been released on a weekday.

There are also some drawbacks in trying to get publicity through Sunday newspaper exclusives. If the information is not given adequate prominence, it may well be ignored by other reporters. As a result, an organisation which reserves information for Sunday journalists may not only fail to benefit from what was intended to be exclusive, but also lose the opportunity to present its case to the rest of the news media.

However, in the pit dispute the risk of an occasional failure did not deter Mr Walker, as he knew that the NCB and the government faced a long haul in their campaign to persuade miners to return to work. Soon after the start of the strike, Mr Walker began arranging regular briefings for the editors of those Sunday and national daily newspapers whose editorial policies supported the objectives of the NCB and the government. It was important to explain the government's thinking, so that the editors would be in a better position to monitor the news stories that their reporters and correspondents submitted. In return for the access that he provided, the editors kept Mr Walker informed of the latest developments in the strike, which allowed him an opportunity to advise the newspapers and to interpret the importance of whatever might have happened. He had long practical experience of briefing political correspondents, having assiduously cultivated those whom he believed would be of most use. In view of the importance of weekend news coverage during the strike, he frequently took telephone calls on Saturday morning, either at home or in his constituency office in Worcester. And while he was briefing the political correspondents, the coal board was providing the same facility for Sunday industrial journalists, arranging Friday or Saturday briefings with either Ian MacGregor or other members of management.

Political and industrial journalists working on a Sunday newspaper have a closer working relationship than those on a daily paper. As most of their inquiries have to be made on Friday and Saturday, frequently on different aspects of the same news story, their work has a tendency to overlap, and because of pressure of space their stories often have to be pooled to make one report. During the miners' dispute, Mr Walker did his best to make sure the political journalists had the better news story, as this was likely to make the lead and be more favourable to the government and NCB than a report by a labour or industrial correspondent who would be anxious to give equal space to the views of the NUM.

Only Sunday papers were invited to send representatives to the Friday and Saturday news conferences given by the NCB. Journalists from radio and television services were specifically excluded, even though they customarily broadcast news stories on Sundays. The principal British news agency, the Press Association, was also refused admission until later in the strike, when after repeated protests by David Chipp, the editor-in-chief, limited access was allowed, but only for the agency's industrial correspondents. By giving exclusive information to the Sunday newspapers, the NCB believed it stood a better chance of receiving useful publicity. As the miners' strike was of such national importance, the management assumed, quite correctly, that other journalists were hardly likely to ignore the Sunday reports. Indeed, if a substantial development were revealed there was every likelihood that it would be followed up immediately in weekend radio and television news bulletins, as well as in Monday's national newspapers.

Equal thought had to be given to the task of encouraging the broadcasting organisations to follow up favourable newspaper reports in the most advantageous way. Mr Walker and the Department of Energy worked closely with the NCB to make sure that either a government minister or a member of management was available early on weekday mornings, especially on Mondays. By careful planning, maximum morning exposure could be obtained through as many as four separate live interviews – on BBC Breakfast Television, TV-AM, BBC radio's Today programme and on LBC, the independent London radio news station. As all four were in competition with each other, it was possible to play off one programme against another and choose the most suitable time slots in which to be interviewed. Such appearances had to be synchronised so as to prevent any possibility of a minister or member of management giving conflicting statements on the same day.

Peter Walker was playing an increasingly dominant role in co-ordinating the presentation of the government's case against the strike, although the Department of Energy publicly denied any direct involvement, referring most journalists' inquiries to the coal board. When industrial correspondents employed by the national dailies, radio or television approached the NCB, they found the staff in the public relations department tended to know progressively less about management's position. The press statements which were issued became selective in content and open to doubt.

The dearth of official information was largely due to Mr MacGregor's decision to follow the advice of his private publicity consultants rather than the board's public relations director, Geoffrey Kirk. Tim Bell of Saatchi and Saatchi was among those who guided Mr MacGregor on the rare public statements that he was prepared to make. Mr Bell also provided a link with those political correspondents and Fleet Street journalists with whom Mr MacGregor was willing to speak (sometimes he was prepared to take telephone calls at home from certain journalists).

Both Mr Walker and Mr MacGregor appeared well satisfied with these arrangements, as the information that they supplied rarely seemed to be challenged or scrutinised before publication. Mr Walker's briefings continued to be mainly restricted to political correspondents, and Mr MacGregor was holding fewer on-the-record news conferences open to all sections of the media. The publicity emphasis remained the same: Mr Walker tried to convey the futility of the strike and the strength of the government's position, while the NCB briefings reinforced the thrust of the Sundays' political reports by revealing new measures or incentives designed to reassure the working miners and encourage more of the strikers to return to work.

The labour and industrial correspondents employed by both Sunday and national daily papers were well aware of the lengths to which government and management were prepared to go in order to secure publicity for their efforts to end the strike. Specialist correspondents were often exasperated to find that their editors had been given a fuller briefing by Mr Walker than they themselves had been able to obtain in a whole day's work. However hard a reporter might try to produce a balanced report, his efforts could easily be side-stepped. Stories that gave prominence to the position of the NUM could simply be omitted from the newspaper, shortened, or submerged into another report. In such cases there was little a correspondent could do to defend his reputation, other than ask the editor to remove his by-line. That, at least, would indicate to the correspondent's contacts and regular readers that he was not responsible for what had been printed.

On more than one occasion in the early stages of the strike Donald Macintyre, labour editor of the *Sunday Times*, asked for his name to be removed from stories. *Sunday Times* editor Andrew Neil agreed to this, and the phrase '*Sunday Times* reporters' was inserted instead. Mr Macintyre sometimes found that his news stories had been upstaged by copy submitted by the political editor Michael Jones or by information that Mr Neil had apparently obtained himself. For instance, early in the strike, when Mr Macintyre had an exclusive report predicting that the NUM would hold a special delegate conference rather than a pit-head ballot, his story was given a new introduction and the headline, 'Government scent victory in pit battle.' There was little in the report that appeared to substantiate the headline, except for the opening sentence: 'After what it regards as a disastrous week for Arthur Scargill, the government senses victory in its confrontation with the coal miners' (*Sunday Times*, 8 April 1984).

Mr Walker did little to hide his dislike of the labour and industrial correspondents, and sometimes complained in his conversations with newspaper editors about unhelpful stories which were being written by 'left-wing industrial reporters'. This was brought home to me on one occasion by the head of information at the Department of Energy, Ian Gillis, who in response to an inquiry I was making retorted: 'What new mischief are you causing today?' Mr Walker's views seemed to be shared by some newspaper editors, including Andrew Neil, who was himself a former labour editor on *The Economist*. He had also worked for the Conservative Party's research department during the early 1970s, serving as political adviser to Mr Walker, who was then Secretary of State for the Environment. In the third month of the miners' strike a leading article in the *Sunday Times* reflected one of the criticisms which Mr Walker had been expressing about the reporting of the dispute: 'The strike, of course, still continues. Rumours of peace breaking out should be treated sceptically: they are put about by obliging industrial correspondents on behalf of certain coal board officials, miners' leaders and Labour politicians squirming at Mr Scargill's antics' (*Sunday Times*, 3 June 1984).

In a letter to the *Sunday Times* editor published the following week, the chairman of the Labour and Industrial Correspondents' Group, Michael Edwards, industrial editor of the *Daily Mail*, explained that the industrial journalists were doing no more than use their specialised judgement to map out possible developments in the strike. In performing this task they were not 'obliging' anyone, but merely fulfilling their professional duties. Mr Edwards did not go on to point out that the trade union movement might well have levelled the same criticism against political correspondents who wrote about the miners' strike without any contact with the NUM, or against newspaper editors who relied solely on briefings from government ministers.

Several other methods were used by the editors of a number of popular national dailies to generate publicity against the strike. One tactic employed quite frequently was to ask a reporter or feature writer, rather than the industrial correspondent, to prepare a story attacking the miners' union or its leadership. This was usually done without any consultation whatever with the paper's own industrial specialists, who would only discover what had happened when they read the paper the following morning. Some industrial journalists preferred not to know what their papers intended to print, so that if they were challenged they could honestly deny any knowledge of it.

Two of the popular papers that regularly printed stories critical of Arthur Scargill were the *Sun* and the *Daily Express*. A leader-page feature, entitled 'Scargill's seven shadows', was published in the *Daily Express* on 3 April 1984, listing the seven 'militant left-wingers' who were said to keep the Scargill show on the road. The article was written by a freelance journalist, Rodney Tyler, whose work was subsequently featured on 1 May in the *Sun*, in the form of a full-page interview that he had obtained with Ian MacGregor, under the headline 'Scargill doesn't scare me.' Mr Tyler had written several exclusive reports in the past about the Prime Minister and other members of the Thatcher family. He obtained his *Sun* interview with Mr MacGregor without the knowledge either of the newspaper's own industrial correspondent, Tom Condon, or of the coal board's director of public relations, Geoffrey Kirk. The first either Mr Condon or Mr Kirk knew of Mr Tyler's interview with the NCB chariman was when they opened their copy of the *Sun* that Tuesday morning.

As we saw in chapter 4, the repeated publication of virulent personal attacks on Mr Scargill by several of the popular tabloids resulted in large sections of the miners' union refusing to give information to the papers' representatives. The long-standing relationship with the NUM, established during the years when Joe Gormley was president, was virtually destroyed overnight for Barrie Devney, industrial editor of the *Daily Express*, when his newspaper published in May 1984 the mock speech by Mr Scargill in which he 'confessed' to having lied to the membership (see pp. 85–6). After the publication of that one article in which he had played no part, Mr Devney encountered such hostility that he concluded there was rarely anything to be gained in joining the other correspondents lobbying NUM executive meetings in Sheffield.

The miners' strike proved an exceptional one for many of the labour and industrial journalists, because they met antagonism on all sides – from union, management and government. And the difficulties that they encountered received little acknowledgement from specialist writers in the news media. One regular critic was the *Spectator*'s columnist Paul Johnson, who believed industrial correspondents showed an 'appalling disregard' for accuracy and a 'sheep-like propensity' to move in flocks, because of their heavy dependence on the official union machines as their only source of information. Mr Johnson's description of a cosy partnership, in which 'one or two' of the industrial correspondents lived 'in the pockets of the union bosses', failed to recognise the day-to-day problems that arose while reporting the strike.

Mr Scargill and the union's general secretary, Peter Heathfield, were invariably infuriated by the Sunday newspaper coverage, yet despite the importance of weekend news reporting the NUM still took no specific steps to improve communications with the journalists. The radio and television appearances of the president and the general secretary showed a lack of internal co-operation and forward planning that underlined the absence of any kind of overall communications strategy. With the approach of autumn and the NCB's redoubled efforts to encourage more strikers to return to work each Monday morning, the union desperately needed to be able to communicate quickly and effectively with reporters, if it was to counter the information that was being supplied by the board and the government.

If, at weekends, the NUM's press officer Nell Myers was unobtainable on her London telephone number, the only alternative was for journalists to try telephoning those NUM officials who would take calls at home, although they often tended to be away on speaking engagements. Many of the journalists who did weekend duty during the strike would also ring the NUM's headquarters in Sheffield, on the off-chance that a senior official who was prepared to answer questions might be there. The strike operations room was manned on Saturday and Sunday; if Mr Scargill was in the office, he would answer the telephone himself, sometimes disguising his voice and only revealing his identity once he knew who was calling and after he had heard the question.

The NUM's need for more professional advice and support had been recognised by the National Union of Journalists, which was anxious to assist – despite having had to wait for some months for a reply to its request for a meeting with the miners' leadership to discuss their complaints about alleged picket-line violence. After providing an initial donation to the hardship fund, the NUJ's national executive decided in July to allocate to the NUM sufficient money to finance the appointment of temporary press officers, who could help provide publicity for the miners and explain the case against pit closures. Ken Ashton, then general secretary of the NUJ, wrote to the *Guardian* suggesting how the miners, in their turn, could assist the journalists:

> It is tempting for the journalists' trade union to keep its head down and stay silent, because if we speak out, it will either be to anger our own members or to alienate other trade unionists. Yet to stay silent is the one thing, in conscience, we cannot do. Whatever the government's intentions, the result will not be simply to win an industrial dispute: it will be to destroy the miners' trade union. If it succeeds, other unions, including ours, will be weakened . . . Mr Scargill ought to acknowledge, though, that many journalists and many news organisations are trying to do an honest job of reporting the news . . . I hope the NUM will make greater efforts to get its side of the story to the media. My union is willing to do all it can to help. Many journalists will welcome a better flow of information from the NUM side.
>
> (Ken Ashton, Letters to the Editor, *Guardian*, 31 August 1984)

However, the offer to pay for temporary press officers was not taken up nationally, and the journalists' leaders did not get a satisfactory opportunity to meet the miners' leadership to discuss the union's precise needs. Only one NUM area, Durham, took advantage of the NUJ's proposal, appointing an unemployed journalist, Ross Forbes, as area press officer on 17 September. Mr Forbes served as press officer for the 11,500 miners in the thirteen pits in the Durham area at a cost of £6,000 to the NUJ. He had no authority to speak or give guidance on national policy, and worked virtually in isolation: there being no national publicity strategy, each area retained considerable autonomy. The NUJ allocated a further £8,000 towards the cost of local publicity campaigns in the Yorkshire, South Wales and Kent areas, but no other temporary press officers were appointed.

Mr Scargill's objection to the appointment of temporary press officers was that the NUM's head office could not take on part-time or unemployed journalists who were not known to the union and who could not, therefore, be trusted. But the NUJ had taken this point into account, and two possible candidates suggested informally were Glen Allan and Maggie Brittain. Both had been declared redundant in 1983, but were known personally to Mr Scargill and many other NUM leaders. They had worked in London for United Newspapers, providing news copy for the *Yorkshire Post*, *Yorkshire Evening Post* and *Lancashire Evening Post*, which circulated in mining areas. Mr Allan had already notified Peter Heathfield that he was available if needed.

The NUJ, like the Labour and Industrial Correspondents' Group, had effectively failed in its attempt to convince the NUM's leadership of the need to adopt an open policy towards journalists, by providing regular information. The Campaign for Press and Broadcasting Freedom, which was equally anxious to give practical assistance, could not understand why the leadership persisted in its refusal to take constructive steps towards establishing a closer working relationship with the news media. Mr Scargill had also been reluctant to accept the Campaign's advice when the printworkers had obtained space in the national newspapers, giving the miners' union the right of reply (see p. 90). Instead of taking the opportunity to present a structured case against media bias, which the Campaign believed could only strengthen the NUM's case by promoting the need for fairer news coverage in all industrial disputes, the president had chosen to devote most of the space to a restatement of the argument against pit closures.

Another unexpected development, in view of the offers of help from media workers and print unions, was the leadership's decision to halve the print run of *The Miner*. During the early months of the summer about 400,000 copies were being printed almost every week, which was more than twice the number needed for the membership. Production had been increased largely at the request of the miners' support groups, which had been established all over the country and which were asking for information and publicity material to back up the fight against pit closures. Volunteers often sold copies of the paper on the streets of

London and other big cities, in order to raise money for the hardship fund.

Whenever possible, Maurice Jones, the editor, tried to feature the other side of picket-line violence by publishing photographs of policemen restraining pickets and demonstrators. He believed that the union's coverage of the dispute, especially on issues like police conduct, was managing to challenge the version being offered by Fleet Street. Mr Jones kept up his efforts to undermine the credibility of the national newspapers, reporting gleefully on one picket-line ceremony called the 'Sundance' which required strikers to roll up old copies of the *Sun* and use them like a baton to beat out the tune for a Morris dance routine, which ended with the newspapers being opened up and trampled on by the pickets.

In an attempt to match the propaganda of the coal board and government, *The Miner* launched its own publicity campaigns which, it hoped, would be taken up by support groups and other trade unions. In preparation for the approach of autumn, the paper encouraged NUM members and supporters to 'switch on at six'. If domestic electrical appliances were all turned on together throughout the country at 6 p.m., the union believed, this would create an early evening peak in demand which would force the generating board to keep more of its coal-fired power stations in operation, thus increasing the possibility of power cuts.

The decision late in August to scale down the size and frequency of *The Miner*'s print run was explained on the grounds of cost. From then on issues were produced fortnightly instead of weekly, and the print run was reduced to around 230,000, which was enough to cover the NUM's membership and those support groups which were able to pay in advance for their copies. However, *The Miner* had become the only regular line of communication to the union's members and supporters, and it was having to compete for attention with the NCB's *Coal News*, which, as we have noted, was being posted every month to the home of each striker, and often supplemented by special issues carrying major announcements from the management. As the union could not afford the cost of postage, the only way of distributing *The Miner* during the dispute was to deliver copies to each of the strike and welfare centres which served hot meals, handed out food parcels and had become the one place in each community where the union could pass on information. The centres were also used as the main distribution point for NUM area newspapers like the *Yorkshire Miner*.

The union's reliance on groups in each mining community to distribute *The Miner* proved ineffective in Nottinghamshire, where 80 per cent of the miners were working and where a majority of the area leaders were against the strike. The bundles of newspapers delivered to the Nottinghamshire area office were not opened or distributed to the pits, since the local leadership believed *The Miner* represented only the views of Mr Scargill.

The area secretary Henry Richardson, who supported the strike and who was later dismissed by the area executive, did what he could to get *The Miner* circulated. One reason for his eventual dismissal was his refusal to stop the distribution of information from the NUM head office. Mr Richardson told me afterwards that it became the established practice during the strike for other area officials to order bundles of the newspaper to be removed from the office with the rest of the waste paper.

Even if the union could have afforded the postage, it would have been unable to mail copies of *The Miner* to its members, because, like so many manual unions, it had no complete central record of the home addresses of its members. Some areas did maintain lists of addresses, but their accuracy depended on the efficiency of local pit officials and the degree of co-operation received from management. Because of the 'check-off' system of collecting union subscriptions – they were now deducted automatically by the board, who handed over the money to the union at the end of each month – the NUM did not need to maintain an up-to-date record of home addresses. All internal union communications went through the local branch office at each pit, which also conducted pit-head ballots and distributed *The Miner*. So as with British Leyland, British Rail, and British Steel, it was the National Coal Board that had the monopoly when it came to the possession of personal information about employees.

The inadequacy of this arrangement only became apparent during a lengthy strike. By handing the responsibility for collecting subscriptions over to the employer, the union had lost what was often its only point of direct contact with many members. The previous system had required volunteers to collect the subscriptions, and these men had provided a pool of activists who were in a position to build up a personal relationship with each union member, and had acted as a channel for information and for the distribution of union newspapers. Because it now had no means of contacting the miners, the union was in no position to prevent the steps being progressively taken by the NCB to encourage the strikers to return to work. And it was unable to challenge with any degree of accuracy the board's figures for the number of miners who were said to have given up the strike and returned to work – a crucial propaganda advantage for management.

Attempts were made by the NUM to establish the identity of miners reporting for work. The task was relatively easy in small mining communities where the men all lived in close proximity to the pits, but many collieries are situated in or near major conurbations, drawing their workforce from a wide geographical area. The union could estimate only by attempting to count men entering or leaving each pit, which was difficult when they arrived in buses and vans. In some areas buses taking working miners to their homes were followed, as part of the union's attempt to establish how many members were defying the strike.

The first concerted attempt to break the strike was organised in the North Derbyshire coalfield, where the area director Ken Moses worked with almost military precision, making full use of the home addresses of the area's 10,000 miners. Inside the board's local office, maps were displayed showing the streets and villages where the men lived. North Derbyshire was ideally placed for an offensive by management, as it lies just to the north of Nottinghamshire where the miners were working. Bolsover, one of the ten pits under Mr Moses' control, provided a base from which to start since it was manned by members of the Notts branch of the union and had worked throughout the strike.

Towards the end of June Mr Moses wrote to all North Derbyshire miners, offering to arrange transport for any men prepared to report for work. Each pit manager followed this up with a personal letter, after which three management teams began visiting miners at their homes to see if the NCB could promote a faster return to work. The visits started around Shirebrook colliery. The pit manager, Bill Steel, concentrated his initial efforts on making contact with those miners whose homes were furthest away from the immediate vicinity of the pit, as he found that the greater the distance from the mine, the less likelihood there was that miners and their families would fear intimidation. By the end of the month 300 members of the North Derbyshire NUM were at work in the area, rising to 500 in early July. Within a week the board began a similar operation at pits in Scotland and the north-east of England.

Trying to prepare accurate reports on the number of miners at work continued throughout the strike to be a problem for journalists, since management gave no detailed breakdown and even working coalfields like Nottinghamshire simply quoted a percentage for those not on strike. Towards the end of July, NCB national newspaper advertisements claimed that more than '60,000 people' were still working in the coal industry. The union complained, accusing the board of playing with figures, for many of the 60,000 were neither members of the NUM nor had they been called out on strike. On the NCB's own admission, the 60,000 included a large proportion of the 17,000 members of the National Association of Colliery Overmen, Deputies and Shotfirers (NACODS), plus the 15,000 members of the British Association of Colliery Management, neither of which were at that time in dispute with the board. Nonetheless, the Energy Secretary Peter Walker put the same gloss on the figures as the NCB's advertisements, when he wrote a newspaper article outlining Mr Scargill's 'remarkable' list of failures:

First came the failure to unite the miners. Almost all of those coalfields that had a ballot, in accordance with the traditions of their union, have been at work – 60,000 men, or nearly one third of the workforce, daily do their jobs despite intense intimidation and organised mob violence. They have continued to produce coal and, as the weeks have gone by, slowly but steadily, more men have joined them, and more pits have started producing coal again.

(Peter Walker, *The Times*, 20 July 1984)

The return of a few hundred strikers in North Derbyshire and Scotland did little to alarm the NUM leadership, as most collieries had fixed holiday fortnights during July and August when the pits would be closed and when any figures the NCB might publish would be unrealistic. Despite the strike, a holiday atmosphere lasted for much of the summer in the mining communities. Children were taken away on holidays and outings; lorry-loads of provisions and household goods arrived at the strike centres from all over the country. The food had been purchased or collected by other trade unions and by the miners' support groups which flourished in many towns, including some deep in the south-east of England, the heartland of Conservative Party support. Strikers who were active in the union were spending days away from home either on picket-line duty or raising money for the hardship fund. Most had been in the pits since their teens, and even among those who wanted to return there were many who seemed to be enjoying the opportunity to spend a summer without having to go underground, occupying their time digging gardens and allotments, collecting wood, doing odd jobs or temporary work. One consequence of the summer-time growth in outdoor activities was that fewer of the strikers and their families were at home in the evening to watch television. The leadership believed this had helped maintain morale, as much of the news coverage was regarded as hostile to the union, and tended to depress the strike families. After four months away from the pits local miners' leaders were proudly declaring that their members had passed through the pain barrier: they were busy preparing for the winter, when the real battle would start.

As autumn approached, the NUM leadership was encouraged by a series of incidents in which Ian MacGregor undermined his own credibility as head of a nationalised industry through needless and insensitive over-exposure in the news media. On each occasion he had insisted on entering the fray in an attempt to take on Mr Scargill, against the advice of the board's public relations department. One senior coal board director told me that the need to satisfy Mr MacGregor's ego was becoming as great a problem as it appeared to be with Mr Scargill; indeed, the chairman did seem as unwilling as the NUM president to delegate to anyone else any part of the responsibility for conducting radio and television interviews.

Mr MacGregor's limitations as a communicator were cruelly illustrated when he decided, at the very last moment, to take part in his first television debate with Mr Scargill. The discussion, to be broadcast as part of the evening Channel 4 News on 22 August, was scheduled to take place between Mr Scargill and the NCB's director-general of industrial relations, Ned Smith. That afternoon there was a disagreement within the board over the conditions under which management was prepared to take part in the programme, as Channel 4 had changed the format the previous day. Because Mr MacGregor was against Mr Smith conducting a wide-ranging discussion, the NCB withdrew from the programme and at 4 p.m. Mr Smith left the office to catch the train home to Kent. However, after a last-minute intervention by ITN's editor-in-chief David Nicholas, Mr MacGregor agreed to appear. An improvised studio had been prepared in the NCB's headquarters, and Mr MacGregor arrived together with the deputy chairman James Cowan and several other aides. The board's industrial and public relations departments had spent much of the week preparing statistics on the number of miners at work, which Mr Smith had intended to use to counter the NUM's claim that most of its members were still on strike.

While the NCB's internal drama unfolded in London, Mr Scargill was at NUM headquarters in Sheffield busily preparing for the debate. He arrived at a studio in Leeds with plenty of time to assemble the documents that he might need during the discussion.

It was not until five minutes before the start of the programme that he was finally informed that Mr MacGregor, and not Mr Smith, would be representing the NCB in London. As expected, much of the discussion centred on a disagreement over statistics. According to Mr MacGregor, 49,400 NUM members were at work, and in order to back up his claim that the strike was crumbling he declared that the NCB's figures were open to public inspection, as they were based on the payroll. Mr Scargill disagreed with him, declaring that 147,000 miners were on strike – or 80 per cent of the union's 180,000 members; the number of pits on strike was 130, and not the 114 maintained by the board. Although Mr MacGregor had difficulty in finding some of his words, as if reading from a badly typed script, he remained calm while Mr Scargill reeled off his statistics. But then, half-way through the twenty-minute debate, Mr MacGregor began to show increasing signs of tetchiness, finally accusing the NUM president of giving a monologue and speaking balderdash.

As in so many of his previous interviews, Mr Scargill accused Mr MacGregor of departing from the Labour government's 1974 Plan for Coal, quoting from the documents that he had in front of him. At this Mr MacGregor began to flounder. His aides had brought along the latest statistics for the number of miners at work but not, it seemed, a copy of the Plan for Coal – although this would have been a wise precaution in view of Mr Scargill's ability to read into the plan what the NCB said did not exist. ITN's presenter Peter Sissons, who chaired the discussion, was also unable to produce a copy, so Mr Scargill's interpretation of the Plan for Coal again seemed to carry the day. At one point Mr MacGregor started to rise from his seat, saying, 'Well, Mr Sissons, thank you for this programme and I will say goodnight.' But he was brought back by another intervention by Mr Scargill who, when finally thanked by Mr Sissons for taking part replied, 'It's been a pleasure.'

For the first time in the strike Ian MacGregor seemed, during that interview, to be too old for the job. Viewers who telephoned the NCB's public relations department expressed pity: why, asked several callers, hadn't the board used a younger member of the management to present its case? The chairman's performance caused widespread embarrassment within the government and other nationalised industries, because it appeared to give credence to Arthur Scargill's regular suggestion that the Prime Minister ought to pension off Mr MacGregor and send him to a retirement home in Florida. One senior government press officer told me later that Mr MacGregor's behaviour was inexplicable. Ministers and chairmen were always advised not to enter television debates with union leaders during critical disputes. Mr MacGregor's rather 'flip' American attitude had been no match for Mr Scargill: the chairman had simply appeared flustered, which had inevitably led some viewers to question his capability to take policy decisions.

Frequent appearances on radio and television can diminish the authority of the person involved and the strength of his argument. Here was a further danger in Mr MacGregor's over-exposure. Other industrialists said that if he had restricted the number of interviews he gave, his statements might have carried more weight. Sir Terence Beckett, director-general of the CBI, was among those who believed it was time Mr MacGregor withdrew from the public spotlight and concentrated instead on strategy. He was deserted, too, by another staunch supporter, the *Daily Express*: 'Last night's great TV debate – Scargill v. the coal board – was a futile exercise . . . The coal board was foolish beyond belief to indulge Scargill's gimmickry in the first place. Doubly foolish to fall in with his last-minute demand that Ian MacGregor join this silly stunt' (*Daily Express*, 23 August 1984).

One of Mr MacGregor's aides during the Channel 4 debate was David Hart – property developer, political adviser to the Prime Minister and occasional columnist in *The Times*. Mr Hart had become a regular visitor to Hobart House, and had frequently been observed making his way to the chairman's office without having to produce identification to the NCB commissionaire or give prior notification to the receptionist. At one point during the Channel 4 programme, he was seen by ITN staff to hold up a piece of paper containing information that was apparently intended to help Mr MacGregor answer one of the questions. Mr Hart was also among those who attended the inaugural meetings of the National Working Miners' Committee, which was formed in an attempt to organise opposition to the strike.

On 30 August, on the return journey from one of his visits to leaders of the working miners, Mr MacGregor joined the London train at Nottingham. His presence was noticed by three industrial correspondents who were also returning to London after a meeting of the NUM executive. Mr MacGregor did not seem at all perturbed by the unfavourable publicity he had received in the wake of the Channel 4 programme the week before; indeed, he seemed full of confidence, explaining to the correspondents that his optimism was based on the findings of the board's private opinion polls, which had been carried out since the start of the strike. They were had previously made no public reference to the existence of these opinion polls, which ahd been carried out since the start of the strike. They were conducted by Opinion Research and Communication, whose founder Tommy Thompson had carried out similar surveys for British Rail during the 1982 rail strikes (see page 34), when he had advised Sir Peter Parker on the composition of the personal letters which the BR chairman was to write to the railway workers. The polls for the NCB involved questioning miners, trade unionists and other members of the public in the mining areas. Mr MacGregor continued ordering new polls, although he was told by his industrial relations department that they were a waste of money, and that there was no point in asking miners and their families whether they thought it was Mr MacGregor or Mr Scargill who was telling the truth, since they would inevitably give answers that they thought would have some influence on management. However, when it came to seeking the views of a cross-section of miners, the opinion pollsters were again in a stronger position than the leadership of the NUM, as it was management which had instant access to all the necessary names and addresses.

Mr MacGregor had been so heartened by the findings of the board's latest surveys, that the day after his chance encounter with the three industrial correspondents he began preparing an open letter which he hoped would be considered by delegates at the annual conference of the Trades Union Congress in Brighton the following week. When he had finished the letter, the chairman gave strict instructions that it should be sent immediately to every Fleet Street editor, but should not be sent to the news agencies, radio or television services.

Mr MacGregor was advised by the board's public relations department not to send the letter, as it might be regarded as an unnecessary interference in the TUC's internal affairs and could embarrass unions like the electricians' and power station engineers', which were against the conference giving its support to the miners. The chairman was also told that Friday evening was an unsatisfactory time to issue a press release, especially if his intention was to gain publicity, because the Saturday morning newspapers invariably had less space for news than weekday ones and there were fewer radio and television news programmes on Saturday mornings. Nonetheless he insisted on going ahead with the letter, because he was confident, he said, that he had influence with the editors of the national newspapers. In fact, the chairman had established certain contacts with Fleet Street: he was known to have complained on several occasions to the editor of the *Financial Times* about the paper's coverage of the strike, claiming that its industrial editor John Lloyd was 'soft' on the miners. (Mr Lloyd was later named journalist of the year by Granada Television for his reporting of the pit dispute.)

This open letter to the TUC delegates was one of several publicity initiatives launched by Mr MacGregor against the advice of the board's public relations department. It was rather overshadowed on the Saturday morning by an exclusive report in the *Daily Mirror* saying that there would be new peace talks in the dispute once the TUC conference was over. But, the *Daily Telegraph* did publish the full text of the letter, in which Mr MacGregor asked TUC delegates to consider which of the miners deserved their support. Should they be assisting those miners who wanted the strike to continue, or 'the many who had a ballot and are working and the tens of thousands more who would like to work, but are too frightened to return?' The TUC made no public response to the letter.

On the fourth day of the TUC conference, Mr MacGregor was again to embarrass the board. On this occasion he was giving a news briefing in London. When asked by reporters for his views on Mr Scargill's suggestion the day before that it was perhaps time he took a long rest, he said he thought the comment was misplaced; he had been on holiday for much of August and was confident that he was in the best of health. 'I am about as interesting as an old barn door. There is no medical interest in me whatsoever,' he said in reply to one journalist. During an interview afterwards, a BBC radio reporter, Graeme McLagan, again asked the chairman about his health:

MacGregor	I have never felt better in my life.
McLagan	You don't need a long rest?
MacGregor	No sir.
McLagan	What about Mr Scargill?
MacGregor	Ah, I am concerned about him. He has been working much too hard, long hours. I am concerned about his health, yes.
McLagan	Mental health or physical health?
MacGregor	Both, yes, yes, indeed, the stresses must be very great on him.
	(BBC Radio 4, PM programme, 6 September 1984)

When Mr McLagan checked back on the tape-recording of his interview, the other journalists who were present immediately seized on Mr MacGregor's remark about Mr Scargill's mental health. Ned Smith, director-general of industrial relations, was horrified by what the chairman had said. The board immediately denied that Mr MacGregor had ever intended to suggest that Mr Scargill was mentally ill. The denial came too late, as the reporters were already filing their stories. Next morning the *Sun*'s front page headline asked: 'Is Arthur cracking up?' The *Daily Star* used one word: 'Bonkers!'.

The miners' objective at the TUC conference was to persuade the rest of the trade union movement to stop fuel deliveries to the power stations. This, the NUM leadership believed, would quickly result in power cuts once the cold weather arrived. Throughout the early months of the strike, the NUM leaders had virtually ingnored the TUC general council, indicating quite clearly that they were not prepared to accept any advice or interference by other union leaders or by Len Murray, the retiring general secretary. There was so little contact that Mr Murray had not even been given Arthur Scargill's home telephone number, although later in the strike it was supplied to Norman Willis, who took over as general secretary at the end of the conference. Mr Scargill was particularly sensitive about his (ex-directory) home phone number, having insisted that it should not be given under any circumstances to any journalist. As far as I knew no member of the Labour and Industrial Correspondents' Group had the number, or succeeded in ringing Mr Scargill at home during the strike.

When the TUC delegates debated the miners' strike on the opening day of the conference, there was overwhelming support for a statement that had been hastily agreed with the NUM leadership only three days earlier: in an attempt to make the dispute more effective, all unions were asked to observe NUM picket lines and not to move or use coal, coke or substitute oil.

The TUC statement was not an instruction, and the miners' union was asked to acknowledge that the general council would have to discuss the practical implementation of any moves to support the strike with the unions directly concerned, three of which had voted against the TUC proposals, including the electricians' and power station engineers'. The two principal general secretaries concerned, Eric Hammond of the EETPU and John Lyons of the Engineers' and Managers' Association, both warned the TUC that their members in the power stations were not prepared to take the action that the conference had agreed. However, these reservations were swept aside by other major unions like the Transport and General Workers', the Amalgamated Union of Engineering Workers and the General, Municipal, Boilermakers and Allied Trades, whose leaders predicted that there could be power cuts within weeks if there was full support for the TUC's guidelines to stop coal and oil movements.

By giving a display of unity, even though some unions regarded it as an empty gesture, the TUC had hoped to strengthen the NUM's negotiating hand at a new round of discussions with the NCB which were to start in

Edinburgh on the Sunday immediately after conference. These were the first talks for over seven weeks – since the breakdown in mid-July – and much of the TUC conference had been overshadowed by a protracted exchange of letters and telephone calls as union and management worked out the final conditions for the meeting. One intermediary who had done what he could to help arrange a reopening of negotiations was Robert Maxwell, publisher of Mirror Group Newspapers.

Mr Maxwell appeared to regard himself as more than a newspaper publisher – rather as a major public figure with wide interests and a responsibility to exercise his influence for the benefit of others, especially on those occasions when his personal intervention in a major news event might also help promote the *Daily Mirror.* The impasse that had persisted all summer was an opportunity for him to try his hand as an independent negotiator, a task of which he could claim some knowledge because of the numerous printing industry disputes in which he had been involved. Within a short space of time Mr Maxwell was proclaiming his inside knowledge of developments in the miners' strike. He confidently used the first names of the principal participants, while desribing himself as being on this occasion no more than the 'messenger boy'.

He had kept in constant touch with his labour and industrial journalists, and frequently suggested what he thought were appropriate lines of inquiry. The access that he had gained was reflected in the news coverage of the *Daily Mirror,* which had been able to scoop the rest of Fleet Street on 1 September with an exclusive report of a new peace initiative under the headline, 'Miners: TUC ray of hope'. Another exclusive on the talks had followed on 3 September, the opening day of the TUC conference. When the new negotiations finally began in Edinburgh a week later, the *Daily Mirror*'s report on the opening session was another exclusive story. It carried the headline 'Scargill to ballot miners', and was under the by-line of the industrial reporter Terry Pattinson:

> Peace talks aimed at settling the miners' strike ended after only two hours last night. But the *Daily Mirror* can exclusively reveal that whatever the outcome, miners will be asked to vote on the coal board's final offer . . . The union bosses have always resisted a ballot on the six-month-old strike. But they are now ready to recommend a vote on the coal board's final terms.
>
> (*Daily Mirror*, 10 September 1984)

The story surprised the rest of the industrial reporters who were with Mr Pattinson in Edinburgh covering the miners' talks, unaware that he had such a dramatic exclusive. London news editors on other Fleet Street newspapers were on the telephone immediately the first editions had been published the evening before, asking their correspondents to follow up this new development.

One group of industrial journalists were in a restaurant in Edinburgh when the *Sun* newsdesk telephoned, asking to speak to its industrial correspondent, Tom Condon. But there was some confusion, and by mistake the call was taken by Tom McGhie, industrial editor of the *Daily Star*, who assumed he was speaking to his London office. When the newsdesk representative said that he wanted Tom to file the miners' ballot story, Mr McGhie protested, saying he did not believe it was true. He was told he would have to write it anyway, at which he protested again. In the end he discovered that he was speaking not to the *Daily Star*, but to the *Sun*. Later editions of the *Sun* carried the *Daily Mirror*'s story under Tom Condon's by-line, with the headline 'Miners set for peace ballot'.

Inquiries later that evening by other newsmen indicated that there was no foundation for the *Daily Mirror*'s exclusive or for the *Sun*'s follow-up, and no likelihood whatever of the NUM holding a pit-head ballot. As no other reporter had the story in as much detail as Mr Pattinson, he was much in demand the following morning, being interviewed live on TV-AM and the Today programme on BBC radio, staunchly defending the accuracy of his newspaper's story. Later in the day, colleagues in the Labour and Industrial Correspondents' Group discovered that Mr Pattinson had not written the *Daily Mirror*'s story himself, and that he had no personal knowledge of any plan by the miners' union to hold a ballot. When he had been interviewed for radio and television, he did not even know that his by-line had been used on the London editions of the *Daily Mirror*. He had backed up his paper's 'exclusive' in his interviews because he knew that the story would almost certainly have been inspired by Robert Maxwell, and could possibly have been correct, as there had been close contact between his publisher and Arthur Scargill the previous week at the TUC conference. When Mr Pattinson returned to London he was unable to discover who wrote the *Mirror* story under his by-line.

On the morning of the *Daily Mirror*'s 'exclusive', the national newspapers all had pictures of Ian MacGregor's arrival the previous afternoon at the Norton House Hotel on the outskirts of Edinburgh. The NCB chairman was shown walking from his car towards the front door, his face covered by a green plastic carrier-bag. He could be seen peering through the handle hole in the bag and was heard by waiting reporters to mutter, 'I've nothing to say.'

Mr MacGregor felt the need for this protective device following the pursuit of his car by reporters and photographers who were anxious to find out where the next round of talks would take place. Having waited outside his country home at Cairnbaan in Argyll, the newsmen had given chase when they saw him drive away in a green Jaguar. They managed to keep up with him for a considerable distance but lost sight of him north of Glasgow. Other journalists and cameramen were waiting in Edinburgh, checking the airport and various hotels in the hope of seeing either Mr

DAILY Mirror

THREE WAYS TO WIN A £MILLION **16p** PAGE SEVEN

Monday, September 10, 1984 FORWARD WITH BRITAIN ★ 16p

Peace talks are halted after two hours

Scargill to ballot miners
ON FINAL OFFER

SCARGILL: Talks

MacGREGOR: Success?

By TERRY PATTINSON

PEACE talks aimed at settling the miners' strike ended after only two hours last night.

But the Mirror can exclusively reveal that whatever the outcome, miners will be asked to vote on the Coal Board's final offer.

Both sides were non-committal after last night's talks at a hotel outside Edinburgh.

Coal Board chairman Ian MacGregor would only say: "All talks are successful, but some are more successful than others."

Mick McGahey, vice president of the NUM, said: "No comment—that's final."

Ned Smith, the Coal Board's industrial relations director, was believed to be continuing private talks with miners' leader Arthur Scargill last night.

The union bosses have always resisted a ballot on the six-month-old strike.

But they are now ready to recommend a vote on the Coal Board's final terms.

● Pit Ballot—Page 2

COAL boss Ian MacGregor clowned with a supermarket carrier bag when he arrived for last night's vital talks.

He hid his face behind it, peered through the handle holes and muttered: "I've nothing to say."

IN THE BAG . .

SEB COE'S 'NEW LOVE' See Page 3

Plate 12 NCB chairman Ian MacGregor, his face covered by a plastic carrier-bag, arriving in Edinburgh on 10 September for another round of negotiations with the NUM. The Daily Mirror's front-page story surprised the rest of the labour and industrial correspondents covering the talks, as they knew nothing of the supposed about-turn by the NUM over a pit-head ballot. Later the story was proved to be without foundation.

MacGregor or leaders of the miners' union and discovering where the talks were taking place.

One radio reporter, Kenny Macintyre of BBC Radio Scotland, had just checked the Norton House Hotel and was returning to the airport when he met Mr MacGregor's car approaching him in a hurry down the narrow road leading to the hotel. Mr Macintyre had swerved to avoid him, he said, and ended up in the ditch, and as Mr MacGregor had stopped to see what had happened, Mr Macintyre walked across to his car and asked him whether, as one Argyllshire man to another, he would say where the talks were taking place. Mr MacGregor suggested that Mr Macintyre should try following Arthur Scargill instead. A few minutes later Mr MacGregor reached the hotel entrance and stepped from his car, Mr Macintyre having warned him that there would be quite a welcoming party of newsmen waiting for him.

Mr MacGregor should hardly have been annoyed by the newsmen's efforts to keep track of his movements, because his attempt to hide behind a plastic carrier bag was just the kind of bizarre reaction that photographers lie in wait for. Public figures have used many devices in the past when trying to evade photographers, but here was Mr MacGregor adopting a truly novel form of protection. His arrival at the Norton House Hotel seemed more akin to the kind of hurried exit made by the accused after a court appearance, his head under a blanket. Whatever his motive, the NCB chairman had unwittingly provided Fleet Street and television cameramen with one of those unexpected pictures that give the cartoonists and comedians a field-day.

Early that evening when Mr MacGregor and his team of negotiators left the hotel on their way to meet the miners' leaders, their cars were given a police escort. At one point police cars blocked the road to allow the party to get clear of a posse of about fifteen journalists' and photographers' cars. When Mr MacGregor's car disappeared from view, the reporters had no alternative but to begin checking each of the likely hotels in the Edinburgh area. The talks were soon located at the Ellersly House Hotel, where it so happened that the *Daily Telegraph*'s industrial correspondent John Richards had booked in for the night.

The talks in Edinburgh, which lasted for three days, marked another low point in relations with the news media. Neither board nor union had much to say at the end of each negotiating session. Ellersly House was busy with summer guests, including some American visitors, who became increasingly bemused each morning, lunchtime and evening as the reporters, photographers and television crews jostled with each other in the entrance, trying to film and interview the miners' leaders and management.

The refusal of both sides to speak to reporters was partly the result of an official protest which the NUM had lodged at the end of TUC conference week, when it asked management to ensure that all future negotiations were conducted with the NUM and not through the news media. In a letter to the NCB, the union claimed that the outcome of the negotiations had been jeopardised by the way Mr MacGregor had turned the run-up to the talks into a 'media event'. It was a point with which the industrial relations director obviously concurred. When asked, at the end of the third day of talks, whether any progress had been made, Ned Smith replied that the 'road show' was still, just about, on the road. His remark seemed oddly timed in view of the fact that Mr MacGregor and the rest of the directors flew back to London that very evening, saying that there would be more talks the following day at another undisclosed location.

Early next morning Mr Scargill and his team set off south by car. The president refused to say where they were going. The correspondents paid their hotel bills and debated what to do. Little did they know that the Edinburgh talks, which had begun on Sunday with Mr MacGregor's dramatic entrance, would end five days later, 400 miles away in London, after a week which, from start to finish, verged on high farce.

Journalists assigned to cover the miners' talks periodically faced what might be termed a game of cat and mouse, as the principal participants moved around the country to new venues, hoping each time to throw off their pursuers. Negotiations with the miners' union are usually held at Hobart House in London, where the NCB has an extensive suite of conference rooms, well protected from unwelcome intrusion by the news media. During strikes, however, many unions prefer all discussions to be held on neutral territory, and this was what the NUM insisted on from the start of the miners' dispute, not least because the union had placed a picket line on the entrance to Hobart House which no member of the leadership was prepared to cross. Therefore the two sides had no alternative but to use hotel meeting-rooms and to hope that by keeping the locations secret the talks might take place in some degree of privacy.

Secrecy is always difficult to achieve during well publicised negotiations involving well known personalities. If there is a rumour of talks taking place journalists start telephoning or visiting likely hotels and conference rooms. Tip-offs are frequently given to news oganisations by hotel staff or by the public, who may think they will be rewarded with a suitable fee. Occasionally hotel managements reveal the whereabouts of important meetings in order to gain free publicity. Once the news media discover where talks are taking place word spreads quickly, and within a short space of time a hotel lounge can fill up with reporters, photographers and television crews. If the hotel manager protests at the invasion, the journalists respond by ordering coffee and sandwiches or by moving into the bar. By installing themselves as paying customers, and as long as they behave well, there is little a proprietor can do, they hope, to eject them. Nevertheless the sight of journalists waiting near the location of negotiations can cause annoyance, particularly when there are frequent adjournments involving the participants in moving from room to room through areas open to the public.

Only rarely do trade unions or employers seem to understand why photographers and television crews need to get as close as possible to private meetings, even watching the very door that leads to the meeting-room. In fact, it derives in part from the off-hand and cavalier way in which some union leaders and management treat the media. If discussions have lasted many hours and have ended late at night, the participants may or may not want to make a statement. They may decide to hold joint or separate news conferences, or to issue an agreed statement, in which case the newsmen waiting outside will perform a useful function for them. On the other hand, if the discussions are at a delicate stage or have gone badly, the participants may decide to say nothing at all and try to leave as quickly as possible, sometimes by the back door, without speaking to the reporters. An accurate indication of when a meeting may end is unlikely to be available, so the reporters and cameramen have no alternative but to sit it out.

When news conferences are held in the middle of industrial disputes, often in strained circumstances, the two sides invariably want to make any statements they decide on immediately. Sometimes they complain in public about the time it takes radio reporters and television crews to assemble their equipment or instal sufficient lights for the cameras. On these occasions proximity pays off, as only those newsmen in the immediate vicinity will be able to assemble themselves and their equipment in time for the opening of the proceedings; reporters and cameramen who stay working in their offices and then make a dash for the designated location often arrive too late.

On some occasions, particularly at night, unions and management may in fact be relying on the news media to convey the outcome of a dispute in the next morning's newspapers or on late-night or early-morning news bulletins. The information which the media transmit may frequently determine whether union members report for work the next day or whether factories or public services are able to operate. The experience of most reporters is that even on those occasions when their presence has eventually proved to be of practical value little thought is given to the logistic problems that face them.

No assessment of those working in the news media would be fair or complete without acknowledging that competition between rival news organisations is now the factor that has the greatest influence on behaviour. The expansion that occurred during the late 1970s and early 1980s in the radio and television services, which now provide news programmes from early morning until late at night, has resulted in a limitless demand for news and up-to-date interviews and film. The pressure to find fresh material is so great and the competition so fierce that few news desks can risk waiting for the conclusion of a meeting. Reporters, cameramen and television crews are usually sent to the appropriate location well before the likely starting time, in order to observe or film the arrivals. During particularly controversial disputes union leaders and company chairmen can sometimes awake to find reporters and cameramen waiting outside their homes, ready to capture the first photographs, comments or interviews of the day. If the venue for that day's meeting is not known in advance, motor-cycle despatch riders are frequently deployed by the television services to follow union leaders and management in the hope of discovering the precise location. As Fleet Street had found its traditional role of conveying information increasingly taken over by the immediacy of the electronic media, the popular newspapers have tended to retaliate by concentrating on off-beat stories or pictures, like the 'snatch' photograph mentioned earlier that was obtained by pushing open the door of the July miners' negotiations at the Rubens Hotel.

Mr Scargill has frequently complained about what he calls media harassment, which on occasion, he believes, has amounted to an invasion of his privacy. His presence at a union rally or picket line began commanding the interest of the news media in his early days as leader of the Yorkshire miners. Once he became president of the NUM he was subjected to constant attention, especially by Fleet Street photographers. During the 1983 TUC conference, for example, while he was sitting listening to the debates, a *Daily Mirror* photographer, Alf Markey, spent much of one day taking endless photographs whenever Mr Scargill opened the briefcase which he had on his lap. Mr Markey's persistence was well rewarded, because the following morning under the headline, 'Spray it again, Scargill!', the *Daily Mirror* published an exclusive photograph of Mr Scargill and his opened briefcase: in one corner 'nestling among papers' was a can of hair lacquer, which 'enabled the fiery miners' leader to keep his hair on for a change in blustery Blackpool'.

While the constant attention of one photographer may prove mere annoyance, the patience of those under observation quickly reaches breaking-point if numerous cameramen, television crews and reporters are in hot pursuit, as happened at the 1984 TUC conference in Brighton. Mr Scargill's unpredictability and preoccupation with his own performance did little to calm representatives of the news media, who feared they might miss a sensational picture or startling comment if they allowed the NUM president out of their sight, even for a moment. The miners' strike had turned the conference into a media event that began to equal an American political convention, because there was frequently more happening on the outskirts of the conference than in the debating hall itself.

Showing little regard for the TUC's own proceedings, on the second morning of the conference Mr Scargill chose the middle of the debate on the NGA printworkers' dispute to make a statement on the miners' talks.

The president made his announcement in the entrance hall, which forced the producer of the BBC television live conference coverage hastily to switch transmission from the debating hall. As Mr Scargill moved from one room to another in discussion with colleagues, other delegates looked on in bewilderment at the media circus sweeping by. On several occasions unsuspecting visitors were nearly knocked off their feet as technicians trailing cameras, microphones, lights and cables hurried along corridors or up stairs. Some of the behaviour was inexcusable: one television team waited in the corridor outside Mr Scargill's hotel room; a foreign television crew followed the president, perhaps by mistake, as he walked into the conference lavatories. Some newspaper photographers showed no regard for people standing nearby as they clambered on tables and knocked over furniture in order to take their pictures.

Mr Scargill had already complained about the conduct of the media when speaking at a debate on coverage of the miners' strike at the Edinburgh International Television Festival on 27 August. When challenged about the rough treatment being experienced by some television crews on miners' picket lines, Mr Scargill said it was time the media accepted some of the responsibility. Only the previous week he had been trapped in a doorway by 'a herd' of reporters and cameramen whose behaviour, he said, was such that if it had been seen on a picket line they would have been arrested instantly.

Mr Scargill's experiences the week before at Brighton went some way to explain his impatience with the news media at the resumption of negotiations in the second week of September in Edinburgh. In an effort to secure privacy, on the third day the NUM and NCB decided to move to another location. Mr Scargill's regular driver and lifelong friend Jim Parker was at the wheel as the president's Rover pulled away from the Ellersly House Hotel. Three other cars set off at the same time. Mr Parker had been tailed by newsmen before, and had built up a repertoire of tricks designed to throw pursuers off the trail.

His first substantial encounter with Fleet Street cameramen had been at the 1982 NUM conference in Inverness, three months after Mr Scargill had taken over as president. Several newspapers, including the *Sun*, had ordered their cameramen to photograph Mr Scargill every time he entered or left his hotel or the conference hall. On one occasion Mr Parker became so annoyed that he bundled together some clothes to make it look as if Mr Scargill was sitting on the back seat of his Jaguar, and set off at high speed for Inverness airport. The photographers followed, only realising they had been fooled when they reached the airport. The following week the *Sun* published a half-page spread on 'Arthur's Minder', who was described as the bodyguard for one of Britain's most unpopular men: 'Nobody takes liberties with Big Jim Parker. He is Oddjob in steel-capped clogs. A lovely bloke, really, despite an awesome air of menace' (*Sun*, 13 July 1982).

'Oddjob' enjoyed the drive south from Edinburgh that September. The three cars on his tail included one driven by BBC television reporter Mike Smart, another containing his camera crew, and a third being driven by a newspaper photographer, who gave up after about twenty miles. Mr Smart and his crew had little difficulty keeping up until they reached the A1 in Northumberland, where they lost sight of the president's black Rover, only to see it again further south filling up at a petrol station. Mr Scargill waved good-naturedly when he saw the two television cars were back on his tail. When they reached Newcastle-upon-Tyne, Jim Parker made a determined effort to lose the television cars, repeatedly circling roundabouts and then shooting off unexpectedly at one of the exits. After the brakes failed on the camera crew's car, Mr Smart was on his own, finally losing sight of the president's car south of Newcastle. Mr Parker's efforts to throw off his pursuers were in vain, however, because when the president's party stopped for a break at the County Hotel, Durham, Mr Scargill was spotted by an ITN camera crew which was in the city to cover a murder trial. Mr Scargill tried to explain his presence by telling the ITN crew he was the mystery witness in the court case.

Once other newsmen had been alerted, Mike Smart, who was still driving south, was notified, and he caught up with the president's Rover ten miles south of Durham, only to lose it again near Wetherby in Yorkshire. All was not lost because other reporters had been making inquiries all morning, and when it was discovered that Ian MacGregor and his team had set off north for Yorkshire, the *Yorkshire Post*'s industrial correspondent Robin Morgan staked out Doncaster station. He saw Mr MacGregor arrive, but lost sight of him in the station car park. The next train into Doncaster was from Edinburgh, and from this the NUM vice-president Mick McGahey was seen alighting. Mr Morgan followed in his car as Mr McGahey was driven to the Monk Fryston Hall Hotel, near Selby. BBC radio's northern affairs correspondent Ralph Smith, who had been searching hotels in the Selby area, arrived at Monk Fryston almost simultaneously. The location of the talks was broadcast on BBC radio news at 3 p.m. At the successful conclusion of such a prolonged car chase – this one had lasted nearly six hours – the hunters are naturally reluctant to be baulked of their prey.

Within an hour of the new location being announced, there was a large gathering of reporters, photographers and cameramen inside the entrance hall of the hotel. The presence of cameramen and television crews led to an immediate protest by the hotel management, who asked all the newsmen to wait outside. Several of the correspondents, who had ordered tea and sandwiches, managed to speak to industrial relations director Ned Smith, suggesting that all the reporters should withdraw and wait in a nearby café or public house on condition that the two negotiating teams notified them once the talks were over. Mr Smith asked for an assurance that all reporters and cameramen would behave reasonably in the meantime, but

137

the journalists' delegation admitted that it was in no position to give such an undertaking.

Jim Parker told television crews and cameramen to stay by the front door and not go near the room where the talks were taking place. The car chase notwithstanding, Mr Parker cheerily acknowledged the arrival of Mike Smart. As the afternoon progressed, and the newsmen waited, it soon became clear that all was not well. Mr Parker was soon seen emerging hurriedly through the front door, rushing round to the side of the hotel to demand that Giles Smith and an ITN camera crew get off the lawn, whence they appeared to be filming the room being used for the negotiations.

Shortly after 5 p.m. Mr Scargill and Mr MacGregor appeared together on the hotel steps to announce that their negotiations that afternoon had been 'ruined' by media harassment. Mr MacGregor shared the view of the NUM president that the 'unfortunate intrusion' of the press into their attempt to hold an orderly meeting had made it more difficult for the two sides to solve their mutual problems. At this point the miners' vice-president Mick McGahey was heard to comment: 'This is media violence.'

The joint appearance of Mr Scargill and Mr MacGregor, standing side by side, was a news picture in itself, of course, as the two men had not been photographed together since the 'snatch' picture at the Rubens Hotel. Several newspapers commented that here at last was something on which Mr Scargill and Mr MacGregor appeared to be in agreement. Ned Smith told me later that the one incident that persuaded the NCB chairman to join in the complaint about media harassment was the discovery of a cameraman sitting in a tree next to the hotel. The board had taken a first-floor bedroom where Mr Smith's secretary could prepare documents for the talks. Momentarily in the bathroom, she had looked out of the window only to see the cameraman looking in.

When Mr MacGregor heard of this incident he agreed with Mr Scargill that they should leave. According to Mr Smith, the chairman and president were determined to leave Monk Fryston anyway because they feared that 'limpet' microphones had been stuck on the windows of the negotiating room by one of the television crews in an attempt to record what was being said. They had come to the conclusion that there was not a room left in the hotel where they could negotiate without being seen or overheard by representatives of the news media.

The Monk Fryston episode inevitably caught the attention of commentators on media behaviour. The journalists' response was put by John Lloyd of the *Financial Times*, when he wrote of his personal impressions in an article for the *New Statesman* entitled, 'It's our job to be a nuisance':

When does enthusiastic reporting/filming end and harassment begin? There is no line – it is where the object of the reporting complains of being harassed – and has the ability to stop it. Like most newspaper reporters, I can't stand TV equipment jostling me out of place on doorsteps and at press conferences – and get impatient with the me-first, blunderbuss questions of the TV and radio networks. But I want to see or hear the results of their pushiness, and so do Scargill and MacGregor.

(John Lloyd, *New Statesman*, 21 September 1984)

Within the NUM executive there was less sympathy than usual for Mr Scargill's complaints about media harassment. While few executive members had a good word to say for the journalists, there was a general feeling that the president's entourage were partly to blame for the media circus by driving round the country in Rovers and staying in three-star hotels, when the miners had been on strike for six months.

Monk Fryston was the last hotel used for full-scale negotiations. Once Mr Scargill and Mr MacGregor had made their complaint to the assembled journalists, cameramen and technicians the two negotiating teams left immediately, reconvening later that evening not far away, at the offices of British Ropes in Doncaster. When the reporters arrived there they found the building under a heavy police guard, which stopped them getting any closer than the street outside. The Doncaster talks were again reconvened the following day in London at the former offices of the British Steel Corporation, next-door to the NCB's headquarters. Despite a week of attempting to negotiate, the discussions finally broke down that day without a settlement, so ending a hectic round of meetings, the like of which neither the negotiators nor their pursuers in the news media had previously experienced.

When, ten days later, Ian MacGregor met senior TUC leaders at Congress House to discuss the possibility of further talks, the TUC suggested seeking the assistance of the Advisory, Conciliation and Arbitration Service (ACAS), which had been established by the Labour government in 1974 to act as an independent conciliator during industrial disputes. Although the two sides stayed on for nearly an hour after the meeting, trying to agree a joint statement for the waiting journalists, Mr MacGregor was only prepared to say that the NCB would 'consider' help from ACAS, not 'accept' it as the TUC would have preferred. While TUC leaders were still working on their statement, they saw him being interviewed on his way out by radio and television reporters. He simply told them that there had been an exchange of views, but no agreement or timetable for further talks.

The preparation of statements for the news media often becomes a contentious issue, because presentation is usually of crucial importance during difficult disputes. Sometimes the task of agreeing and writing a statement can take as long as the actual negotiations, and the more other organisations tried to help settle the miners' strike the greater the difficulties became.

The need to find a basis for fresh talks was given futher impetus at the end of that week, when on 28 September the pit deputies' union, the National Association of Colliery Overmen, Deputies and Shotfirers (NACODS), announced an overwhelming 82.5 per cent vote in favour of strike action. The result looked like changing the whole emphasis of the dispute, because NACODS members are responsible for the safety inspections which must be carried out before miners can work underground. If the deputies were to stop work, coal production would cease throughout the country and would halt output in Nottinghamshire and other working coalfields. No date had been set for the strike, as NACODS had asked for a meeting with the NCB at the offices of ACAS in order to discuss its grievances. Relations with management had broken down earlier in the summer, when the NCB ordered colliery managers not to pay pit deputies who refused to cross NUM picket lines. Although the board had offered to suspend the instruction, this was insufficient for the NACODS leadership, which had also urged strike action in protest at the board's decision to cut capacity and close pits.

The threat of widening strike action came on the eve of the Labour Party conference at Blackpool which, like the TUC conference the month before, was to be largely overshadowed by the miners' dispute. Arthur Scargill's every move was followed all the week by the news media, which succeeded in annoying the president before the official proceedings had even started. As the reporters, cameramen and television crews waited in a foyer at the Winter Gardens on the Sunday morning before the conference opened, a BBC television lighting technician started shining his lights through the glass door into the room where the miners were meeting. Within seconds there were protests from Jim Parker at this interruption of a 'private meeting', to which the technician replied that he was simply testing his equipment.

On the first day of the conference there was overwhelming support for a resolution which blamed the miners' strike on the 'total dishonesty' of the Conservative government, and accused the police of being responsible for 'organised violence' against pickets and their families. Next day the *Daily Mirror* described it as 'Scargill's hour of triumph', the conference having put its weight unconditionally behind the 'Scargill strike tactics'. The *Daily Mail*, under the headline 'Kinnock's humiliation', said that the Labour leader had seen his party 'stolen from under his nose', while he sat by 'grinning sheepishly' as Mr Scargill was treated to a 'coronation ceremony'.

The following day, after Labour's energy spokesman Stan Orme was seen mid-morning in the conference foyer recording a television interview with Ian Ross of ITN for that evening's Channel 4 News, there were suggestions that a new formula had been found for a reopening of talks. As Mr Kinnock was due to give his conference speech that afternoon, Mr Orme's involvement was a further indication that a new initiative seemed likely. Earlier, the miners' delegates had been seen crowding round Mr Scargill while he read to them what he said was part of Mr Kinnock's speech, obtained in advance.

When news of the Labour leader's likely initiative was reported later that morning on BBC radio and the BBC's teletext service, Ceefax, Norman Willis telephoned Mr Kinnock and asked him not to make any mention of new talks, as premature disclosure might endanger the moves that were under way. But twenty minutes earlier, Mr Kinnock's press secretary, Patricia Hewitt, had circulated copies of his remarks to lobby correspondents on five evening newspapers. When she asked for the copies to be returned, the industrial correspondents had already begun preparing their reports. Later Mr Scargill blamed the leak on the Labour Party, but the whole incident was an illustration of the complex procedures operating behind the scenes.

One newspaper scoop, which appeared on the second day of the Labour Party conference, sparked off sustained criticism of media behaviour. The *Daily Express* had published an exclusive picture taken by photographer Michael McKeown, showing the very moment when a private detective handed a writ for contempt of court to Mr Scargill as he sat listening to a debate. The previous Friday, 28 September, Mr Justice Nicholls had ruled in favour of two Manton miners who were against the strike, Robert Taylor and Kenneth Foulstone, declaring that the stoppage in the Yorkshire area was unlawful because it was started without a ballot. The two miners obtained the writ for contempt after Mr Scargill had appeared on Channel 4 News, within seven hours of the High Court ruling. During an interview with Peter Sissons the NUM president had again said that the strike was official, being in accordance with the NUM's Rule 41 which allows a strike to be declared official by the national executive on application by an area of the union.

The incident produced an immediate protest, which prompted the conference organisers to launch an investigation to discover how it had been possible for a court writ to be served on the conference floor, where admission could be gained only through possession of a delegate's or visitor's pass. Moss Evans, general secretary of the Transport and General Workers' Union, said it had to be more than a coincidence that the *Daily Express* was the only newspaper to have photographed what had happened. Some delegates demanded that all the paper's photographers and reporters be ordered to leave the conference. Later the organisers announced that they had been unable to discover how the writ-server gained access, but the *Daily Express* had known what was happening and did have its photographer alongside. The conference then decided to withdraw the press credentials issued to the *Daily Express* editor Sir Larry

Lamb, who, while confirming that his photographer had entered the conference hall with the writ-server, had denied there had been any collusion. Next day Sir Larry gave his version of his expulsion:

> I am quite proud to be barred from conference for standing by my staff in their achievement of a significant scoop in obtaining the only picture of the writ being served upon Arthur Scargill . . . This is the way the Labour Party behaves these days. There is no charge, no evidence, no trial. The conference organisers, who have been themselves satisfied with my assurance on Tuesday evening, have now bowed to the pressures of the mob.
>
> (Sir Larry Lamb, *Daily Express*, 4 October 1984)

As the conference continued, Mr Scargill assumed an increasingly higher profile in the news media. On the Monday evening, after he had been served the court order, he spoke to a fringe meeting in the Winter Gardens, brandishing the writ for the benefit of photographers and television cameras, and acknowledging that he might have to go to prison. He had been ordered to appear in court on 4 October, the Thursday of the conference, but instead he stayed in Blackpool.

When the contempt hearing took place – in his absence – the sole evidence against Mr Scargill was the Channel 4 interview. Three television sets had been installed in the court, one in front of the judge, another for counsel and a third for reporters sitting on the press bench. When Mr Justice Nicholls asked whether Mr Scargill was simply disagreeing with the order, rather than disobeying it, a recording of the interview was shown on the three television sets. At the point where Mr Scargill had said that no High Court judge would take away the democratic rights of the NUM, Mr Justice Nicholls leaned forward and switched off his set. Although he described what had happened as a 'grave state of affairs', the judge adjourned the hearing in the hope that the NUM and its president would reflect on their position and reconsider the desirability of being represented.

News of the adjournment reached Blackpool just before the conference lunch-break. As delegates left the hall Mr Scargill was instantly surrounded by television crews, radio reporters and journalists, all asking for his comment on the court's decision. As Mr Scargill walked up the stairs from the conference floor an unseemly mêlée developed, in which elderly delegates and visitors were pushed aside by the cameras and cables of the television crews. The pressure on radio and television staff had been considerable, as all the networks wanted to hear Mr Scargill's reaction to what had been said in court. Soon the confusion bordered on panic, and several delegates thought the jostling might have been caused by police officers trying to arrest Mr Scargill.

The conference week had been one in which the NUM had concentrated all its efforts on securing the fullest possible support from its traditional allies in the Labour Party, while the public spotlight had stayed firmly on Mr Scargill because of the court case and the possible penalty of imprisonment for contempt. There had been little opportunity for the union to make a broader appeal to the public by diverting the focus of attention to its case against pit closures. One chance that did arise was mishandled by the union because of its continued failure, seven months into the strike, to make adequate allowance for the operational requirements of substantial sections of the news media.

This missed opportunity concerned the publication of a study on the economics of the coal industry. In order to challenge the NCB's argument that certain pits were 'uneconomic', the NUM had commissioned the study from Andrew Glyn, a lecturer at Corpus Christi College, Oxford. The first that most labour and industrial correspondents heard of the imminent publication of this document was during the morning of 3 October, the third day of the conference. Nell Myers had told them that a new report on the industry would be released by the union for general publication later that evening, but not until after its contents had been revealed exclusively on BBC television's Newsnight programme at 10.50 p.m. Correspondents were asked to assemble by the tea bar in the Winter Gardens at the end of the afternoon session, where advance copies would be available. Mr Scargill would be there to answer questions.

When the correspondents arrived they found there were many other reporters, delegates and visitors in the vicinity of the tea bar, some asking questions of Mr Scargill. Nell Myers gave those correspondents she knew a copy of the eighteen-page document, accompanied by a short press release explaining that the contents were embargoed and were not for use until after 11.45 p.m. Mr Scargill had insisted on the documents being distributed discreetly, as, he said, one of the reporters responsible for the exclusive item to be broadcast on Newsnight, Vincent Hanna, had asked him if he would restrict the circulation of the advance copies. Production staff on the programme feared a rival news bulletin might broadcast Mr Glyn's findings before Newsnight was transmitted.

Few of the national newspaper correspondents had time to ask many questions. Keith Harper, labour editor of the *Guardian*, had precisely half an hour in which to read Mr Glyn's complex conclusions before phoning his story for the first editions of the next day's paper. Because of the 11.45 p.m. embargo, the report could not be mentioned that day on any of the tea-time or early evening radio or television news programmes. The next day, however, the BBC did broadcast a report by its labour correspondent, summarising the findings on the 7 a.m. news on Radio 4. The *Morning Star* led its front page with a report on the study, and Keith Harper's story became the lead on page 2 of the *Guardian*. It was also the lead on the labour page of the *Financial Times*, secured nine paragraphs on page 2 of the *Daily Telegraph*, and was summarised in two paragraphs in *The Times*. But the document was largely ignored by the Fleet Street popular newspapers and the broadcasting services.

Arthur Scargill and Nell Myers were dissatisfied with the news coverage that the report had received, and began quoting it as an example of the way the news media had ignored the NUM's case. Equally, however, the NUM could be said to have ignored all the precautions which organisations usually follow when distributing complex documents to representatives of the news media. In order to assist the assimilation of the information, it is usual for such a document to be issued a day or more in advance, under an embargo – which gives an opportunity to quality newspapers to assess how much space to devote to it, to television programmes to consider ways of illustrating it, and to radio programmes to plan interviews or perhaps a studio discussion. Journalists are then invited to a news conference at which the author can be interviewed.

My own subsequent inquiries indicated that the NUM had issued just two copies of the Glyn report in advance of the general distribution to correspondents at the Winter Gardens tea bar. Vincent Hanna told me that Newsnight had received its copy on the previous Sunday, and Mick Costello, industrial correspondent of the *Morning Star*, said his paper had obtained a copy on the previous Monday, which had enabled it to give the report extensive coverage. But if the Glyn report was regarded by Mr Scargill as a document that deserved wide publicity, the NUM would have been well advised to have provided all newspapers, radio and television programmes with the same advance information that had been supplied to Newsnight and the *Morning Star*. Mr Scargill might even have revealed part or all of one conclusion, promising more at the weekend, ready, say, for Monday morning's newspapers and news programmes. Many organisations adopt the tactic of trailing major reports in the hope of building up interest and gaining maximum publicity when the full report is published. If a proper news conference had been arranged, the news media would also have been able to interview Mr Glyn about his findings, rather than having to accept Mr Scargill's interpretation. And here was another opportunity for the NUM to project someone other than Mr Scargill. Alternatively, in view of the correspondents' preoccupation with the Labour conference, the NUM could have waited until the following weekend before releasing advance copies of the report, and then arranged a structured news conference where Mr Glyn and Mr Scargill could have answered questions.

The NUM had chosen the worst possible moment to issue the Glyn report. Most of the correspondents who were in Blackpool were there to report the Labour Party conference, not the miners' strike. As mentioned earlier, late afternoon is always a risky time to issue a major report, as it is too close to the copy deadlines of the national newspapers. Then, to have allowed Newsnight to reveal the contents as an exclusive a day before the rest of the news media, could hardly have been regarded as the most diplomatic way of encouraging rival organisations to give prominence to the report. Mr Scargill believed that Andrew Glyn's conclusions could have been incorporated in later news reports, and could have changed the assumptions that the news media were making when referring to 'uneconomic' pits. These views may have some justification, but given that labour and industrial correspondents working for the serious national newspapers, radio and television were anxious to provide balanced coverage, if the NUM was intent on maximising the report's publicity opportunities it should have paid at least some attention to the time constraints under which news organisations operate, and recognised that if the union wanted to pick and choose, by supplying information exclusively to certain programmes or papers, it ran the risk of jeopardising wider coverage.

The NUM's apparent failure to think through a communications strategy had alerted the National Union of Journalists and other organisations that were prepared to assist; their advice went unheeded, as we have seen. As the final months of the strike approached, the National Coal Board and the government both had clearly defined publicity objectives. The NCB was preparing for the propaganda advantage that would accrue from the moment when they could claim that half the miners were back at work. The Secretary of State for Energy, Peter Walker, was facing another challenge in media management: he wanted to keep all mention of the power stations out of the news in order not to antagonise those trade union members who were ignoring the TUC's conference decision and allowing maximum electricity output. For much of the strike Ian MacGregor had been one of the NUM's greatest assets, an aunt sally at which the miners could hurl abuse. Within a few weeks the NCB chairman would make his wounded retreat from the public spotlight.

SIX

The Height of the Offensive

The last five months of the strike began with a succession of bewildering incidents and changes in management personnel which were, without doubt, the clearest illustration during the dispute of the strong undercurrent of political interference that shaped the National Coal Board's relationship with the news media. At one point a fierce clash of personalities, involving Ian MacGregor, looked like nullifying many of the endeavours of pit managers to encourage a return to work. As we have seen, through much of the strike Mr MacGregor had insisted that he alone should present the board's case, just as Arthur Scargill had said he should be the only official spokesman for the National Union of Mineworkers. When Mr MacGregor finally stopped trying to compete with Mr Scargill for the attention of the media, the government and coal board found it easier to exploit Peter Walker's contacts in Fleet Street and the skills of management's publicity advisers in putting the best possible interpretation on the return-to-work figures. Mr MacGregor's withdrawal from the spotlight exposed the union's lack of communications strategy and the inherent danger in allowing one man to have sole responsibility for the preparation of press statements.

But any shortcomings in communications or publicity might well have seemed irrelevant when set against the achievements of the mining communities themselves. In early October, as the union approached the seventh month of the dispute, there were almost a hundred pits where not a single miner had worked since early March. In the heartlands of the strike in Yorkshire, South Wales, Scotland, Durham, Northumberland and Kent there were less than five hundred miners in total reporting for work each day, out of a combined NUM membership for those areas of 107,000 men. It was a remarkable example of solidarity. Arthur Scargill was leading a strike which had become unique in the history of the British trade union movement: it was the first sustained use of industrial action on a national basis in defence of jobs.

There had been repeated attempts by management and government to break the strike. According to Media Expenditure Analysis Ltd, the

National Coal Board had spent, in the twenty-nine weeks to 30 September, a total of £1,750,300 on national newspaper advertisements as part of its campaign to persuade the miners to return to work. The miners had faced an unprecedented security operation designed to stop mass pickets, but the combined efforts of the coal board, government and police seemed only to strengthen their resolve. Mr Scargill, his enthusiasm hardly dented, had the British establishment worried: his sheer unpredictability had generated unease and uncertainty in management and Whitehall. A grudging sense of admiration could be observed in the columns of some of the newspapers that had been most critical of the miners' leader:

> He is the newsmaker, the man the media wants to question. No other union leader comes within a mile of him . . . His belief in himself, his granitic determination to get his way, is awesome. No one else in our public life has it in the same degree, with the one exception of Margaret Thatcher.
>
> (Paul Johnson, *Daily Mail*, 7 September 1984)

> Scargill is one of the most remarkable, instinctive exploiters of publicity in British politics. Neither the National Coal Board nor the government has anything to match.
>
> (Simon Jenkins, *The Times*, 5 November)

Mr Scargill had brilliantly exploited the discussions that had taken place with the coal board. All of the twelve negotiating sessions that had taken place in the last four months had ended in failure, but he had used each new meeting to help sustain the resolve of his members. The perpetual prospect of a negotiated settlement had gone a long way to stem the trickle back to work since the men preferred to wait for an agreement, not wanting to be the first to go back or to join those who were already being accused of disloyalty.

However, once the summer holidays were over there were a number of well publicised attempts to bring about a return to work. Towards the end of August a poster campaign was launched by a group described as the Moderate Miners' Wives, under the leadership of Mrs Irene McGibbon. Her husband Robert, a face-worker at Betteshanger pit in Kent, was one of thirty miners who returned to work on 3 September in a coalfield that had previously given solid support to the strike. The following month Mrs McGibbon, a Conservative Party committee member at Deal in Kent, was given a standing ovation at the Conservatives' annual conference in Brighton, after she had spoken of the wives' back-to-work campaign. But the vast majority of the 2,200 Kent miners stayed loyal to the NUM throughout the strike, and as Christmas approached only 2 per cent were back at work.

Nevertheless, there was one strike-bound area which, against the national trend, was reporting a noticeable drift back. The persistence of the local management in North Derbyshire (see page 122) was beginning to pay off and achieve national prominence. By the fourth week of September the number of men at work in the area had topped 1,000 for the first time since March, representing exactly a tenth of the local workforce. The North Derbyshire director, Ken Moses, was the first to open his books for public inspection, as promised by Mr MacGregor in the televised debate with Mr Scargill broadcast by Channel 4 News on 22 August. A report in the *Daily Telegraph* on the 24th described how the colliery manager's daily attendance record at the Shirebrook pit had 'well thumbed' pages, filled up in different pens and writing styles, indicating that it had been compiled by colliery officials over a long period. There was no positive proof that 158 men were working at Shirebrook, but the reporter said that against the entry for each man was the name of his town or village. The North Derbyshire management gave wide publicity to its increasing return-to-work figures, taking full-page advertisements in the local newspapers.

The communication techniques employed by the area director and his staff, which included regular letters and visits to the homes of strikers, prepared the way for a slow but relentless erosion of support for the strike in North Derbyshire. As his area had set the pace for the other coalfields, Mr Moses was naturally concerned at the prospect of strike action by the pit deputies' union NACODS, which threatened to shut every pit in the country. Area directors rarely commented, however obliquely, on the conduct of senior management in national disputes, but on 23 September Mr Moses admitted that the disagreement with NACODS was of critical importance; if the deputies went on strike it would bring all coal production to a halt. He hoped this new dispute would be quickly resolved.

Mr Moses' warning seemed to have angered Mr MacGregor and the deputy chairman, James Cowan. They would hardly have needed reminding by a colleague of the way they had mishandled the NACODS dispute, by announcing on 15 August that deputies would not be paid unless they crossed NUM picket lines. The board's decision had been greeted with indignation by the Fleet Street leader-writers. Now the whole issue had been revived, and the day after the blunt words of Mr Moses, the *Daily Mail* declared that Mr MacGregor's provocation of the pit deputies was 'by far his most serious tactical blunder'. The NCB chairman was told to give a clear signal to NACODS that he had made a 'mistake'. One director told me that Mr MacGreor, however, was ready to take on the pit deputies as well as the miners. Knowing full well that they had a statutory responsibility to make safety inspections which, if not completed, would prevent miners from going underground, he had nonetheless asked his colleagues about the possibility of trying to continue coal production in the working coalfields without the deputies. He even inquired whether working miners could be asked to take on the deputies' jobs. Some of the directors feared Ian MacGregor might seek to dispense with the deputies, just as Ronald Reagan had dismissed 11,500 American air traffic controllers during a strike in 1981.

Other senior members of management indicated in private conversations their dissatisfaction with Mr MacGregor's conduct. From my contacts with other directors, it was clear that Ken Moses was virtually *persona non grata* within the board, because of the way he had spoken out publicly on the threat of a NACODS strike. All the other directors were told not to speak or give interviews to the news media without first getting clearance from the deputy chairman, who was said to be conducting what was described by his colleagues as a 'witch hunt' to determine who was responsible for some of the leaks of information from within the board. The nervousness among senior management was heightened by Mrs Thatcher's comments during a BBC radio interview on the Jimmy Young programme on 19 September. In reply to one question, she said it did not matter how long the strike continued: it could go on for a year or longer, but the uneconomic pits would have to be closed. She did not seek to correct Mr Young when he suggested that Mr Scargill seemed to have upstaged Mr MacGregor in the propaganda battle. According to one director, the Prime Minister's remarks sent a shiver through the board.

There seemed a general feeling within management that the week of talks with the NUM that started in Edinburgh and ended in London did get close to an agreement, but the government had ordered the NCB to pull back as they thought that management had gone too far and were on the point of allowing sufficient concessions to the union for Mr Scargill to claim a victory. The tension within the board was heightened by the approach of the Conservative Party conference, and the evident wish of Mrs Thatcher and other ministers to avoid any adverse publicity or criticism from within the party on their handling of the strike.

Help was at hand, because conciliation staff at ACAS had been busy for days preparing the ground for a new initiative, which resulted, on the eve of the Conservative conference, in an announcement that representatives of the miners' union and coal board would be invited, for the first time in the dispute, to attend joint talks at the ACAS offices in St James' Square. Once the invitation had been accepted by the NCB, the government could safely deflect any possible criticism from conference delegates by requesting that nothing should be said to jeopardise the ACAS talks. Also, in order to assist negotiations, the pit deputies had agreed to suspend their threat of strike action. The NACODS' leaders had been assured that they would be consulted in any discussion on colliery review procedure, which the union believed had been breached by the NCB's 6 March closure announcement, and which it wanted strengthened by an independent appeals body. At a cabinet meeting the previous Thursday, in an attempt to head off a pit deputies' strike, the government had agreed to allow the appointment of an independent advisory committee to examine future colliery closures.

When the ACAS talks opened on 11 October, there was renewed hope that the concession to be offered to NACODS might pave the way to an overall settlement of the pit dispute. The ACAS chairman Pat Lowry was conscious of the challenge he faced in trying to conciliate between miners' leaders and management, since previously the two sides had spurned all suggestion of an ACAS intervention. From long personal experience Mr Lowry knew that if the talks were to succeed they might last for days if not weeks, and this would necessitate great tact and secrecy in order to prevent any unnecessary speculation in the news media about the negotiating positions of the various parties.

Because of the sensitive nature of its work ACAS has taken care to restrict the access afforded to representatives of the news media, while at the same time providing all the facilities that journalists could possibly expect, including telephones. A large room, approached immediately off the entrance hall, has been allocated for the media, where reporters, cameramen and technicians can wait while talks take place. ACAS has its own press officers who alert reporters when talks are about to finish, and provide what limited information is thought appropriate.

Two days before the start of the ACAS talks the NCB announced that its director-general of industrial relations, Ned Smith, had been suspended from duty on health grounds. Mr Smith had a serious back complaint, and would not return until fully recovered. But Mr Smith had in effect been relieved of his duties, the public relations director, Geoffrey Kirk, told me. It would be wrong to say he had been suspended because of his known disagreements with Mr MacGregor, but equally, said Mr Kirk, it would be wrong to say all was 'harmony and light' in his relationship with the chairman. Mr Smith, who was fifty-nine at the time, had previously indicated that he would retire once the strike was settled; but his sudden suspension, almost on the eve of the ACAS talks, was the first public confirmation of the deep differences within the board, which had briefly surfaced on 22 August, the night of the Channel 4 programme, when Mr Smith had been replaced at the last moment by Mr MacGregor.

The first round of negotiations at ACAS lasted until early evening. The management was under the impression that both sides had agreed, in view of the adjournment, not to make any comment to the reporters waiting downstairs. Mr MacGregor, the first to leave, made no statement. When Mr Scargill left a little later, however, he went straight to the press room to announce what he said was an important development: the NUM was prepared to accept new, independent proposals which could provide the basis for a settlement to the strike. However, he said, these suggestions had already been rejected by the NCB.

Mr Scargill's remarks were right on time for the Nine O'clock News on

BBC television. When management saw the NUM president make his announcement, there was consternation at coal board headquarters. The 'independent' proposals were in fact, according to Mr Lowry of ACAS, no more than suggestions which the NUM had made itself, but Mr Scargill had adroitly used Mr MacGregor's decision to leave without commenting as an opportunity to seize the initiative. He was able to take the credit for having made what appeared a conciliatory move, while at the same time putting the NCB in the dock, at the very moment when the government might have expected Mr MacGregor to have been explaining the management's willingness to allow pit closures to be considered by an independent body. The NCB's public relations staff immediately advised Mr MacGregor to regain the advantage by at least giving radio and television interviews to explain the NCB's position. In the end the chairman decided against this, saying there should be no more than a short written statement, which was finally issued at around 11 p.m. That evening's television news bulletins had also been seen by government ministers attending the Conservative conference in Brighton. How was it, they asked, that Mr Scargill was receiving all the publicity, when it was the government that had made the concession?

When the public relations director Geoffrey Kirk left for home shortly after 11 p.m., he was still saying, in accordance with the instructions he had been given, that Mr MacGregor was not prepared to give interviews. So he was somewhat surprised early next morning to hear the chairman being interviewed live on the telephone on the BBC's Today programme.

It appeared that just before 1 a.m., the overnight production team on the Today programme in London received a call from the programme's producer at the Conservative conference, giving a telephone number on which the NCB chairman was prepared to be interviewed shortly after 7 a.m. that morning. The producer in Brighton had been given the message by Sir Robin Day, who told me he had simply passed on the message at the request of Gordon Reece (later Sir Gordon), who is the publicity adviser credited with the successful softening of Mrs Thatcher's image in time for the 1979 general election, and was then standing in as the Conservative Party's director of press and publicity.

The chairman's Today interview did not achieve quite the impact that Mr Reece might have hoped for, because at 3 a.m. that same morning a bomb had exploded at the Grand Hotel in Brighton, where Mrs Thatcher and her ministers were staying. Throughout the morning the television and radio news programmes were dominated by pictures and eye-witness reports of dramatic scenes of the Brighton seafront. Events had again overtaken Mr MacGregor; he had lost the opportunity to counter the publicity that Mr Scargill had gained the night before.

Later that morning, after the Today interview, Mr Kirk asked me how the programme had managed to get hold of Mr MacGregor, as the public relations department was still under instructions to say that he would not speak to radio or television. I told him what I knew, including the telephone number the Today progamme had used to contact Mr MacGregor. Several days later Mr Kirk told me that he had asked Mr MacGregor about the interview, and that the number was in fact that of Mrs MacGregor's private telephone in the chairman's London flat; however the chairman had not revealed why he had changed his mind, after Geoffrey Kirk had left NCB headquarters, between 11 p.m. and 1 a.m. that night. The whole incident illustrated the growing exasperation within the government and Conservative Party at the way Mr Scargill was still capturing the headlines, seven months into the strike.

The involvement of the Conservative Party's acting publicity director, Gordon Reece, indicated the invidious position that Geoffrey Kirk found himself in: his advice was no longer being accepted, and his department was being ignored even when it came to some of the day-to-day arrangements for the chairman's interviews. Peter Walker had been closely monitoring the NCB's publicity operation for some months, and by the autumn it seemed that friends and consultants from outside – including Mr Reece, and Tim Bell from Saatchi and Saatchi – had gained the chairman's total confidence. The apparent consensus among them was that it was time to 'soften' Mr MacGregor's image: it would be done not by trying to improve his own effectiveness as a communicator, but by bringing in a new 'voice' to speak on behalf of the coal board. Within a week of the Conservative conference Michael Eaton, the NCB's North Yorkshire director, was named as the board's new public spokesman, with the task of assisting Mr MacGregor in 'co-ordinating communications within the board and with the public presentation of the facts'. The announcement was carefully timed as an exclusive for the Sunday newspapers.

The first Mr Eaton knew of his move to London was when he received a telephone call from the chairman on 18 October, two days before his appointment was announced. There was much to commend in the chairman's choice, not least of all because Mr Eaton, at fifty, was considerably younger than Mr MacGregor, who by then was seventy-two. In fact Mr Eaton was the youngest man to have been appointed an area director, having served as Barnsley director for three years and then for ten years in North Yorkshire, which had brought him into regular contact as a negotiator with Mr Scargill, throughout the years he was leader of the Yorkshire miners. Mr Eaton had started in the coal industry on leaving school at sixteen, when he joined as an apprentice at the Frickley pit. After winning an NCB scholarship to Nottingham University and qualifying as a mining engineer, he rose rapidly through the management ranks. This long association with the coal board contrasted sharply with Mr MacGregor's thirteen-month spell as chairman. Mr Eaton had a hesitant, almost apologetic approach when answering questions on radio or

Plate 13   Fleet Street cartoonists took full advantage of Michael Eaton's appointment on 20 October as public spokesman for the NCB. Nearly a year after Gibbard's cartoon was published in the Guardian *when Mr Eaton unexpectedly sought early retirement in September 1985, Mrs Thatcher paid tribute to his work in communicating the board's case.*

television; in terms of public presentation he could clearly be portrayed as the acceptable face of management.

There were plenty of favourable headlines in the Sunday newspapers on 21 October. The *News of the World* reported that Mr MacGregor had brought in a 'Mr Nice Guy', quoting the new public spokesman as saying that when the miners saw his face on television he hoped it would go some way to restore the loss of confidence there had been between the NCB and the men. The *Sunday Telegraph* said the move was welcomed in Whitehall, as the government had been disappointed by Mr MacGregor's failure to communicate with the miners, which had left ministers with no alternative but to handle the publicity campaign themselves. Mr MacGregor told reporters it was his idea to appoint Mr Eaton, as it was time to bring in one of the industry's top men to put over the NCB's case.

After the Sunday headlines, Monday's national papers began to express greater interest in the tactical reasons behind the appointment. The *Guardian* interpreted the board's decision to 'send in a professional' as an indication that Mr MacGregor 'has been shuffled (or has elected to shuffle himself) sideways'. The *Daily Mail* described the appointment as a 'dire gamble at a critical juncture', and it warned the NCB against conceding 'one fraction more of substance' to the NUM or NACODS. Its leading article was entitled 'The muzzling of MacGregor':

Now you hear him. Now you don't. For Ian MacGregor to have his public address system switched off at this, the most decisive moment in the struggle, has to be an admission of inadequacy . . . Enter Michael Eaton, the new front man for the Coal Board's case, whose own manner is as comforting as a pint of Yorkshire ale . . . The singer has had to be changed. The song must not.

(*Daily Mail*, 22 October 1984)

Mr MacGregor seemed annoyed that some of the newspaper reports interpreted the appointment of a new public spokesman for the duration of the strike as perhaps the first step towards some diminution in his own role as chairman. His sensitivity over the publicity Mr Eaton was receiving was shared to a degree at No. 10 Downing Street, where the Prime Minister's chief press secretary Bernard Ingham was telling lobby correspondents that Mrs Thatcher had received no advance warning of Mr MacGregor's announcement. The attempt at news management which surrounded the Eaton appointment illustrated the confusion that can occur when separate briefings are given by a nationalised industry, by the minister responsible and by No. 10 Downing Street.

I first heard about Mr Eaton's new job on Friday, 19 October, when Geoffrey Kirk telephoned to say that the board would be holding a news briefing the next morning for industrial correspondents on the Sunday newspapers. A new public spokesman was to be appointed, he said, but the announcement was embargoed until Sunday morning, and I was only being informed out of courtesy; the briefing would be restricted to Sunday journalists, and Mr Eaton would not be available for radio or television interviews until Sunday lunchtime.

After going to Mr Eaton's Saturday briefing, which Mr MacGregor did not attend himself, the Sunday newspaper correspondents began asking if there was any political significance in the announcement. Lobby correspondents then started ringing No. 10 Downing Street; Mr Ingham said afterwards that that was the moment when he first heard of Mr Eaton's appointment. But the coal board's public relations department had, at least, informed the Department of Energy on the Friday that Mr Eaton would be giving the Saturday-morning news briefing – during which the public relations staff were telephoned by the Department, and asked if Mr Eaton was making it clear that he had been given the job by MacGregor, and that the appointment had nothing to do with the government.

Once Downing Street heard that some journalists were likely to imply that Mr MacGregor seemed to be on the way out, there were some hurried consultations. Several Sunday journalists said that Peter Walker spent some time that Saturday phoning correspondents to tell them that the Sunday papers should get it right: Eaton was not a new MacGregor, simply a 'front' man for the coal board. Eventually all the correspondents had been given the same information: as Mr MacGregor was aware of the government's criticism of his handling of the media, he had decided it was time the coal board was represented on television and radio by someone who had his roots in the industry and who looked and sounded more like a miner.

Mr MacGregor lost no time in indicating the limit of Mr Eaton's responsibilities. Although the new public spokesman had referred in his weekend interviews to the continuing dispute with the pit deputies, he was pointedly not included in the management team that began talks at ACAS the following Tuesday. However, the industrial relations director Ned Smith did return unexpectedly, rejoining the negotiators only a fortnight after being suspended 'on health grounds'. Mr Smith was later to explain that when he had been ordered to leave he in effect resigned, but he had then been telephoned at home by Mr Cowan and told that the chairman wanted him to return, in order to help with the negotiations. Mr Smith's presence was a reflection of the importance of the latest talks, because NACODS had renewed its threat of strike action, announcing that its 17,000 members would stop work on 25 October. After the failure earlier in the month of the ACAS negotiations involving the miners' union, the pit deputies' leaders sensed the strength of their position and were determined to exact the maximum safeguards against pit closures, and the strongest possible colliery review procedure.

The threat of strike action by the pit deputies prompted a switch in the coal board's advertising, with full-page advertisements in the national newspapers, set out like a letter and addressed, 'Members of NACODS'. A full explanation was given on the state of the negotiations under the headline, 'Let's find a way to end this dispute, not prolong it.' Mr Walker had been telling lobby correspondents for some weeks that he was confident the deputies would not strike, but the negotiations continued nearly to the deadline, partly, perhaps, because both coal board and government were anxious not to be seen in any hurry to make concessions, which might only have hardened the resolve of the miners. When a final agreement was eventually reached, NACODS called off the strike the day before it was due to start. The TUC would have preferred the deputies to have simply suspended it as that would have kept up the pressure on the board and the government.

Although the miners' union was left to fight on alone, the NACODS leadership believed it had gained significant concessions. The original closure proposals would be 'completely reconsidered'; the five pits that had been the subject of the first closure threat would remain open, to be considered along with any other colliery closures; and there would, as indicated, be a new independent review body which could hear the views of the unions and the mining communities when pits were named for closure.

Mr Scargill described the NACODS formula as 'completely unacceptable' to the NUM, insisting that the miners' strike would continue; but within the coal board and Whitehall the sighs of relief were almost audible. The settlement with the pit deputies had effectively removed the only likely cause of power cuts that winter. So long as the working coalfields in the East Midlands continued operating, the government was confident that coal stocks would last well into the New Year.

Four days after the NACODS settlement, Mr Scargill received one of the severest propaganda setbacks of the strike, when the *Sunday Times* revealed that the union's chief executive, Roger Windsor, had been sent as the NUM's representative to meet the Libyan leader Colonel Gaddafi in Tripoli. News of this visit, five months after woman police constable Yvonne Fletcher had been shot outside Libya's London embassy, led to a storm of protest. Senior TUC leaders were at the forefront of the general condemnation, one saying that the NUM's free flight to Libya must have been the most counter-productive made by any union. The next day, instead of exploiting the NUM's embarrassment, Mr MacGregor ended up scoring what the *Daily Express* described as 'yet another own goal' which equalised the damage done by 'Scargill's monumental blunder' over Libya. The NCB chairman had chosen the day of maximum discomfort for the miners' union to silence his new public spokesman, cancelling all Mr Eaton's appointments with the news media on the grounds that the 'sensational developments' arising from the miners' Libyan adventure had changed the whole situation. Mr MacGregor believed that stopping all press statements and interviews by Mr Eaton would help focus attention on the miners' union, but the abruptness of his action had only drawn attention to the internal rivalries within the board, which had been inflamed by his own appointment of a public spokesman.

Mr Eaton had apparently been excluded from the management team that negotiated the NACODS agreement the week before at the specific insistence of the deputy chairman Mr Cowan, who was supported by the board member for personnel, Merrik Spanton. As the two men had been involved in the original refusal to pay the pit deputies, they were both said to have been more than a little disconcerted when, on the day his appointment was announced, Mr Eaton described the deputies' dispute as the kind of mistake that, he believed, the board could avoid once Mr MacGregor started receiving better advice. At one point Mr Cowan and Mr Spanton were both said to have threatened to resign unless the public spokesman was barred from the negotiating team. Mr Eaton's remarks did little to enhance his reputation with the chairman, either: when the Opposition's energy spokesman, Stan Orme, had approached Mr Eaton, on the assumption that he had some influence, Mr MacGregor had reminded Mr Orme that all approaches should be made first to the chairman's office and not to Mr Eaton, who was 'just the PR man'.

The news that Mr Eaton had been silenced, only eight days after his appointment, emerged during the morning of Monday, 29 October, in time for the lunchtime news programmes. The World at One on BBC radio reported the anger felt by some of Mr Eaton's colleagues in Yorkshire, who had told me that the new public spokesman feared he was on the point of being relieved of his job and of being sent back north on the next train. One close associate said that he knew he had been 'kicked into touch'.

The sudden switch in the attention of the news media, away from Mr Scargill's discomfort over Libya to the internal feuding in the coal board, embarrassed the government but delighted Labour MPs. During energy questions that afternoon in the House of Commons, Peter Walker tried to play down the disagreement, declaring that Mr Eaton 'happily remains' at his duties, confident that it was 'perfectly right' of the chairman to have cancelled his press engagements while the board re-examined its position following the disclosures over the miners' Libyan connection.

At the moment when Michael Eaton was officially 'silenced' he was actually being interviewed by the *Guardian*'s labour editor, Keith Harper. During the discussion the public relations director Geoffrey Kirk, who was sitting in on the interview, was summoned to the chairman's office to be told that all the board's contacts with the news media should cease forthwith. Mr Kirk returned to the Eaton–Harper interview and quickly drew the conversation to a close. He then cancelled the other news interviews that had been arranged that day for Mr Eaton, and asked his staff to call off a buffet lunch which was being organised for the following day for Mr Eaton and about thirty industrial correspondents at a public house in Whitehall.

While Mr Kirk and his staff were busy cancelling, he discovered that a reporter from Independent Radio News had obtained an interview that morning with Mr MacGregor, by telephoning direct to the chairman's office. When the interview was broadcast, Mr Kirk protested that it seemed inconsistent with the chairman's directive that press contacts should stop. The argument that ensued was to be the last in a long line of disagreements between the chairman and his public relations director. Next day Mr Kirk had departed, or, as Mr MacGregor put it, was 'on vacation'.

Ten days before his departure Mr Kirk had been involved in a major disagreement with Mr MacGregor over the advertising campaign aimed at persuading miners to give up the strike, which was costing the NCB around £400,000 a month. The NACODS dispute had required new advertisements, and these were now being prepared by the board's advertising agency, CM Partnership. When, on Friday, 19 October, Mr Kirk said, he was handed new copy for the advertisements by Mr MacGregor, he was told that in future all advertising over the strike should be conducted by another agency, Lowe Howard–Spink Campbell–Ewald. Mr Kirk protested unsuccessfully at the decision, maintaining that it was unwise to switch agencies in the middle of the strike, as Lowe Howard–Spink had not prepared advertisements for the board before. Three months after the change in agencies, Mr MacGregor's advertising and communications consultant Tim Bell was to leave Saatchi and Saatchi, becoming chief executive of Lowe Howard–Spink in January 1985.

Tuesday's national newspapers were still disgesting the silencing of Mr Eaton – which the *Daily Express* had headlined 'The farce of Mr Fixit' – when the *Daily Mirror*'s industrial editor Geoffrey Goodman, a long-standing friend of Mr Kirk, heard reports of his disagreement with Mr MacGregor. On Wednesday morning Mr Goodman had an exclusive report headlined 'Chaos in the coal board', which described how Mr Kirk had apparently been dismissed in circumstances that he described as 'a total shambles'. Mr Goodman's report made much of the fact that during Prime Minister's questions in the Commons the day before, Mrs Thatcher had pointedly evaded questions from the Labour leader, Mr Kinnock, as to whether she still had 'full confidence' in Mr MacGregor.

One theory for Mrs Thatcher's refusal that day to repeat her usual endorsement of Mr MacGregor, was that her press secretary Bernard Ingham, another long-standing acquaintance of Mr Kirk, had been among the first to know of his sudden departure. (Before becoming a government press officer Mr Ingham had been a labour correspondent on the *Guardian* and had established a close working relationship with Mr Kirk, who had been the coal board's public relations director for twenty-four years.) Later Mr Ingham told lobby correspondents of his distress at what had happened, acknowledging that he would have preferred Mr MacGregor to have made greater use of Mr Kirk, rather than rely on advice from consultants like Tim Bell.

On 6 November after a week's 'leave', Mr Kirk, who was then sixty-three, returned to the coal board for a two-hour meeting with the deputy chairman Mr Cowan, where he was offered reinstatement and the opportunity to continue as public relations director until the end of the year, when he had intended to retire in any case. Mr Kirk asked if the board was prepared to offer an apology for the unnecessary embarrass-ment which, he believed, had been caused to his wife and family. Mr Cowan left the meeting to put this request to the chairman, returning with the message that Mr MacGregor would allow Mr Kirk his apology, but it would be up to Mr Kirk to announce it; the board was not prepared to issue its own public apology. On hearing this, Mr Kirk told me, he decided to retire immediately, and it was agreed that he should leave at the end of the week.

Later that day Geoffrey Kirk held a news conference at Hobart House to announce his departure, at which he accused the board of lying when it had said the previous week that he had gone on holiday: 'Going on holiday is voluntary: being sent on leave is not. I have been given no explanation as to why they lied.'

The news conference itself was another odd twist in an already bizarre sequence of events: here was Mr Kirk, who had another three days to serve as public relations director, telling reporters inside the coal board's headquarters of his disagreements with the chairman. In the space of ten days there had been four arguments, most of which seemed to have arisen over his dissatisfaction with the way Mr MacGregor was treating his public spokesman: Mr Kirk felt that he was wrong to have barred Mr Eaton from the negotiations at ACAS, and then to have silenced him the following week. Mr MacGregor had in turn blamed Mr Kirk for the adverse publicity that the board had received.

Mr Kirk had obviously been offended by the chairman's failure to take his professional advice, not least of all in the sphere of publicity. He did not know the precise function of the consultants that Mr MacGregor had employed, he said, but three had been active: Tim Bell of Saatchi and Saatchi, David Hart, a freelance journalist who had been writing for *The Times* about the National Working Miners' Committee, and Gordon Reece, then standing in as the Conservative Party's director of press and publicity. Mr Kirk had seen Mr Hart twice, and had been surprised on one occasion to find that Mr Reece was advising Mr MacGregor during a News at Ten interview for ITN. Later, in a letter he wrote to the Labour MP Austin Mitchell, Mr MacGregor had said that Mr Hart and Mr Reece were personal friends; only Mr Bell had been retained as a consultant.

In mid-December the labour and industrial correspondents held a farewell dinner for Mr Kirk, where he predicted that it would be the following March before the strike would be over and most of the miners back at work. Then, five months after the dinner, came news that he had drowned in a boating accident off the Isle of Skye.

The disagreement between Ian MacGregor and Geoffrey Kirk overshadowed what turned out to be the final round of full-scale negotiations between the coal board and the miners' union. On the very morning that news broke of Mr Kirk's sudden departure, talks had begun at ACAS as a follow-up to the agreement reached the previous week with the pit deputies. As the miners' union had already rejected the NACODS formula, there seemed little prospect of the two sides reaching a settlement. Mr MacGregor's own commitment to the talks also appeared open to doubt, as he had suggested to his colleagues that the board should consider withdrawing from all negotiations with the union as a protest at the NUM's visit to Libya.

After ten hours the ACAS discussions broke down. Mr MacGregor declared the time for talking was over: the NUM, he said, had 'refused to move' from the position it had adopted in March, and the board believed the union had no intention of seeking to resolve the dispute by negotiation. Mr Scargill maintained it was the NCB, acting on government instructions, that was unwilling to negotiate. Over a period of four weeks the ACAS chairman Pat Lowry (later Sir Pat) and his advisers had made a valiant attempt to try to settle the dispute; their assistance had helped to avert a stoppage by the pit deputies, but when it came to the miners' strike the conciliation staff found their work had been hindered by the high public profile which Mr MacGregor and Mr Scargill had insisted on maintaining.

If, when discussions are still in progress, each side continues to give hostile interviews about the other on the steps of the ACAS headquarters, then the conciliators and waiting journalists usually deduce that the protagonists are still more interested in propaganda than negotiation. Conversely, as we have seen, one indication of possible progress is the refusal of union leaders and management, on either their arrival or their departure, to comment to newsmen. Throughout the ACAS talks the NUM and NCB vied for publicity; the rivalry was so intense, and their eagerness to follow the news so great, that the negotiating teams even competed with each other for the one portable television set provided for those times when all the negotiators can do is to while away the hours in separate rooms, as Mr Lowry and his staff pursue the path of conciliation.

Often news interviews were given by Mr Scargill or Mr MacGregor when the other side was already in the ACAS building. It was on these occasions that there was the greatest pressure to see or hear what the other side had been saying at the front door. Mr Lowry tried hard to prevent such distractions, believing it would be better if the negotiators did not give interviews or divert their attention by watching or listening to the news, as this tended to generate yet more statements to the news media and was not conducive to a calm negotiating atmosphere.

The final round of the ACAS talks finished on 31 October at 8.30 p.m. Mr MacGregor ordered an immediate news conference at Hobart House where, in an attempt to repair the shattered image of the management, the chairman was flanked by James Cowan and Ned Smith. When reporters inquired about Geoffrey Kirk's unexpected departure the day before, Mr MacGregor indicated that he would not answer any further questions and started to walk from the room, but retraced his steps when Mr Cowan insisted that the public relations director had not been dismissed. A second news conference was called next morning, when the board again displayed its full negotiating team in another show of managerial unity. The message was the same. The NCB was about to change course: there would be no more talks with the NUM, and instead there would be new moves to encourage a return to work.

Within days of the failure of the ACAS talks, Michael Eaton was restored as official spokesman. The chairman had finally relinquished his role as the coal board's principal communicator. His withdrawal opened the way for a carefully controlled propaganda offensive which would make a significant contribution to the ultimate defeat of the miners' leadership.

From then on three clear themes began to emerge in the coal board's advertisements, press statements and interviews. The greatest emphasis was placed on telling miners of the bonus and holiday money for which they could qualify by returning to work. This was backed up by two constantly repeated messages: there would be no more talks with the NUM, and even if the strike did continue into the following year there would be no power cuts that winter. The word that kept recurring in the interviews and statements given by the Secretary of State for Energy, Peter Walker, was 'senseless' – it was now a 'senseless' strike.

From early November the coal board and the government demonstrated the effectiveness of their efforts to co-ordinate publicity. The joint campaign would build up relentlessly until the day when management could claim that half the miners were back at work – the most decisive moment of all in terms of propaganda, because the government would then be able to say that after having been denied a pit-head ballot, a majority of miners had voted with their feet and given up the strike.

From the moment the pit deputies had reached their agreement in October, the government had believed that it would only be a question of time before the miners drifted back to work. By agreeing to silence himself Mr MacGregor was free to concentrate on strategy. The growing sense of confidence, which began to emerge at Hobart House and Westminster, was also reflected in Fleet Street. Labour and industrial correspondents on the newspapers that supported Mr MacGregor and Mrs Thatcher were among the first to detect an easier working atmosphere. They found that their editors had suddenly become much more relaxed about the miners' dispute. One correspondent told me that from the moment the pit deputies called off their threat of strike action, the internal office memos stopped; his editor was no longer giving him almost daily instructions about news coverage of the dispute. Another correspondent described how his editor had been called to Downing Street for a meeting with the Prime Minister, who was concerned about the tone of some of the newspaper's reporting; but once the pit deputies settled, that editor too had taken the pressure off his staff.

Within two days of the final breakdown in the ACAS negotiations, the coal board was ready to launch its greatest publicity offensive yet, announcing on Friday, 2 November that miners who were back at their pits by the 19th would qualify for bonus and holiday payments which could provide total pay packets of up to £650 in the week before Christmas. By making the announcement on the Friday, the board knew there was every likelihood that the publicity could be sustained over the weekend, ensuring a big drift back the following Monday morning. Correspondents on the Sunday newspapers were given fresh calculations by the NCB: any miner returning to work by Monday could earn £1,400 in the seven weeks leading up to Christmas. For many men their first pay packets would be tax-free, as they had not earned any money in that financial year and therefore had not reached their tax threshold.

In several coalfields, including Lancashire and Staffordshire, the board sent out letters to the homes of every striker, outlining the maximum potential earnings. The letters, which were signed by individual colliery managers, emphasised that negotiations had finished. The November issue of *Coal News*, which was again posted to all miners, reinforced the thrust of the board's publicity with a bold front-page headline declaring 'End of the talks'.

On the morning of Monday 5 November the board claimed a record return to work, stating that there were 868 'new starters' back that day for the first time since March. By Friday the board was claiming that 2,177 miners had resumed work that week – six times the previous weekly record. The largest single increase was in North Derbyshire, which reported 2,282 men at work – up by more than 1,000 on the previous week. In South Wales the board maintained that thirty-three strikers had crossed the picket lines, which represented the first breach in the solidarity that had been shown for so long by the 20,000 miners employed in the coalfield.

Record attendances were reported in each of the following two weeks. After 5,016 miners had returned in the five days ending on 16 November, Michael Eaton predicted that more than half the miners would be back at work by Christmas. On the following Monday, 19 November, another 2,282 miners gave up the strike, rising to 5,700 by the end of the week. However, once the deadline passed for Christmas holiday payments, the 'surge' back tailed off dramatically, dropping to 975 on Monday 26 November. Mr Eaton's brave prediction looked more than a little premature, and the board's public spokesman was careful not to commit himself again.

Press officers from the coal board were on duty from early each morning in the NCB's six regional headquarters. Several areas had their first estimate of the daily return ready in time for the 8 a.m. news bulletins on radio and television. In a matter of days, it seemed, the early-morning reporters and press officers had formulated their own jargon. Strikers reporting for work were described as 'new faces' – a phrase which subsequently began appearing in some news reports and, although it drew criticism from the NUM, did neatly illustrate the pressures being exerted: the pit managers wanted to indicate as early as possible each morning the number of men abandoning the strike, to the news gatherers waiting with their deadlines.

The board knew the tactical advantage in giving its estimate for the return to work as early as possible, well before the union could respond. Often there was no time for a detailed check of the attendance records, so the pit managers could do no more than run their eye over the miners reporting for work, and add up the number of men they had not seen before. This figure would then be telephoned through to the regional headquarters, where a press officer would be waiting in the control room ready to give journalists the first instant assessment. Later in the day, once the attendance records had been checked, the board was able to give detailed figures for both morning and afternoon shifts.

By broadcasting and publishing these return-to-work figures, journalists met fresh hostility from the miners' leadership, who believed that the news media should not have been so ready to accept unsubstantiated information from management. Mr Scargill disputed figures, insisting that nearly 80 per cent of the NUM's members were still on strike. He rarely gave a detailed breakdown to back his assertions, and there was no effective internal communications system within the union to produce daily figures. Many journalists tried to balance their reports with up-to-date statistics from the union, but it was difficult to give an accurate overall asessment. While Mr Scargill was ready to accuse the NCB of manipulation, neither the NUM headquarters in Sheffield nor the area offices seemed either capable or prepared to give a pit-by-pit breakdown on the same lines as the NCB.

The figures were only part of the drama that was unfolding in the coalfields. There on the television news each day was film of cars and coaches taking men to work through the picket lines. Some of the former strikers were prepared to give their reasons for going back. Such interviews made compelling viewing and listening, especially on those occasions when a family was split – when a father returned to work but not his son, or when one brother went back and not the other. At Ellington colliery in Northumberland, the NUM branch secretary, John Cunningham, returned to work on 19 November amid considerable publicity, despite protests from his son who stayed out on strike, declaring that he would not speak to his father again.

On 5 November, when the board reported its first major breakthrough in the return to work, the NUM had issued its own brief statement – namely, that 800 miners who had previously provided voluntary safety cover had been withdrawn from the pits. But there had been little other information forthcoming from the union, until, at the end of the second week of the November 'surge' back, it produced a comprehensive area breakdown for those on strike and at work, which for most journalists was the most detailed they had received from the union since the start of the dispute. Apparently, 49,235 NUM members were at work in the week ending 16 November, and not 59,000 as claimed by the board. There was a wide measure of agreement between the NUM and the NCB on attendance in areas like Yorkshire, South Wales and Kent. The largest discrepancy arose in the working coalfields of Nottinghamshire, Leicestershire and South Derbyshire, where the board claimed that 5,500 more men were at work than acknowledged by the union. Throughout the build-up in the return to work, the board had refused to give pit-by-pit figures for Nottinghamshire and some of the other working coalfields, which reinforced the union's suspicions of manipulation. Even so, the attention of the news media was firmly focused on areas like North Derbyshire, where on the union's own figures 3,500 NUM members had given up the strike.

When journalists attempted to do their own calculations, they frequently came unstuck. The *Sun* did so in spectacular style on 20 November, by publishing a table entitled 'The flood back to work'. When the first edition was published, the paper gave the total at work as 47,631 – which was well down on the 60,000 claimed by the board, and fewer even than the NUM's own estimate of 49,235 published the week before. In later editions the *Sun* had added 15,000 'ancillary workers', giving a new total of 62,631, which was in line with the board's most recent estimate. Later the board denied there was any group known as 'ancillary workers', suggesting that the *Sun*'s original miscalculation had arisen through the omission of miners on certain shifts and the failure to allow for illness and absenteeism.

The two tables were reproduced in *The Miner*, which said that the *Sun*'s adjustment in the 'scab figures' was a naked attempt to influence opinion and weaken the strike. *The Miner* gave its own version of what happened that night at the *Sun*:

editor Kelvin MacKenzie stopped the presses in the middle of the November 20th print run and added another 15,000 to the scab figures. He was afraid that the lesser number would aid the strike. Small wonder that Fleet Street, TV and radio now enjoy the same sort of trust among miners as people felt towards Hitler 50 years ago.

(*The Miner*, 11 December 1984)

The confusion over the total for the number at work stemmed from the misleading phraseology that the NCB had adopted during the summer, when *Coal News* stated in its July issue that 'a total of 57,000 people were working', rising to 'more than 60,000' in the August issue. The impression was given that the total was for miners at work, but when pressed to substantiate the figures the NCB agreed that not all those mentioned were NUM members, as some belonged to the other mining unions. In the September issue of *Coal News* the NCB had tried to be precise, claiming that '50,000 NUM members' were not on strike; the figure rose to 'more than 52,000' in November. However, the board's belated attempt to qualify its own figures had only drawn attention to the way it had changed the definition. Under the banner headline 'Bloody liars', *The Miner* on 21 November made much of the fact that on the NCB's own estimate, the total for those at work was over 7,000 less than in August, yet the November issue of *Coal News* was claiming a 'surge of ex-strikers' returning to work. The change in the figures was described by *The Miner* as 'cast-iron proof of how the National Coal Board lies through its teeth'.

Throughout November and December, the coal board's national newspaper advertisements gave further publicity to the return-to-work figures – now clearly stating that they referred to NUM members. Tim Bell hoped the advertisements would encourage more men to give up the strike, while at the same time reassuring those who had gone back that they had made the right decision. As the return to work gathered pace the advertisements were changed each week, featuring first the NCB's final offer on pit closures, then the following Sunday, 11 November, the money that miners could earn by Christmas if they abandoned the strike.

On 22 November new advertisements gave the figures for the number of men who had abandoned the strike in the previous two weeks, in the form of a table under the headline, 'If you turn up for work this week, you won't be alone.' The next in the series appeared in the Sundays of 2 December, and showed two men asking, 'What's the difference between a working miner and a striking miner?' It went on to explain that a working miner knew that 'more than 68,000 NUM members' had given up the strike, and their number was 'growing daily'. The following Sunday the advertisements were changed again, this time featuring a double-page spread: on one side was a list of the twenty-seven pits where no miners were at work, and on the opposite page was a list of the 147 pits where miners were said to be reporting for duty. In the three months to the end of December, Media Expenditure Analysis Ltd estimated that the NCB spent £1,284,060 on national newspaper advertising, which took the total estimated expenditure on press advertising in the forty-two weeks since the start of the strike to £3,035,360.

If the NUM was to succeed in regaining the publicity initiative, it had to find some way to demonstrate the determination of the strikers. It needed a strategy aimed at persuading the news media to focus its attention on those statistics that would help reinforce the solidarity of the mining communities. Ross Forbes, the one (temporary) press officer in the union, who was acting as spokesman for the Durham miners, had found it virtually impossible to compete against the barrage of coal board figures. Although the number of men going back in the Durham coalfield in the first week of November was well under one per cent of the workforce, he noticed that any statements he made on behalf of the NUM were simply tagged on to the end of news stories in what he regarded as no more than a token attempt at balance. Mr Forbes was disappointed by his experience, but while critical of most journalists for following the NCB's figures, he acknowledged the superiority of the board's public relations department and the failure of area NUM leaders to give sufficient priority to the preparation of information for the news media. The board was succeeding each day in setting the news agenda, in the same way that British Rail had

WHAT'S THE DIFFERENCE BETWEEN A WORKING MINER AND A STRIKING MINER?

He knows that the Coal Board has made its last offer.

He wants to protect his job and safeguard his pit.

He wants the whole industry to have a good long-term future.

He believes his Union should carry out the wishes of its members.

He knows that it's always been a fact of life in mining that pits have to close.

He wants more money invested in modernising old pits and opening new ones.

He knows that more than 68,000 NUM members are not on strike, and their numbers are growing daily.

He's working.

He knows that the Coal Board has made its last offer.

He wants to protect his job and safeguard his pit.

He wants the whole industry to have a good long-term future.

He believes his Union should carry out the wishes of its members.

He knows that it's always been a fact of life in mining that pits have to close.

He wants more money invested in modernising old pits and opening new ones.

He knows that more than 68,000 NUM members are not on strike, and their numbers are growing daily.

He's on strike.

NCB

Management are doing all they can to keep the pits open.
Help us secure your future.

held the advantage in the summer of 1982 when it received widespread publicity for its attempt to run a limited train service in the face of the ASLEF strike (see p. 33).

It was not only newspaper, radio and television reporters who were having difficulty in obtaining accurate national statistics, but also editors of trade union journals, whose coverage would almost certainly have been sympathetic to the miners. Some reporters wanted an indication of the number of pickets that had been injured, in order to counterbalance the official police casualty figures; others were trying to keep track of the number of miners who had been sacked by management or who had appeared in court for picket-line offences. But the NUM continued to make little effort to co-ordinate such information in a form suitable for the news media, even though regularly available national figures could have been used by the union to considerable effect.

Organisations that raised money to help relieve hardship among the miners' families did receive widespread publicity for their efforts, especially in the run-up to Christmas. Street collections were organised throughout the country; there were frequent newspaper, radio and television reports of more outings and parties for miners' children, and the donations of food and household goods continued to arrive. Early in October the NUM press office had given several days' advance notice of the arrival at Dover of a convoy of thirty-five lorries carrying food from the French trade union federation the CGT, and of the docking at Hull of a ship chartered by the Danish seamen's union, carrying foodstuffs and children's clothing.

While the leadership did all it could to promote individual acts of generosity towards the miners and their families, it drew a veil of secrecy over its own finances and those of the Miners' Solidarity Fund in Sheffield. From the earliest days of the strike, Arthur Scargill had spoken with pride and confidence of the steps he had taken to protect the NUM's assets. However, after the union had refused to pay the £200,000 fine for contempt (see p. 141), imposed when it had continued to declare the strike official against the ruling of the High Court, sequestrators were appointed. After a month's investigation the sequestrators announced, on 28 November, that £4.6 million of the union's money had been traced in Luxembourg, £2.7 million in Dublin and £500,000 in Zurich. It was at the

Plate 14   One objective of the NCB's advertising campaign was to reassure those miners who had given up the strike that they had made the correct decision and were not alone. In this Sunday Express *advertisement, published on 2 December, the NCB had chosen its words carefully so as to avert another collision with the NUM over figures. By claiming that 68,000 were 'not on strike' the NCB had also avoided saying that all these NUM members were at work – in fact an undisclosed number were sick or absent each day.*

end of that week, after another High Court hearing, that a receiver was appointed to replace Mr Scargill and the other NUM trustees.

In the face of such concerted legal action, the leadership believed it had no alternative but to prevent all public disclosure of information about the union's finances. The wish for secrecy was shared in the mining communities, where there were widespread fears that publicity about financial assistance for the miners' families might lead to deductions in the social security payments being made to wives and children. Some of the trade unions which were providing the NUM with loans and donations feared that their money, too, could be seized by the courts; some union leaders met criticism from their members for donating to the NUM. Vast sums were involved. The Transport and General Workers' Union made a national contribution of £1 million, and estimated that its regions and branches donated another £3 million to help hardship funds in the coalfields. Fleet Street printworkers raised over £2 million, and collections organised by over 300 support groups throughout the country brought in another £2 million. Some of the largest amounts were collected well away from the coalfields: the Isle of Wight support group raised about £1,000 a week. Money also came from abroad, for the strike had sparked off international support and interest of a kind not seen for any post-war British industrial dispute. Trade unions in Scandinavia collected £350,000; according to the NUM vice-president Mick McGahey, the Soviet Union sent £900,000; and at a ceremony in London a cheque for £10,000 was handed over on behalf of Afghan trade unionists.

The letters accompanying these donations had deeply moved the union's general secretary, Peter Heathfield, but he, like Mr Scargill, refused to answer any questions about the finances of either the union or the support funds. The NUM was fully justified in thinking that the publication of any financial information was fraught with danger, but again there was no overall strategy; many donations went unreported, and the union failed to gain the maximum possible publicity from these unparalleled demonstrations of solidarity and generosity.

Some of the money was raised at the showing of the 'Miners' Campaign Tapes' – six short films on the background to the dispute, available on video cassette. These tapes had been produced for the NUM as a gesture of solidarity by workers at ten of the film and video workshops accredited by the Association of Cinematograph, Television and Allied Technicians, in response to what they felt was a dearth of information sympathetic to the miners' fight against pit closures. The first tape was called 'Not just tea and sandwiches: miners' wives speak out.' Two tapes dealt with the facts and figures behind colliery closures and redundancies. Another entitled 'The lie machine: media coverage of the strike', examined the role of newspapers, radio and television. The cassettes were shown first in the mining communities, but as the strike continued requests were received from other trade unions, from support groups throughout the country and then from trade union activists overseas. Over 2,000 copies were eventually shown throughout the world. Two NUM members took tapes to Australia, returning with £20,000 in donations; shipbuilding workers in Denmark raised £3,000 after showing them in local shipyards; in Germany the NUM's supporters went to the trouble of giving the films a German soundtrack. The organisers were overwhelmed by the response.

As we have seen management had been using video as a form of communication for some years. Ian MacGregor had recorded a video tape for workers at British Steel in 1980 (see p. 46), and at the start of the miners' strike the coal board had attempted, without success, to arrange showings of a video message from Mr MacGregor to the miners (see p. 99). The six tapes produced for the NUM were regarded as a breakthrough in trade union communications. Video had never before been used on anything like this scale to communicate with the membership and maintain morale during an industrial dispute. The dedication of the film-makers, and the co-operation they received from the mining communities, were recognised three months after the strike when the Miners' Campaign Tapes were awarded the British Film Institute's John Grierson award for innovative documentary work.

As Christmas 1984 approached, Arthur Scargill reminded readers of *The Miner* that even if 51,000 NUM members were reporting for duty, as claimed by management, very few of them were the key underground workers whose presence was needed before the board could produce coal in quantity. Painting pit-head gear or sweeping up did nothing to fuel the power stations; all the union needed, said Mr Scargill, was for 'General Winter to do his job over the next few weeks', and the aims of the strike would be achieved. But the president's brave promise could only be fulfilled if the trade unions representing workers at the power stations implemented the overwhelming decision of the TUC conference, by asking their members to observe NUM picket lines and stop the delivery and use of coal or substitute oil.

In the wake of the conference vote there were many warnings of the likely impact on the electricity industry. One of the most explicit predictions was given by Gavin Laird, general secretary of the Amalgamated Union of Engineering Workers, who said on TV–AM on 25 September that power cuts would start 'within six to eight weeks at the outside'. Only the week before, the Prime Minister had declared emphatically that the miners' strike would have no effect on power supplies, either 'this side' or 'the other side' of Christmas. Her confidence stemmed in part from the failure of the electricity industry unions to reach any agreement on the implementation of the TUC's pledge of support. As we saw in chapter 5, leaders of the power station engineers and the electricians had both indicated that their members would not be taking industrial action to back the miners. The general secretary of the EETPU,

169

Eric Hammond, had been roundly condemned by TUC delegates at Brighton for his criticism of the strike. Mr Hammond's stand was vindicated on 19 October when the EETPU announced that its members in the electricity industry had voted by 84 per cent in a postal ballot against supporting the NUM.

This reluctance to back the miners prompted the TUC chairman Jack Eccles to suggest that it was time the union movement prepared a realistic assessment of what it could deliver. Mr Eccles also believed that the 'fatal hour' was fast approaching when the TUC would have to make its own judgement on what would constitute a reasonable settlement to the strike. Although the views of the TUC chairman were an accurate reflection of what many union leaders had been saying in private, the TUC considered he had overstepped his brief, and he was told not to attend any further meetings of the liaison group responsible for monitoring relations with the NUM. But Mr Eccles had apparently been determined to speak out. His original statement, calling on the TUC to reassess its 'narrow and blinkered' support for the strike, was part of an interview that he had pre-recorded for The World at One on BBC radio on the morning of 30 October, before setting off for London. He was obviously forewarned of the reception that would be awaiting him later that afternoon at Congress House, because shortly before The World at One was to be broadcast at 1 p.m., he rang the BBC from Crewe station to say that he was sticking by what he had said, but would be grateful if the programme could stress that the comments he had made were his own and not those of the TUC.

A fortnight later the miners' frustration and anger at the TUC's failure to stop coal and oil deliveries was met head-on by Norman Willis, who had spent his first two months as TUC general secretary trying to drum up support for conference policy. Mr Willis had been invited to address a rally of South Wales miners at Aberavon. He faced a capacity audience, knowing he would have to refer to the TUC's difficulties in trying to deliver support, as well as to the concern of the wider trade union movement over the violence that had again been seen on the picket lines. The TUC, he said, was not an army, and the general secretary was not a field marshal. He wished he could guarantee the miners every bit of support they needed, but other workers were concerned over their own future and had reservations about the strike. When, after having condemned what he said were 'scenes of unprovoked police aggression', Mr Willis turned to the subject of picket-line violence, he was met by boos and shouts that turned into a slow handclap when he declared that he had never marched in front of a miners' banner that had praised 'the brick, the bolt and the petrol bomb'.

A few minutes later a hangman's noose descended from the ceiling in front of Mr Willis as he stood speaking on the platform. A group of men had gained access to a gantry in the roof, where they had found a coiled-up rope which was to have been used, once the speech was over, to lower the television lights installed in the hall. Thus the news media had inadvertently provided the prop for an impromptu protest which was seen throughout the country and produced some of the most riveting television pictures of the week.

Throughout the rally there were calls from local NUM leaders for solidarity, and for a show of unity on the picket lines aimed at persuading the eighty or so South Wales miners who were working to rejoin the strike. There was also a hero's welcome for Arthur Scargill, who told the audience that he would not be commenting on allegations about picket-line violence as he knew it was the police who were responsible. His only wish, said Mr Scargill, was that labour and trade union leaders would turn their venom not on the miners' union but on the 'hyenas' of Fleet Street. Next morning the car of a BBC Radio Cymru reporter, Hefin Wyn, was overturned outside the Celynen South pit, and several other BBC journalists in South Wales were attacked that week in picket-line incidents. Later that same month a South Wales taxi driver, David Wilkie, was killed when a concrete block was dropped from a road bridge, smashing through the windscreen of his taxi as he was taking a working miner to Merthyr Vale colliery.

The day after the Aberavon rally Mr Scargill was in the Midlands, visiting the small South Staffordshire coalfield, where management claimed that over 80 per cent of the miners were back at work. As the president was speaking to six hundred strikers crowded inside the miners' welfare at Lea Hall, steam blew across from the cooling towers of Rugeley power station, close to the pit; in the road outside a lorry passed every thirty seconds, taking another load of coal past the picket line and on into the power station. Mr Scargill seemed undaunted by the obvious lack of local support for the strike.

The following week, on 21 November, *The Miner* declared that power cuts were already taking place. Apparently a 3 per cent voltage reduction had lasted for half an hour in much of southern England, but the effects were being hidden, it said, as the government feared the news would act as 'a big boost to the morale of strikers'. In a survey of Yorkshire power stations, *The Miner* claimed that coal supplies were running out as power workers had to scrape 'the bottom of the pile'. The paper was correct in its observation that coal stocks were low in Yorkshire, but it had overlooked, as had most independent analysts, the scale of the switch that had been made from coal- to oil-fired power stations.

From the very start of the strike, the Secretary of State for Energy had ordered a virtual news blackout on the operations of the Central Electricity Generating Board. Mr Walker was to prove as effective in his news management of the electicity industry as the power stations were in meeting the demand from consumers. As management was only too willing to co-operate, Mr Walker was able to exercise tight control over the flow of information. Demonstrating the meticulous planning that is required for a successful communications strategy, he was later, by careful timing, to deliver a body blow to Arthur Scargill's propaganda at the very moment when the NUM was already starting to slide towards defeat.

Mr Walker had strong reasons for ensuring the utmost secrecy over the precise level of fuel supplies and the output from individual power stations. His first priority was to avoid any repetition of the public debate about coal stocks that had arisen during the 1974 miners' strike, when industry had been put on a three-day week. If accurate information was not available, then any assessment by the miners' union or other, independent, analysts on the length of time coal stocks would last, was more than likely to be unreliable.

As the months went by, Mr Walker must have been increasingly amused by the succession of city stockbrokers and academics who were still warning of the possibility of power cuts. He knew that his own confident prediction that coal stocks would last well into 1985 could not be challenged, as the share of the load being shouldered by the oil-fired stations had been increasing steadily, and oil was also being used in many of the coal-burning stations. By late autumn the amount of electricity being generated from oil was the equivalent of what would have taken a million tons of coal a week. The switch was almost sufficient for the generating board to dispense with the services of the big power stations in Yorkshire.

Secrecy was also desirable so as to avoid disruption of the build-up in oil-fired and nuclear electricity generation by industrial action in support of the miners. If attention was not drawn to those stations where output had increased, the government believed it would lessen the likelihood of sympathetic action. Once winter approached and power station workers began ignoring the TUC's call for a ban on coal and oil deliveries, there was a third reason for secrecy. The government knew it had to proceed with even greater caution, because the last thing Mr Walker wanted to do was to embarrass those union members who had refused to back the miners. This was why it was so important for the government to play down the success of the electricity industry in beating the effects of the strike.

Before it was known that it would be possible to achieve a three-fold increase in the oil burn, the government had reacted quickly when it heard that the *Sunday Telegraph* intended publishing on 25 March 1984 a report suggesting that the cabinet was about to consider contingency plans for the introduction of power cuts. John Kesby, the *Sunday Telegraph*'s industrial correspondent, had reported that the government's plans 'could mean rationing of power supplies to domestic consumers and industry to conserve energy for a long battle with the miners'. However, on the evening of Saturday, 24 March, even before the first edition of the newspaper had been printed, the press office at No. 10 Downing Street had telephoned the *Sunday Telegraph* to say that the story was inaccurate: there were no plans for the weekly cabinet meeting to consider contingency measures for power cuts. Although it was too late to stop or alter the first edition, John Kesby's story was removed from later editions of the paper.

The government's sensitivity on the question of power cuts, coupled with the refusal to give up-to-date information about coal stocks, did give the miners' union the chance to gain maximum publicity from its warnings of imminent power cuts. During the first two months Arthur Scargill had made regular predictions on how long coal supplies would last, maintaining that power station stocks had fallen to no more than eight weeks' supply. As spring turned to summer and the Nottinghamshire miners kept on working, Mr Scargill drew back from making any further forecasts, as his earlier predictions had been ridiculed repeatedly by Peter Walker. Instead the NUM president tried a light-hearted approach. His favourite joke at the time was that the heaps of coal at the power stations were rather like his own head of hair: hollow in the middle. When reporters asked what had happened to his confident predictions about power cuts, Mr Scargill suggested it was time the journalists hired a plane and flew over the power stations so that they could report on the true state of the coal stocks.

With the approach of the summer holidays Mr Scargill could see the danger in making further predictions, but he knew that, once the autumn arrived, the miners and their supporters had to be reassured about their expectation of power cuts. After having avoided for some weeks pronouncing anything that could be regarded as a forecast, Mr Scargill suddenly changed his tactics when, on 26 June, in an address to the annual conference of the National Union of Railwaymen, he again gave his estimate of coal stocks:

> I have received information a few hours ago about the stock position in the power stations, slightly different from the public position. They've only got a little over fifteen million tons of coal on the ground, and I can tell you that the CEGB, in conjunction with the government, are preparing for presentation to Parliament emergency measures for power cuts on a rota basis as they go into August and September.
>
> (Arthur Scargill, NUR conference, Llandudno, 26 June 1984)

After his speech I asked Mr Scargill why he had chosen that moment to deliver this unexpected warning about possible power cuts. He smiled, acknowledging that he had not made a similar prediction for some weeks, but said his address at Llandudno had been the appropriate moment to return to the subject. He had delivered his warning in the middle of the afternoon, as though timing it precisely for the early evening news bulletins on radio and television, which all reported his speech. Peter Walker's staff were among those who took a careful note of what Mr Scargill had said.

The following month, on 22 July, the *Sunday Telegraph* printed an exclusive report based on an interview with Mr Walker, in which he forecast for the first time that the government would get through the winter without having to make any power cuts. He was at ease when briefing political correspondents, and, unlike some ministers, was quite prepared to have discussions with journalists in his private office at the Department of Energy without having a government press officer in attendance – his skills in news management were readily acknowledged within the civil service. When Ian Gillis, head of information at the Department of Energy, retired at the end of July, he paid his own tribute to the Secretary of State. Much to the amusement of the assembled guests, Mr Gillis remarked at his retirement party that Mr Walker had been the best press officer who had ever worked for him.

The government's success in avoiding power cuts was due to a combination of careful planning, skilful management and good fortune. Contingency arrangements in case of a strike were being made by the generating board as early as 1982. Once the miners' overtime ban began in November 1983, the board made no attempt to import coal in case this provoked sympathetic strike action within the power stations. Instead, the industry was told to burn as much oil as it needed, whatever the cost. By mid-summer the bill was running at £20 million a week, and was estimated to have reached twice that figure by the middle of the winter.

The industry was fortunate because many of the power station operators at the Trent Valley stations, which kept working with coal from Nottinghamshire, were members of the General, Municipal, Boilermakers and Allied Trades Union, which had not taken a hard line over trying to enforce support for the strike. By contrast, in Yorkshire, more of the power station workers belonged to the Transport and General Workers' Union, which had issued specific instructions to its members not to handle new deliveries of coal or oil. However, the Yorkshire stations were not receiving coal anyway, as all production had stopped at the surrounding pits. So, by a simple geographical accident, the workers of those stations nearest to the working coalfields were prepared to take delivery of what would be termed in other areas 'scab' coal. Then, because of the successful build-up in the generation of electricity at the big oil-fired stations in southern England, like Fawley and the Isle of Grain, the management did not have to force the issue in Yorkshire by trying to bring in coal from outside.

As the whole operation was so complex, management was as anxious as Peter Walker to ensure the lowest possible public profile for the power stations. The industry already had a long tradition of restricting the amount of information supplied to the news media, especially when pay negotiations were being conducted by the Electricity Council (see p. 22). After the strike the Council's central director for public relations, Ray Dafter, told me that relations with the news media during the strike had effectively been under the overall influence of Mr Walker, who had been guiding the industry on what it did and did not say.

Each statement made by the generating board or the Electricity Council was examined by both management and Mr Walker, in order to prevent any comment that might suggest that the industry was biased against the miners. Mr Walker was careful to give radio and television interviews only on those occasions which were thought appropriate; he often hurried away or refused to comment if questioned unexpectedly by labour and industrial correspondents about the strike or about coal stocks. All reference was avoided to a possible 'Scargill surcharge' to meet the additional cost of burning oil, in case this implied that the management had taken sides. Although the power station workers could see for themselves that electricity supplies could be maintained without interruption, no attempt was made within the industry to challenge the NUM's predictions about power cuts; the management wanted Mr Scargill's propaganda to bounce back in his own face.

Mr Walker had the same objective, but waited until the ninth month of the strike before dealing his body blow to Mr Scargill. He chose that lean period for the news – immediately after Christmas – when newspapers, radio and television will devour the slightest morsel. His propaganda initiative took the form of a New Year message, issued on 29 December ready for the Sunday newspapers next day and guaranteeing that there would be no power cuts throughout the whole of 1985. Mr Walker said he had been given an assurance the previous week by the generating board that fuel stocks were so plentiful that the power stations would be able to step up the use of coal and reduce their oil burn. The message was part of a publicity build-up prepared jointly by the government and the coal board, demonstrating that even if the men stayed out for another year it would have no effect, and aimed at encouraging a further acceleration in the number of miners returning to work after the Christmas and New Year holiday.

Mr Scargill seemed caught off guard by the timing of Mr Walker's statement. In an interview that evening, on ITN News, he replied: 'Of course, Mr Walker has been making various claims throughout the dispute. Taking into account that I have never suggested there would be power cuts anyway, I am not surprised he would make this comment.' Consternation immediately broke out among his supporters, as Mr Scargill's remarks were immediately regarded as an admission by the NUM that there would not be power cuts that winter, despite all the union had said. By denying that the NUM had any remaining expectation of power cuts, Mr Scargill had, it seemed, destroyed the whole point of the strike; he had handed a propaganda advantage over to the government.

Mr Walker, determined to keep the initiative, issued an immediate response to the ITN interview in which he accused Mr Scargill of 'telling a total lie' in claiming that he had never suggested there would be power cuts. Referring back to the warning the NUM president had given at the NUR conference in June, the Secretary of State accused Mr Scargill of lying in order to evade the exposure of his 'false predictions' about coal stocks and power cuts.

There were other repercussions to what many in the union regarded as a serious blunder. Mr Scargill was about to be criticised from within for the unthinkable: of being beaten at propaganda. The most damaging response came from South Wales, which for so long had been a stronghold of the strike but had become disillusioned with Mr Scargill's leadership. Although only 126 out of 20,000 miners were at work, the last thing the strikers had wanted to hear was a demoralising admission from their own president, said Kim Howells, research officer for the South Wales area of the NUM. As the union had been 'badly beaten' by Peter Walker's propaganda, there would have to be new initiatives from the leadership if the strike was to remain solid. And three days later, after the Labour Party leader, Neil Kinnock, had paid a New Year constituency visit to a picket line at the Celynen South pit, he remarked on the disappointment he had detected among the strikers over Mr Scargill's acknowledgement of the unlikelihood of power cuts. It was evident, by the way he drew attention to the annoyance felt in South Wales, that Mr Kinnock relished the opportunity for some public point-scoring against the NUM president.

Despite one of the coldest winters for years, the generating board was able to drive home its propaganda advantage against the miners by announcing on 8 January that it had met a new record in the demand for electricity in England and Wales. In the half hour up to 5 p.m. that day, demand had reached 44,748 megawatts, beating the previous record peak of 44,225 megawatts recorded in January 1980. The board would not say how many power stations were in use, but the statement underlined the credibility of what Mr Walker had said a few days earlier. As the cold weather continued, the board established over the succeeding nine days another three production records.

Mr Walker's New Year message had been timed to coincide with a new national newspaper advertising campaign by the coal board, which was intended to provide 'something for every miner on strike to think about over the New Year'. The advertisements urged each man to make up his own mind by asking himself one question: 'What more can I gain by staying out on strike?' Then came a reminder of the fact that most miners would not have to pay tax until April, and that after four weeks' work they would qualify for holiday pay and other entitlements, enabling them to take home up to £1,000 tax-free during January. At the end of each advertisement miners were given instructions on what to do: they were to call their pit manager to hear about the transport and other arrangements that would enable them to return to work and join the '70,000 NUM members who are not on strike'.

At the same time, Mr Walker informed political correspondents that he had told the cabinet just before Christmas of his prediction that 15,000 miners would return to work in January. Once this figure was reached, Mr Walker said, the management would be able to declare that half the men were back at work. In similar vein Ian MacGregor, breaking his long public silence by giving an interview to TV–AM on 6 January, said that it would need only another 10,000 to 15,000 miners to return to put the strikers in a minority.

Despite the combined efforts of government and coal board, the vast majority of the miners remained loyal to the union. Only 368 men had given up the strike on 2 January 1985, which for many pits was the first day back after the holiday. When the return to work had failed to reach the management's expectations, the board predicted that there would be a big increase the following Monday, 7 January, which was the start of the first full week. But although 1,203 miners had abandoned the strike that day, the total had been well down on the record figures in November. This failure to achieve the breakthrough that had been heralded so frequently was all the more disappointing to management after the adjustments they had made in the figures in order to present them in the best possible light.

At the start of the strike the board had said that it had 195,800 NUM members on its books. By December 1984, *Coal News* put the total at 189,000, falling to 188,000 by January. No reason was given for the change in the figures, nor was there any explanation as to why the number of NUM members at work was shown in the January issue of *Coal News* as 70,000, when a simple addition of the figures given in the December and January issues showed that the actual total was 69,545. The reason for the adjustments only became clear in the small print: the board had started to represent those at work as a percentage – 36 per cent in December, rising to 37 per cent in January. Yet, on the figures given in *Coal News*, only 1,545 miners had returned during the intervening four weeks, which was less than a one per cent increase. By rounding up the return-to-work figures and rounding down the total of NUM members, the board was hastening the day when it would be able to claim that half the miners were back at work.

When I explained on the BBC's Today programme on 8 January how management was succeeding in putting the best possible interpretation on the figures, the board's public relations department immediately protested. During an interview broadcast the following morning, the public spokesman Michael Eaton denied there had been any misrepresentation. The total number of NUM members employed by the board had fallen since the start of the strike through natural wastage and voluntary redundancy. The return-to-work figures, he said, had been the latest available at the time of publication. There was no immediate response to my suggestion that there should have been an explanation alongside the figures. However, I did hear later from journalists on *Coal News* of their own reservations about the presentation of some of the figures. Apparently, the board's industrial relations department always had the final say over return-to-work statistics printed in *Coal News*. One case in point was North Derbyshire, which claimed that 137 miners had returned to work on 2 January. When this total was checked by *Coal News* it appeared to be a twenty-four-hour figure that 'stretched back' from the morning of 2 January to the afternoon of the last working day before Christmas. There were other inconsistencies, too. In Yorkshire the management gave a twenty-four-hour figure, while in London the board quoted only those returning that morning – so the local figure was invariably higher.

Throughout January government ministers virtually tripped over themselves in a headlong rush to talk up the figures. On 25 January the Prime minister told the Commons at question time that 77,000 miners were working; when interviewed that evening by Sir Alastair Burnet on TV Eye, she said that the figure was 78,000. At 10.45 a.m. on 28 January Peter Walker stated that 'more that 700' miners had returned that morning, yet the figure being given by the coal board was 629, which was quoted on BBC radio news at 11 a.m. The following day the Under-Secretary of State for Energy, David Hunt, claimed that nearly 79,000 NUM members were at work (42 per cent) while the coal board's official figure was 78,000 (41 per cent).

Although the rate of the return to work in January did not equal that of November, more men than before were crossing the picket lines in former strongholds of the strike in Yorkshire, the north east and Scotland. At the Kiveton Park pit in South Yorkshire, 157 men walked back together on the morning of 21 January. By the middle of the month the board was claiming that 4,600 miners were working in Northumberland and Durham, where there had been only twenty-six in October. The North Derbyshire coalfield had also continued to maintain a strong drift back, claiming that 630 men returned in the first three working days of January, taking total percentage at work comfortably over the half-way mark to 52 per cent.

The management in North Derbyshire had regularly used local advertising as part of its campaign to encourage a return to work, and now it followed through its success with some of the most explicit newspaper advertisements published during the strike. In November the board's advertisements in the *Derbyshire Times* were giving the weekly figures for the men at work in the four pits which had the largest attendance. Once well over half the men were back at work, the board took a double-page spread in the paper: on the left it listed the nineteen local authority districts in the area where NUM members lived, giving the number of men on the books and the number at work, and on the right each pit was named, again giving the number of men at work. The information in the advertisements was so detailed that one could readily identify those villages or districts which had a significant proportion of men on strike or at work. The advertisement in the *Derbyshire Times* of 25 January, for example, showed that seventy-four NUM members lived at Wingerworth and Ashover and that fifty-four of them were at work (73 per cent). But at Killamarsh, which was also in the North-East Derbyshire district, only seventy-three of the 329 NUM members were working (22 per cent). The advertisements were yet another indication of the precision with which the area management had appoached its task of encouraging miners back to work.

Each coal board area took an individual approach to its local newspaper advertising. At the end of the North Derbyshire advertisements came the message, 'When are YOU coming back to work?' – reminiscent of the famous First World War recruiting poster with Lord Kitchener saying, 'Your country needs YOU!' As North Derbyshire had been at the forefront of the board's campaign to encourage a return to work, its advertising had been closely scrutinised by the local NUM leadership and their supporters. These included Betty Heathfield, wife of the union's general secretary and a member of Chesterfield women's action group. A frequent speaker on behalf of the union, she referred regularly to what she called the deception being carried out by the board in a 'relentless and remorseless' fashion:

> In our local newspapers, day in, day out, not just one newspaper, but every local newspaper, there are advertisements aimed at demoralising the men who are going on picket lines every morning. It reminds me of when I was a child when the war was on. The Nazis tried a similar thing to demoralise us. Now we have the same thing, the same language. 'The NUM leadership are unable to resolve this dispute. Negotiations are at an end. Further hardship is to no avail. Your families come first.' I have got this leaflet from the British Museum, issued by the Nazis: 'Your pals are waiting for you in Germany. You will live in peace and complete safety. Come on over. Stop fighting.' We don't believe what we read in these rags. We screw them up and chuck them in the bin.
>
> (Betty Heathfield, Liaison Committee for Defence of Trade Unions conference, London, 12 January 1985)

When the coal board had begun its New Year publicity offensive, there had seemed little prospect of a negotiated settlement to the strike. Peter Walker said it was 'incredible' to hear Arthur Scargill suggesting more talks, when the NUM was still refusing to give any commitment to negotiate on the central issue of the closure of uneconomic pits. In the previous nine months there had been seven rounds of negotiations at

179

National Coal Board,
NORTH DERBYSHIRE AREA.

TO NORTH DERBYSHIRE
MINEWORKERS
ABSENT FROM WORK

**By the end of last week 65.6% of all NUM Industrial Workers
employed in the North Derbyshire Area had abandoned this futile strike.**

Numbers by Main Local Authority locations* are as follows:

LOCATION	MEN ON BOOKS	AT WORK	%
Bolsover DC			
Bolsover Area	1049	775	**74%**
Glapwell	132	102	**77%**
Pleasley/New Houghton	276	84	**30%**
Shirebrook	1058	757	**72%**
Tibshelf/Blackwell	83	64	**77%**
South Normanton/Pinxton	117	90	**77%**
Whitwell/Barlborough/Clowne	690	332	**48%**
Chesterfield BC			
Chesterfield District	917	687	**75%**
Brimington/Staveley/Inkersall	1160	559	**48%**
N.E. Derbys. DC			
North Wingfield Area	291	219	**75%**
Clay Cross	257	150	**58%**
Unstone/Dronfield/Eckington/Renishaw	577	168	**29%**
Killamarsh	329	73	**22%**
Mickley/Stretton	106	82	**77%**
Calow/Duckmanton	351	220	**63%**
Wingerworth/Ashover	74	54	**73%**
Grassmoor/Hasland	376	233	**62%**
Mansfield District			
Mansfield/Mansfield Woodhouse	457	357	**78%**
Langwith/Langwith Junction	664	375	**56%**

Last week 7074 Derbyshire Miners received wages.

When are YOU coming back to work?

* The figures given above do not include mineworkers living outside the above districts.

National Coal Board
NORTH DERBYSHIRE AREA
21st January, 1985

Plate 15   Advertisements like this one in the Derbyshire Times *of 25 January 1985
gave information so precise that it was possible to identify at a glance the villages and
districts where the men were working or on strike. The campaign in North Derbyshire had
been mounted with almost military precision: ordnance survey maps, pinned up at the*

National Coal Board,
NORTH DERBYSHIRE AREA.

TO NORTH DERBYSHIRE MINEWORKERS ABSENT FROM WORK

On Friday 25th January 1985,
7074 Derbyshire mineworkers will receive pay.

*This represents 65.6% of all NUM Industrial Members
employed in North Derbyshire Area*

The numbers of NUM Industrial members at each unit are shown below

COLLIERY/UNIT	NUM ON BOOKS	NUM AT WORK		%
Arkwright	604	427	=	70.7%
High Moor	553	98	=	17.7%
Ireland	666	181	=	27.2%
Markham	2046	1252	=	61.2%
Renishaw Park	529	190	=	35.9%
Shirebrook	1947	1533	=	78.7%
Warsop	1174	911	=	77.6%
Whitwell	727	369	=	50.8%
Williamthorpe	274	248	=	90.5%
Duckmanton Workshops	581	431	=	74.2%
Blackwell Workshops	250	209	=	83.6%
Road Transport	154	129	=	83.8%
Other Activities	380	321	=	84.5%
Total Derbys. NUM	**9885**	**6299**	=	**63.7%**
Bolsover - Notts. NUM	**896**	**775**	=	**86.5%**
Total Area (NUM)	**10781**	**7074**	=	**65.6%**

On Monday day shift 21st January a further
184 NUM members returned to work.

When are YOU coming back to work?

National Coal Board.
NORTH DERBYSHIRE AREA.
21st January 1985

*offices of the area headquarters, indicated the very streets and villages where miners lived.
This attention to detail paid off: North Derbyshire had a faster rate of return than any other
coalfield.*

which the coal board had 'sought agreement on every occasion', yet, said Mr Walker, when the talks had ended each time in failure, Mr Scargill had boasted that he had not shifted an inch from his – according to Mr Walker – 'absurd and impossible' demand that every pit should be kept in being until the last ton of coal was exhausted or the pit was unsafe.

Despite the bleak prospect, the TUC's monitoring group continued its efforts to find a basis for negotiations. Then, on 21 January, within a week of his final retirement, the coal board's reinstated director-general of industrial relations, Ned Smith, held an unexpected meeting with the NUM's general secretary, Peter Heathfield. As it was the first face-to-face meeting between management and union since the previous October, there was speculation that the two sides might be ready to reopen negotiations. However, as had happened so often in the past, the meeting only led to more recriminations, this time over the publicity.

The two men had met at the Cavendish Hotel in London, but for once the news media were not in attendance. Therefore when Mr Heathfield left the hotel at 3.15, on completing his discussions with Mr Smith, he was somewhat surprised to find that the London *Standard* was already saying that the talks had failed. As Mr Heathfield had not been informed that a press statement had been issued, he was puzzled by what he read.

In fact, there had been only the briefest statement that day from the coal board, which had simply announced, shortly before 1 p.m., that contact had been established with Mr Heathfield. Because of the sensitive nature of Mr Smith's initiative, the board was not prepared to reveal any further details about the meeting. And in order to prevent any possibility of premature disclosure, Michael Eaton cancelled all his briefings that day with reporters, including a prearranged meeting with Tom McGhie, industrial editor of the *Daily Star*.

However, Mr Eaton's precautions proved in vain, because well before the coal board was ready to comment on the outcome of the talks, 'guidance' had been given to political journalists by the press office at No. 10 Downing Street. The Prime Minister's press secretary Bernard Ingham had told members of the lobby that the talks had got nowhere. The government would stand firm until half the miners were back at work, he said – a view in line with Mrs Thatcher's, which she had made clear on several previous occasions. On discovering that Mr Ingham had been giving briefings to political journalists, Mr Eaton asked me if I could find out exactly when the lobby correspondents were first told that the initiative had failed. My inquiries revealed that many of them knew from about 3 p.m. Mr Eaton blamed Mrs Thatcher for having blocked progress. (After the strike when I asked Mr Ingham about his briefings to political journalists during the dispute, he said he had no intention of breaking the silence which he always maintained about the nature of his work.)

Three days later the labour editor of *The Times*, Paul Routledge, published a detailed report on what had been discussed at the Smith–

Heathfield meeting. It appeared that the two men had considered a tentative twelve-point plan which was intended to form the basis of a draft peace agreement, and according to Mr Routledge the NUM had, for the first time, accepted that pits had closed in the past on economic grounds. A similar but less detailed report was carried in the *Morning Star*, which also suggested that there was now a possible formula under which management and union could side-step the contentious issue of uneconomic pit closures. Mr Heathfield told me the next day that he was dismayed by what he had read in *The Times*, because it was clear that Mr Routledge had seen a copy of the minutes of the meeting which, on the union side, had been made available only to himself, Arthur Scargill and Mick McGahey. Later, Mr Scargill expressed similar annoyance, telling me he was convinced the leak had come from within the union. But Mr McGahey said it was an 'outrageous and monstrous' lie to suggest that anyone in the union would leak the contents of the minutes when it was 'obviously' the work of the government, which had wanted to sabotage the talks. As Mr Routledge refused to reveal his source there was no way of saying exactly what had happened, but the detailed disclosure in *The Times* brought the initiative to a sudden halt, illustrating the pitfalls of premature publicity.

Speculation over the possibility of a reopening of negotiations had again had the effect of slowing down the return to work. On Monday, 28 January, 915 miners abandoned the strike, but this was only half the number of the previous week. As the board was determined to prevent the union using the prospect of further talks to stem the drift back, they insisted there was still no basis for new negotiations. The following Monday, 4 February, management claimed a new one-day record of 2,318 miners abandoning the strike, taking the total at work to 81,000, or 43 per cent. More men returned the following day, many walking back in groups of thirty and forty. Although there were still only 364 miners crossing the picket lines in the whole of South Wales, the local leadership feared the men could not hold on much longer and that the strike would begin to crumble in this last major stronghold. There was aleady open talk in the valleys of the South Wales miners returning to work without an agreement.

The first official confirmation that the South Wales NUM was considering the possibility of the strikers going back together was given by area's research officer Kim Howells, in a telephone interview with a BBC radio reporter, Tim Maby. Mr Howells stressed that South Wales had no intention of going back on its own, but the local leadership believed the option of returning without an agreement would have to be considered by the national executive. When BBC Radio News began transmitting the story on the morning of 7 February, Mr Scargill telephoned Mr Howells to remind him that he had no authority to make statements on behalf of the national union: the president was the only official spokesman. A heated argument ensued, which ended when the South Wales vice-president Terry Thomas slammed down the phone after telling Mr Scargill that South Wales would look after its own affairs and that he, Mr Scargill, would be better advised to concentrate his attention in Yorkshire, where 6,000 miners had abandoned the strike.

The possibility of a return to work without an agreement was featured extensively in my own reports that day for BBC radio. The South Wales president Emlyn Williams told me that it was my reporting that had effectively 'stitched up' Mr Howells and 'nailed him to the cross', because the following week he was ordered by the area executive to stop giving press statements and interviews. Although Mr Williams appeared annoyed, he conceded, once the strike was over, that he had in fact been relieved by what had happened, as he believed that Mr Howells' remarks had helped the NUM to make a final decision on the future of the dispute.

In the last few weeks of the strike there were several unsuccessful attempts by the TUC to get a negotiated settlement. Management and government had insisted as a precondition that the union would first have to put in writing, in 'a form of words acceptable to the board', that it would discuss uneconomic pits. Mrs Thatcher had said she wanted a 'dead straight answer, not a fudged statement'. Despite the obstacles, the TUC general secretary Norman Willis persevered, holding a series of meetings with Ian MacGregor.

The talks resulted in the preparation of new proposals outlining the need for 'an economically sound industry', and suggesting a revised formula which proposed that uneconomic pits should be closed when the reserves did not provide a 'satisfactory basis' for continued operations. The document remained a 'blueprint' for closures, said Arthur Scargill, and it was rejected by his executive. Mr Willis persisted in his efforts, leading a TUC delegation to see Mrs Thatcher on 19 February. There was another flurry of meetings and yet more amendments to the NCB's proposals, including a commitment by management to establish an independent review body on pit closures by 1 June 1985. Mr Willis thought the changes had strengthened the NUM's position, but Mr Scargill described the new wording as 'infinitely worse' than the proposals submitted the week before. The following day, 21 February, a special delegate conference agreed that the board's terms were still unacceptable. There was nothing further the TUC could do: from then on the NUM was on its own.

The following Monday, 25 February, the board claimed another new record, when 3,807 miners abandoned the strike, taking the number at work to 91,000. By 27 February the total 'exceeded 93,000', which according to the board represented 50.2 per cent of NUM members. The percentage was calculated on the basis of an NUM membership of 186,000 – well down on the 188,000 mentioned the month before in the January issue of *Coal News*, and lower again than the figure of 187,300 quoted in

Coal News at the beginning of February. The board said the figure had needed further adjustment because of natural wastage and voluntary redundancies.

Michael Eaton, as the board's public spokesman, was ready to be interviewed the moment the 'half-way' point was reached, and he described the achievement as a milestone in the long dispute. There had obviously been extensive preparations: the national newspapers next day carried full-page advertisements announcing that 'half of all NUM members' were back at work. Any man still on strike was told to recognise that he could 'lose the support' of the '93,000 NUM members who are getting the industry back on its feet again'. On Arthur Scargill's calculations, however, 61 per cent of the miners were still on strike; Peter Heathfield put the figure at 59 per cent. Next day the national executive agreed to call another delegate conference, which voted by 98 votes to 91 to accept a South Wales resolution recommending a return to work without an agreement.

Most of the strikers went back to work on 5 March. Perhaps the most moving scene of all was at Maerdy, the last pit in the Rhondda Valley, where not one miner had been at work for a year. As dawn broke and the church bells rang out, the colliery band, the miners, their wives and supporters set off from the village with banners held high on the mile-long walk up the valley to the pit gates. The march back by the Maerdy miners presented a vivid picture of trade union comradeship; similar scenes of solidarity were seen that morning at many other pits in South Wales, Yorkshire, the north east and Scotland. By their dignified return to work, the miners probably achieved more public sympathy and understanding in one day than on any other day in the previous twelve months.

Some men in Scotland and Kent stayed out on strike for a time in a vain attempt to force the coal board to reinstate sacked miners. The management was resolute. Ian MacGregor declared that the men whom the board had dismissed were 'now discovering the price of insubordination and insurrection. And boy, are we going to make it stick!' Eventually the last of the strikers returned to work, and the strike was finally over, presenting a new challenge to Arthur Scargill and the rest of the leadership – the task of reuniting and rebuilding the National Union of Mineworkers.

SEVEN

Aftermath

By ending the strike without a negotiated settlement, the miners went back to work with no agreement on the procedure to be followed by the National Coal Board during pit closures, and with no amnesty for up to 700 sacked miners. There were many in the trade union movement who thought the miners would have been wiser to have settled on the terms offered in July 1984, or at least to have concluded the dispute with some form of agreement, which might have given the NUM a base-line from which to fight back.

Within four months of the return to work, the coal board had announced the closure of fifteen pits, with the projected loss of 15,000 jobs. This was in addition to the five pits that had been proposed for closure either before or during the strike. The total planned reduction in jobs was put at 20,000. This cut-back in exhausted and uneconomic capacity was accompanied by a restatement of the board's commitment to the future of the coal industry. Investment in new pits and modernisation had resumed at the rate of £2 million a day. Over 7,000 jobs would be provided within a decade by the development of new coalfields at Selby in Yorkshire and Asfordby in Leicestershire, together with plans for a new mine in south Warwickshire and other investment projects.

The NUM, on the other hand, estimated that in the same four months twenty-five pits had been either nominated for or threatened with closure or merger, with the loss of 25,000 jobs within a year. Arthur Scargill told his annual conference in July 1985 that the closures had violated all established procedures in the industry, proving in his view that the NUM had had no alternative but to strike. It was clear, he said, from the moment Ian MacGregor announced his plans to reduce capacity, that the NUM could either have accepted the original proposals, in the certain knowledge that they would have been the start of a massive closure programme, or taken action and fought 'with dignity and pride for the position we knew to be right'. Mr Scargill was convinced that history would vindicate the strike.

The pit deputies' union, NACODS, was appalled by the speed with which some of the closures were announced and implemented, accusing the board of a clear breach of the agreement reached the previous October at ACAS. In mid-May 1985 the deputies banned overtime for three weeks as a protest. And despite a series of meetings between the board and the mining unions, there was no agreement by the summer of 1985 on either the terms of reference for the modified colliery review procedure or the composition of a new independent review body to consider pit closures.

Management's conduct towards the end of the strike drew a firm rebuke from the former director-general of industrial relations, Ned Smith. His own misgivings had been revealed publicly at the time of his retirement in January 1985, five weeks before the end of the strike, when he had said that a large proportion of the British people disapproved of the way Mrs Thatcher had gone for victory over the miners. When the strike ended, Mr Smith described the final outcome as not the 'most sensible' the management could have achieved. There had, he acknowledged, been a 'dramatic' change during the final three months of the dispute, when the government had started prescribing what the NCB's negotiators could and could not do. He was saddened by the way the board's own spokesmen had supported these preconditions.

Three weeks after the return to work came a swift reorganisation in senior management, which included promotion for Michael Eaton as personnel director to succeed Merrik Spanton, who was retiring. However, as the time approached for his move from North Yorkshire, Mr Eaton appeared increasingly disenchanted with the prospect of a permanent job in London. Then, in September 1985, three weeks before Mr Spanton was due to leave, Mr Eaton revealed that he would not be taking up the appointment: he had decided, at the age of fifty-one, to seek early retirement, for 'personal, family and business' reasons. His resignation statement made no mention of his frequent disagreements with Ian MacGregor, but they had continued after the strike when he had tried without success to persuade the chairman to provide more protection for those miners who had worked during the dispute. Mr Eaton had also seemed confident of becoming the new deputy chairman on the retirement of James Cowan. However, fellow directors had warned him that he could not rely on a politician's promise. It was when he heard that he had not been chosen that he finally announced his resignation, telling friends that he would instead join his two sons in the family building firm. Only a few hours after giving his statement to reporters Mr Eaton was taken to Pontefract Hospital with a suspected perforated ulcer.

Throughout his time as public spokesman for the NCB, Mr Eaton had rarely appeared decisive on radio or television, often giving the impression of not being exactly sure how any sentence he might have started would finish. But he had done what was required during the closing months of the strike, trying each time he was interviewed to convey what he thought was the reasonableness of the board's position. It had been rather like sailing into the eye of the wind with an unsteady helmsman; each time public opinion seemed to be swinging against a return to work, Mr Eaton stepped forward to do his best to get the board back on course. In a generous tribute on his retirement, the Prime Minster congratulated him on doing a 'superb job' in communicating the board's case. She added: 'He is such a nice person and everyone knew that he knew the industry thoroughly. He was the sort of man of whom people said: "If he says it, it's true."' Peter Heathfield believed that Michael Eaton had become no more than the front man in the process of destablising the miners. When talks were held there was always renewed hope that a settlement might be possible, but each time the negotiations broke down morale slumped. The board knew only too well, said Mr Heathfield, that each successive failure would have the effect of encouraging more miners to return to work.

The increasing expertise of management in communicating directly with the strikers had been implemented most aggressively in North Derbyshire, where letters and newspaper advertisements had been followed up with visits to the strikers' homes. Half North Derbyshire's miners were back at work by early January 1985 – a faster rate of return than at any other major coalfield that had given full support to the strike from the start. In the managerial reorganisation that followed the strike, the area director Ken Moses was promoted to become the NCB's new technical director responsible for long-term planning. He had clearly become part of the new cutting edge of the coal board management, having in effect been given the task of preparing a new Plan for Coal.

Of all the communication techniques used by management, newspaper advertising had been by far the most expensive. By the end of March 1985 Media Expenditure Analysis had calculated that the total expenditure by the NCB on newspaper advertisements was £3,683,160. Mr MacGregor's communications consultant Tim Bell would not discuss the cost. However, after persistent questioning in the Commons Select Committee on Energy by the Labour MP Geoffrey Lofthouse, the NCB finally revealed in December 1985 that it had spent £4,266,000 on national advertising plus a further £300,000 locally. Mr Lofthouse said he began inquiring about the cost after seeing 'divisive' advertisements in South Yorkshire the previous December which featured a Christmas tree covered in £ note signs.

There were mixed feelings about the six personal letters sent out by Mr MacGregor during the strike. Some area managements believed they were counter-productive – a view reflected in the board's own internal surveys on communications. While most working miners had been pleased to receive them they were not welcomed by the vast majority of strikers, and it was difficult to gauge the precise impact a letter might have on a striker

Plate 16   The NCB's November advertising campaign was backed up by personal letters sent to the strikers by individual pit managers. Some managers would later telephone the strikers who had returned the tear-off slip, to explain the transport arrangements. At the Denby Grange pit in the Barnsley area, the manager Doug Bulmer told the men to carry white carrier bags as they waited to be picked up in the vans and buses, so that the police could distinguish them from pickets and protect them.

Barnsley

YOU AND WHO ELSE?

Men have started to go back to work at pits in every Area of the Yorkshire Coalfield – including Barnsley.

We know that more would like to join them but, understandably, don't want to face the "aggro" and the intimidation of being in a minority.

At almost every pit in the Area our managers are hearing the same thing, "We're not coming back in one's and two's. It would be different if there were a crowd of us".

Well here's the chance to come back on those terms.

This leaflet includes a Back to Work form and a reply paid envelope. If you genuinely feel that it's time to get back to work and would be willing to come back in a group all you have to do is fill in the form and post it in the envelope provided.

At any pit where there are enough men to form a sizeable group we will get in touch with you and lay on all the necessary arrangements.

ALL REPLIES WILL BE TREATED IN STRICT CONFIDENCE AND NO APPROACHES WILL BE MADE UNTIL WE HAVE ENOUGH NAMES TO MAKE UP A GROUP.

If you start work in the next couple of weeks your pay between now and Christmas (with holiday pay and other entitlements) will add up to more than £1000 for face men and about £800 for surface workers.

- If **YOU** think the strike has gone on long enough
- If **YOU** are fed up with waiting for a national settlement
- If **YOU** are facing mounting debts and dreading the final demands
- If **YOU** want to protect your job, your pit and your family's future,

THEN STAND UP FOR YOUR RIGHT TO WORK

Join the 50,000 British Miners who vote with their feet
at the pit gates every day and

COME BACK TO WORK

- -

To: The Manager .... (insert name of Colliery or Unit)

I am interested in returning to work as part of an organized group.

Name: .... Check No. ....

Address: ....

.... Tel No (if any) ....

Signature: .... Date ....

who was thinking of returning to work. One member of management who questioned the chairman's policy of sending personal letters was the manager of the Denby Grange pit, near Wakefield, Doug Bulmer, who thought it would have been wiser to have left the timing of such communications to the individual colliery managers, as circumstances differed from pit to pit. Despite daily mass pickets, 70 per cent of Denby Grange miners were back at work early in the New Year, and the pit began producing coal on 17 January 1985, which made it the first in the Barnsley area to resume production. Mr Bulmer had written only one letter to the strikers, in December 1984, following it up with telephone calls to those men who had sent back a tear-off slip indicating their wish to return to work. Mr Bulmer thought that the return to work had been facilitated by the fact that the Denby Grange miners did not live in one local, cohesive, community, but were drawn from a wide area south of Leeds.

As for the recorded video messages employed by the chairman, coal board press officers in the working coalfields had reported that response was not encouraging: one said that Mr MacGregor's Christmas video – in which he thanked working miners for their efforts during the first nine months of the strike – had gone down like a lead balloon. The redundancy Freefone operation, however, at the start of the strike, had proved the effectiveness of this communication technique, with 21,000 miners applying within a matter of weeks.

Mr MacGregor did not wait long before commenting on the coal board's conduct during the strike. In an interview published in the *Sunday Telegraph* on 10 March 1985, he revealed the strength of his determination to avoid a compromise with the NUM, describing Ned Smith and 'a hell of a lot of other people' in the management as 'romantics' who were not tuned in to the realities that had faced the board. During a BBC radio interview the same day, the chairman frankly acknowledged his own limitations as a communicator. Asked by Gordon Clough why he had withdrawn from the public spotlight the previous October and appointed Michael Eaton as public spokesman, he replied:

> The simple reason was that managing the strategy of the strike was a twenty-four hour job, without maintaining the communications. It is a well known principle of management to make sure you maintain control of your strategy and delegate those things you can. Anyway, Mr Eaton is a much more articulate person than me. He is a charming man and he is a well known mining engineer, much respected in his community, whereas most people were unfamiliar with my background in mining.
>
> (Ian MacGregor, BBC Radio 4, The World this Weekend,
> 10 March 1985)

The chairman did not go on to explain why it had taken him eight months of dispute to accept that he was not an effective communicator. Although his previous record at the British Steel Corporation had shown he was anything but weak or uncertain, the rest of British management seemed to have noticed within a matter of weeks that in his present role he came across as confused and indecisive.

His insistence on attempting for so long to compete with Mr Scargill for the news headlines seemed to have been caused by a combination of vanity and stubbornness. He had not repeated his own successful communications strategy at British Steel, where he had kept a low public profile; nor had he followed the benign approach which he outlined for himself in March 1983, when he said he was prepared to 'take the stick' which went with the exposed position of NCB chairman. In response to a comment of mine, when the miners had been out for only a fortnight, Mr MacGregor had drily observed that Mr Scargill was a 'resourceful fellow'. And the abuse heaped on his head by the 'resourceful' NUM president had achieved its purpose: the chairman rose to the bait. It was not until Mr MacGregor had taken a back seat that the board could demonstrate the effectiveness of its communications policy.

The return to work had proceeded at what seemed to the chairman a painfully slow rate, but it did develop a steady momentum. Once decisions were taken, they were stuck to. Mr MacGregor had stopped thinking aloud for the benefit of the news media. Four months after the strike, on 28 July, Mr MacGregor complained in another *Sunday Telegraph* interview about government interference during the dispute, remarking that it was not surprising he had sometimes lost his cool because he had frequently been pushed 'beyond the threshold of tolerance'. He recalled one meeting at No. 10 when Mrs Thatcher had been 'extremely relentless' in her criticism of management; on other occasions he had found the Secretary of State for Energy trying to 'steer the boat' by holding private meetings with the pit deputies' general secretary, Peter McNestry. Mr MacGregor concluded that Mr Walker was only interested in 'short-term advantage', and that British politics were 'largely a public relations activity'.

By revealing that such political pressures had continued after the strike as well, Mr MacGregor exposed the sensitivity within Whitehall over the government's handling of the dispute. Although Mrs Thatcher had obtained a clear-cut industrial victory over the NUM, the achievement had not been reflected in an immediate improvement in the government's electoral popularity. Within the NUM itself there seemed to be a sense of grim satisfaction that Mr MacGregor's failure to communicate had eventually forced Mrs Thatcher and her ministers to argue the case for shutting uneconomic pits. In public relations terms, the government was seen to be firmly defending further closures at a time of high unemployment, when the political parties were already having to think ahead to the next general election.

Mr MacGregor's differences with Mr Walker during the strike had been a frequent source of comment within the coal board. One director told me that relations had been particularly strained in January 1985, when the return to work had resumed. Mr Walker had apparently been anxious to ensure that management did all it could to 'encourage' miners to give up the strike, while Mr MacGregor was said to be intent on seeing the men 'driven' back through fear of losing their jobs. Several of those who attended senior managerial meetings recalled the chairman's fondness for quoting from his own experience in the American coal industry, and particularly one strike at an Amax mine in Belle Ayr, Wyoming, where according to Mr MacGregor, the miners ended up 'crawling' back to work.

Although extensive management changes were made soon after the strike, the final readjustment did not take place until 3 October, seven months after the return to work, when Mr Walker took the unusual step, almost a year before Mr MacGregor was due to complete his three-year term, of announcing the appointment of the new NCB chairman – Sir Robert Haslam. Sir Robert, who had succeeded Mr MacGregor as head of the British Steel Corporation in 1983, had at first rejected the new post, but later accepted a three-year appointment from September 1986. However, Mr Walker insisted that Sir Robert should 'take up full-time duties on NCB matters' from the beginning of May 1986, four months before the expiry of Mr MacGregor's term as chairman. Sir Kenneth Couzens, a former permanent under-secretary of the Department of Energy, was appointed deputy chairman. The day after the announcement Mr MacGregor called a news conference to welcome the new team, which he was sure would maintain the 'dramatic' recovery evident in the coal industry since the end of the strike. In reply to questions about his own criticisms of the Secretary of State for Energy, the chairman simply replied that Mr Walker was 'a charming fellow'. When asked whether he intended to complete his term as chairman, he said that the government had no choice in the matter, adding: 'For better or for worse I am here and I am going to stay. Yes indeedy.'

Peter Walker reserved some of his reflections on the strike for a profile which appeared in the *Daily Mail* on 6 March, the day after the return to work. The article was written not by a specialist correspondent but by the editor, Sir David English – which reflected Mr Walker's close links with Fleet Street. Sir David said that the Secretary of State had 'dedicated a year of his life to beating Scargill', and disclosed that Mr Walker was 'contemptuous of the media perception' that the NUM president was a 'master communicator'. Even so, he had prepared himself for his 'battle against Scargill' by studying the president's speeches. Indeed, it seemed he had done his homework so thoroughly that he was using with even greater confidence than Mr Scargill the technique of challenging radio and television interviewers by casting doubt on the validity of their questions.

An instance of this occurred on the evening before the miners finally walked back to work, when Mr Walker had been asked on BBC television by Fred Emery of Panorama whether the coal board was inflicting a double penalty by refusing to reinstate the sacked men. Mr Walker's response was to ask Mr Emery if he was suggesting that the BBC should keep on employees who had smashed up studios during an industrial dispute. When Mr Emery protested that he was only asking the Secretary of State to answer the question, Mr Walker retorted that Mr Emery knew he was wrong to suggest the BBC should keep on an employee who had beaten up a colleague.

Perhaps Mr Walker could be excused for appearing confident and somewhat aggressive. During the previous twelve months he had demonstrated that Mr Scargill's undoubted ability at conveying his own point of view was of no tactical value unless accompanied by a communications strategy that had clearly defined objectives and that paid at least some regard to the operational constraints under which the news media have to work. Mr Walker had immediately identified those sections of the news media that would be of greatest use to the government; his radio and television appearances had been carefully planned in conjunction with the coal board; he had been at pains to avoid contact with industrial or labour correspondents who might ask pertinent or embarrassing questions, and he had identified those aspects of the dispute which should not be publicised.

Mr Walker's policy of restricting his private briefings largely to political correspondents (see p. 115) was confirmed publicly after the strike by Michael Jones, political editor of the *Sunday Times*, in a book on the miners' strike written by the paper's Insight team. During the dispute it had been generally acknowledged in Fleet Street that Mr Walker had perhaps the closest relationship of all with the *Sunday Times*. In an account of the aftermath of the strike Mr Jones recalled how the government was 'suspicious' of industrial correspondents and 'preferred dealing' with Westminster lobby journalists. Andrew Neil, the *Sunday Times* editor, had no doubts about the accuracy of his paper's coverage of the strike. Nor did he appear to have any reservations over the disagreements there had been with his labour editor, Donald Macintyre. In an introduction to the Insight team's book Mr Neil declared:

From the start, the *Sunday Times* took a firm editorial line: for the sake of liberal democracy, economic recovery and the rolling back of union power . . . Scargill and his forces had to be defeated, and would be . . . Our views, however, were kept to where they belong in a quality newspaper: the editorial column. For us the miners' strike was above all a massive reporting and analysing task to give our readers an impartial and well-informed picture of what was

really happening. Our journalists acquitted themselves superbly.
(Andrew Neil in *Strike*, André Deutsch and
Coronet Books, September 1985)

Of all Mr Walker's comments on the strike, perhaps the most revealing was his explanation of the way he controlled his feelings on those occasions when he was angered by Mr Scargill's propaganda: realising he had at all costs to keep cool, he went home and relaxed with his family.

By contrast with Peter Walker, Arthur Scargill had seemed unable to distance himself from the strike, even for a moment. Unlike Mr MacGregor, Mr Scargill had not found it possible to delegate any of his responsibilities as official spokesman, which might perhaps have allowed him more time to prepare an overall communications strategy. Instead of addressing himself to the central problems facing the NUM, he would often appear absorbed in his own performance or in some minor detail of the way the dispute was being presented in the news media. Occasionally he infuriated staff at ACAS and the TUC by what was described to me as almost an obsession with trying to prepare press statements which, it was thought, could do no more than score an inconsequential propaganda point against the coal board or government.

Mr Scargill's preoccupation with the need to project himself took several forms. At the height of the TUC's efforts to obtain a settlement in February 1985, a meeting took place between TUC general secretary Norman Willis and NCB deputy chairman James Cowan, after the NUM executive had decided, apparently aganst Mr Scargill's advice, to recognise the coal board's duty to 'manage the industry efficiently'. While waiting at Congress House for Mr Willis to return from the meeting, he occupied his time by writing out his press statement in the expectation that the TUC's initiative would not succeed because he knew the executive would not accept any reference to the need for 'an economically sound industry'. Later in the evening, after Mr Willis had confirmed that new negotiations were still not possible, Mr Scargill emerged on to the steps of Congress House to tell waiting reporters that he would 'never ever' be a signatory to the closure of any part of the coal industry as long as he was president of the NUM. The following day he told me that he had prepared his statement in advance because he had been convinced all along that the government was determined to prevent a settlement.

On other occasions, if Mr Scargill had given an adroit answer to a journalist's question, or if he had found a particularly neat way to express the union's dilemma, he would take care to observe the use that was made of his replies. Shortly before Christmas 1984, again after a meeting at the TUC, he said in a BBC radio interview that the ultimatum the NUM was facing over pit closures was exactly the same as if a gunman stopped three people and asked which of them would like to agree to be shot. As union president representing miners at every pit in the country, he was in no position to compromise and say: 'Yes, just shoot one of us.' Next day Mr Scargill asked if I had liked his comment about the gunman. When I told him his answer had been used extensively on BBC radio that day, he gave a knowing smile which seemed to reflect both satisfaction with his own performance and his continuing fascination with the news media.

Another illustration of the care with which he studied radio and television news reports is well illustrated in the following incident. One evening in February 1985 I was on the telephone to Mr Scargill, asking him for details about a visit by the NUM executive to the TUC the following day. As he answered, I could tell that he was elated. He asked if I had seen ITN's News at Ten that evening and a report by Giles Smith on a leaked generating board document, which showed that the cost of burning oil during the strike was approaching £2 billion – twice the previous estimate. Giles Smith had finished his report by saying that the latest estimate suggested the Mr Scargill's claim that the strike had cost the country £5 billion 'might not be quite the exaggeration that some ministers have claimed'.

Our conversation took place at 11.45 p.m., and in the hour and a quarter that had elapsed since the end of News at Ten Mr Scargill had already, he said, played back Giles Smith's report seven times on his video. He could not believe that ITN was actually saying that the NUM's estimate might be correct. As he had a calculator with him as we spoke, he proceeded to bring his own estimate up to date, saying the cost of the strike was actually nearer £6 billion than £5 billion.

Mr Scargill often became infuriated if there had been what he thought was undue delay on the part of the broadcasting organisations in using a statement he had issued. He paid particular attention to the teletext news services transmitted on television by Ceefax and Oracle, well aware that although the proportion of viewers who obtain their news from teletext might be small, the output of Ceefax and Oracle is monitored closely during the day by government departments, public relations officers and journalists. The two news services compete with each other to provide the latest information on fast-moving stories like industrial disputes. They also provide some advance indication of the priority of treatment that the main news bulletins on BBC or ITN may give to a particular development – information that can be of critical importance to those organisations directly involved, and to journalists. The significance of the teletext services had not been lost on Mr Scargill.

News reports about the miners' strike which appeared on Ceefax, for example, were prepared either from information submitted by journalists working for the BBC or from news copy supplied by various news agencies, including the principal British agency, the Press Association. Therefore, the text of a statement issued by the NUM could arrive at

Ceefax from several sources. The speed with which it was supplied or appeared on the screen would depend not only on its news significance, but also on a variety of other factors: often BBC journalists or news agency employees might have to clarify or check what the NUM had said before filing their stories, a process which can take time. On a number of occasions Mr Scargill telephoned Ceefax himself to inquire if there was any reason why certain statements were not being used. He was particularly concerned if he considered his statement was a reply to what had been said by the coal board. After one complaint in October 1984, he offered several times to dictate statements himself direct to Ceefax. However, the NUM was advised to supply its statements in the first instance to the BBC's general news service, based at Broadcasting House, which serves the whole of the corporation. This had in fact been the union's practice since the early days of the strike.

Once he had discovered whom to contact, Mr Scargill would insist on being put through to the relevant department, using with confidence the appropriate newsroom terminology such as 'GNS' (the general news service). Not only BBC journalists, but those working for other news organisations as well, were sometimes surprised to find themselves speaking directly to the NUM president, when they happened to answer the telephone at work. Similar persistence is not unknown among public figures, but there are certainly few trade union leaders who have gone to such lengths to acquaint themselves with the internal workings of news organisations in order to obtain publicity.

These recollections and observations are not intended to detract from what I consider was a significant achievement by Mr Scargill in terms of news presentation. He took on the news media virtually single-handed. On many issues he seemed able for months on end to keep one step ahead of the combined resources of Fleet Street, radio and television. While his critics in the rest of the trade union movement say he had no chance of ever winning public sympathy after the NUM's refusal to hold a pit-head ballot and its failure to stop the use of mass pickets, Mr Scargill's skill in seizing the headlines and in keeping the strike in the news did nonetheless often cause despondency at the coal board. From my own conversations with the directors I could detect the perpetual unease generated by the difficulty which they faced in trying to determine exactly what Mr Scargill might do next.

I can only recall one occasion during the strike, early in January 1985, when I found Mr Scargill down at heart; when for once he was not trying to promote a new line of inquiry for the news media to develop. The preceding few weeks had been an exceptionally busy period for the president, as he had been occupied with the legal work that followed sequestration and the appointment of a receiver to control the NUM's assets. Mr Scargill's lengthy consultations with the lawyers had inevitably had the effect of reducing his output of press statements. Indeed, there were several days in December when his name did not appear to have been mentioned once in radio or television news bulletins. Then, immediately after Christmas, Peter Walker's New Year statement that power cuts would not occur during 1985 had provoked the South Wales NUM to criticise the president for being badly beaten at propaganda. When I spoke to Mr Scargill on 5 January after he had addressed a rally in Worksop, I asked him why he had been so slow off the mark. He looked away for a moment, sighed, and then replied that much of his time had been taken up by the legal problems facing the union.

The conversation confirmed what had been apparent for so long: the NUM and its president were trying to fight on too many fronts at once. When Mr Scargill was forced to devote himself to the legal and financial implications of the court rulings, he simply did not have sufficient time to spend on publicity. As he remained the only official spokesman, there was no one who could shoulder any of the responsibility; nor did there seem to be any machinery within the union for bringing forward fresh ideas or new material to take the place of Mr Scargill's own press statements.

Another tendency discernible in the closing weeks of the strike was that Mr Scargill seemed to be more concerned with communicating with his own members than with the public at large. Wanting to demonstrate the strength of his own resolve to those on strike, he spent much of Christmas morning on the picket line at Ferrybridge power station in Yorkshire, where he was filmed for television news. But there were many other activists in the trade union movement who believed Mr Scargill had not paid sufficient attention to the signs of a shift in public opinion. There had been little violence for a month, since the death of the South Wales taxi driver David Wilkie on 30 November, and the NUM's supporters in the wider union movement were encountering a growing public sympathy for the miners. Several advisers on union publicity believed Mr Scargill should have used the Christmas holiday to win wider support, perhaps by visiting the families of strikers or by allowing himself to be seen talking with children or retired miners. In fact, over the pre-Christmas weekend Mr Scargill had already been involved in a children's party at Worsborough miners' welfare, not far from his home. Local reporters and photographers had tried, unsuccessfully, to persuade him to dress up as Father Christmas, but he did agree to take Santa Claus to the party in his car.

Once the strike was over, Mr Scargill indicated that he had no intention of giving any assistance to newspaper reporters or broadcasters who wanted to examine what had happened during the strike. The NUM press officer, Nell Myers, said that the president and general secretary had both taken a policy decision not to co-operate with journalists who were attempting to prepare background reports or write books on the dispute. Mr Scargill's reluctance to allow any investigation of his own actions did not prevent him apportioning blame, however. In his presidential speech at the 1985 annual conference he identified the news media as being one factor in the union's defeat:

> The capitalist media has played a role which would have impressed even Goebbels. Press and broadcasting have smeared and lied about our union, its leadership and its members. It's no good just blaming proprietors and managing editors. Journalists, many of them here today who will say they support the miners, have allowed themselves to be used to attack us every day at every turn, as we fight to protect and sustain our industry.
>
> (Arthur Scargill, NUM conference, Sheffield, 1 July 1985)

The following day, when there was angry reaction to the speeches of those delegates representing the working coalfields, Mr Scargill appealed for order, saying that the last thing the conference should do was provide the 'piranha fish' of the news media with any further opportunity to smear the NUM. As he spoke he pointed to where the journalists were sitting, declaring that they could not tell the truth, even if they 'swilled out their mouths with Dettol'.

One reporter absent from the press bench at the NUM conference was the labour editor of *The Times*, Paul Routledge. When the strike had finished, he had been taken off industrial reporting and sent to Kuala Lumpur as correspondent in the Far East. His departure was widely regarded in Fleet Street as a punishment for the way he had embarrassed his editor, Charles Douglas-Home, by revealing to other journalists a conversation he had had with the Queen during a visit she made to *The Times* on 28 February 1985 to mark the newspaper's bicentenary.

Mr Routledge had intended being in Sheffield that day to report a meeting of the miners' executive, but had been told by his editor to be at his desk for the Queen's tour of the newsroom. When the Queen stopped to talk to him, he had asked what her feelings were on the miners' strike. According to Mr Routledge the Queen had said that the dispute was 'very sad', and had added: 'It's about one person, really.' Soon after the Queen had moved away, a BBC radio reporter, Graeme McLagan, who had been assigned to cover the visit, asked Mr Routledge what the Queen had said, to which he replied: 'I think she felt that the dispute was essentially promoted by Mr Scargill.' Mr Routledge had, apparently, gone on to explain to the Queen that he thought it was a much more complex issue than that.

When Mr McLagan returned with his inteview to the BBC, the radio newsroom waited until they received a comment from the Queen's press secretary, Michael Shea, before broadcasting Mr Routledge's remarks in the lunchtime news bulletins. The news reports were accompanied by a Buckingham Palace statement that any conversation which took place during the visit was private and that the Queen did not take sides during any dispute. Not all Mr Routledge's remarks were broadcast, including one section where McLagan asked him for the Queen's reaction when he had 'put her right' on the strike being more than 'about one person'. Later that day *The Times* apologised to the Queen for what it described as the 'nonsense' that had surrounded her visit. Both Mr Douglas-Home and Mr Routledge issued statements saying that the Queen had not, at any time, said the strike was 'promoted' by Mr Scargill.

The incident provoked considerable controversy, which the rest of Fleet Street seemed thoroughly to enjoy, as it provided an opportunity to chide *The Times* for allowing its labour editor to publicise his conversation with the Queen, thus breaching the long-established convention that conversations on royal visits are private and confidential. Mr Routledge insisted afterwards that he had not been warned in advance of the customary rules. He explained that he had faced a personal dilemma even before he met the Queen: he knew that if he became engaged in conversation he would, as a journalist, want to ask for her views on the strike.

A month before the Queen's visit Paul Routledge had annoyed Arthur Scargill and Peter Heathfield by publishing, on 21 January, an exclusive story on the private meeting between Mr Heathfield and Mr Smith (see p. 182). The accuracy of his report showed both the depth of his contacts in the coal industry and the independence of his reporting, indicating his value to *The Times*. Mr Routledge came from a mining family which for three previous generations had earned a living from the pits. During the strike he gave what financial help he could to miners and their families at a pit in Yorkshire; his wife was a member of a women's support group in Hemel Hempstead which raised money for the miners' hardship fund. After receiving £5,000 in libel damages from the *Daily Express*, which had described him on 3 April 1984 as being one of 'Scargill's seven shadows', he gave half the money to the miners. When I met him shortly before he left for the Far East, he seemed philosophical about his encounter with the Queen and his departure from industrial reporting: 'I shared the same fate as the miners but I suppose I shouldn't grumble. If you are a journalist and see a story in front of your nose you can't just run away.'

EIGHT

Repercussions

Any attempt to examine the use of communications and the role of the news media during the strikes of the late 1970s and early 1980s is fraught with difficulty. It is particularly difficult in the miners' strike, because the dispute was without precedent in British industrial history. After a twelve-month national stoppage which caused such deep divisions within the country, the task of trying to disentangle fact from propaganda is daunting. Even so, almost before the strike was over, a debate began on the NUM's shortcomings in the battle for public opinion, provoking a disagreement which seemed as fundamental as the dispute itself.

Soon after the first criticisms arose, a strong defence of the NUM's record in providing access to the news media was mounted by the union's press officer, Nell Myers. In an article in the *Guardian* on 3 June 1985 she said the union knew, long before the strike began, that those who owned, controlled and managed the means of mass communication 'were, and remain, monolithically marshalled in total opposition to our fight' to protect jobs and the communities which depended on them. The industrial correspondents, along with broadcasting technicians, were basically the 'front-line troops' for the miners' enemies.

An equally forthright condemnation of a 'right-wing monopoly press and subservient broadcast media' was delivered by the Campaign for Press and Broadcasting Freedom in an examination of news coverage of the coal dispute entitled *Media Hits the Pits*. The group believed the news media had clearly been antagonistic, having played an important role in 'consistently reinforcing' the case of the government and the coal board and in 'systematically undermining and demoralising striking miners and their supporters'. Nevertheless, the Campaign concluded that the conduct of the media 'was not itself decisive to the final outcome of the dispute'. This note of caution was reflected in a review of *Media Hits the Pits* published in *The Miner* in June of the same year, which stressed that if accurate and effective communication was stopped, people would simply never hear the message, no matter how brilliant, just or good it might be.

The NUM's vice-president in Scotland, George Bolton, had reached a similar conclusion. In a discussion for *Marxism Today*, published in April 1985, he noted how at the end of the twelve-month strike, despite the 'anti-miners media barrage', a significant percentage of British public opinion either supported or had sympathy for the miners' case. This illustrated, said Mr Bolton, the potential support which the NUM had failed to tap. But although there had been this sympathy and support he still believed, after a year's struggle, that the average person did not know what the strike was about – which only indicated that the NUM had not spent enough time getting its case across to the public.

The most sustained criticism of the shortcomings of the miners' leadership came from within the union, in an assessment written for the *Journalist* in January 1985 by Kim Howells, research officer for the South Wales NUM and a member of the National Union of Journalists. He could understand the bitterness felt by miners and their communities when they discovered that large sections of the news media were controlled by individuals or cabals whose attitude towards the Conservative government was one of 'fawning, craven subservience', and whose rarely disguised desire was to see 'the NUM crushed and Thatcherism triumph'. However, he could not go along with this blanket dismissal of the news media, which had been aided, he thought, by the attitude displayed by 'certain leading NUM figures', who all too often had used the news-gatherers as whipping-boys on whom to vent their frustration at being unable to mobilise wider trade union support. He continued:

> The NUM has displayed extreme symptoms of a malaise which afflicts virtually the whole of the trade union movement. It assumes that, somehow, the 'truth' about the dispute is going to fall out of the sky and land neatly on news desks, ready-packaged for consumption. Union press statements are almost non-existent or often so predictable as to be virtually unusable. Telephone conversations between journalists and local miners' leaders are all too frequently terminated by the leaders with the complaint, 'What's the use of me telling you anything? You won't print what I say anyway.'
>
> Nothing has changed a great deal in this respect thoughout the course of the dispute, despite the fact that it should be transparently obvious that blanket condemnations of news coverage are unwise and insensitive. Instead of attempting to use the systems of mass communication to the best advantage of their members, far too many trade union leaders have turned the systems into great totems, not to be approached at any cost, but, perversely, to be feared and hated almost as primitive tribes feared and hated malevolent gods which could never be overcome.
>
> (Kim Howells, *Journalist*, January 1985)

My own conclusions on the pit strike relate strictly to my examination of the way union, management and government used the news media in their attempt to communicate with miners and members of the public. I have not tried to give an assessment of the news media's own performance in reporting the strike; nor do I venture to make any comment on such controversial issues as the treatment by television of picket-line violence or the editorial policies of Fleet Street newspapers.

As labour correspondent of BBC radio, my task during the strike was to report and assess the decisions taken by the NUM, the NCB and government, and to follow the protracted negotiations. Although I was present during a number of major distrubances, I spent only a limited time on the picket lines and did not cover the mass demonstrations at Orgreave. I acknowledge immediately the dominant impact of television coverage of the dispute, but without having reported the violence myself, I consider that my own observations would perhaps lack substance and authority.

In its booklet *Media Hits the Pits*, the Campaign for Press and Broadcasting Freedom offers little to substantiate its sweeping assertion that the radio services 'ridiculed' the miners' case, or to justify its description of the broadcasters as the 'cheerleaders' for the government. It makes only a few cursory references to BBC radio, and ignores completely the countless hours devoted to the strike by regional radio and local radio stations in the mining areas. When *Media Hits the Pits* was first published, I asked one of the authors, the Campaign's national organiser, Mike Power, how it justified its criticism of the way the radio services had reported the strike:

Power   They ridiculed it by the way they presented the argument; to constantly refer to a 'miners' strike' when it was in fact a 'coal dispute'. There were three parties, miners, coal board and government, yet the whole thing was put on the back of the miners and in general the broadcasting services argued that the problem in British industrial relations is trade unionists, is workers, because they go on strike, never ever taking account of the fact that management very often and consistently mismanage, as MacGregor was shown to be a mismanager.

Jones   I can't find any example of where you feel the radio services ridiculed the miners.

Power   It is referred to in general, the use of language for instance, the way in which the terms of reference are the terms of the coal board – 'uneconomic pits' and not 'so-called uneconomic pits'. There is . . . the way in which miners' communities are seen as unimportant as compared to, say, the needs of government or the coal board to make or save money. In that way people's lives are ridiculed.

202

Jones   But radio stations up and down the country, the national radio services, believe they provided a balance of opportunity for the miners' union, and this blanket criticism, that radio ridiculed the miners, is something which they feel is a case of blatant bias on your part because you have yet to back it up with any evidence.

Power   We talked about it in general in a short pamphlet in which we tried to argue that the broadcasting services and the press lined up behind government and the NCB. We have given plenty of examples – the way in which Scargill was interviewed in a hostile way: 'Oh surely Mr Scargill you are not saying . . . ', whereas to Mr MacGregor it would be 'Mr MacGregor, have you got a point of view on this?' These kind of things indicate the extent to which Fleet Street, run by five multi-national millionaire companies, set down the terms of reference, accepted what the government and NCB said, and radio and television followed it.

Jones   You compliment radio on the access programmes it provided. I would have thought that was the strength of what the radio services did. They did provide access and a balance of opportunity to the miners' union.

Power   We do not accept, for instance, that the broadcasting and press services can be blamed for the outcome of the dispute. There are a number of programmes on television as well as radio which were a lot fairer than the worst, but in general the BBC and ITN lined up with the government, and that is what most people are aware of, and that is what they felt in the mining communities.

(Mike Power, Campaign for Press and Broadcasting Freedom, BBC Radio 4, Today programme, 14 May 1985)

Mr Scargill displayed by his own actions the transparency of some of his regular onslaughts on the conduct of those who work in the news media. When addressing miners' rallies he would denounce all journalists, broadcasters and technicians, declaring that they would always 'go on supporting Mrs Thatcher'. Yet, almost within minutes of making such an attack, he would happily co-operate with the media, arranging yet another live television appearance on Channel 4 News or the BBC's Newsnight. Mr Scargill took the easy way out: he preferred to deal with certain programmes individually, and sometimes exclusively, rather than develop a strategy aimed at capturing the attention of the major news bulletins on radio and television. The NUM was offered, but rejected, outside advice and assistance; Mr Scargill chose instead to remain the union's principal communicator, knowing that to do otherwise would mean relinquishing some of the personal control he exercised over the union. At the annual conference in July 1985 he showed no sign of any doubt or self-criticism over the tactics that had been adopted during the dispute: he told delegates that it was not a failure of mass picketing, but 'a failure to mass picket', that had been the NUM's weakness. The real problem, however, was that at no time had the union sought to devise a strategy based on trying to win public support rather than using industrial muscle.

As a working journalist, I cannot help but be concerned that when I have spoken to young miners and other trade union activists since the pit strike, many have just turned away, seemingly convinced that they will never get a fair hearing from anyone employed in the news media. They often repeat, word for word, the accusations of Mr Scargill. Of all the reasons for writing this book, one of the strongest has been the urge to try to answer some of the criticisms made of journalists. I hope that my examination of the way unions, management and government use communications and the news media may help others to make a fair assessment of the role of the press and broadcasting during industrial disputes.

Could the miners have won the dispute if the NUM's channels of communication to its members and the public had been as extensive, and used as effectively, as those of the coal board and the government? I know that many in the NUM and the wider trade union movement – and some members of the public as well – believe that such a question cannot be answered without an examination of complaints about media bias. However, in the hope of countering such objections, I have modified the question: Would the NUM have stood a better chance of obtaining a secure future for the mining communities if the strike had been accompanied by a campaign that had put as much emphasis on public relations as it did on industrial strength? I feel I am on safer ground with this question, especially in view of the comments that have already been made on the NUM's own shortcomings in publicity and communications.

In the light of my research for this book, I would answer the question in the affirmative. If the NUM had tried at the outset to devise a strategy of mobilising public opinion, the government might indeed have been forced to prepare plans for the expanded use of Britain's coal reserves, which could in turn have provided stronger safeguards for the mining communities and ensured greater investment to ease the transition to newer pits. There can be no doubt that the communications strategy that the coal board and the government evolved was a decisive factor in persuading miners to return to work. The NCB improved on the communication techniques developed at British Leyland, British Rail and British Steel, and used them with great dexterity. The tactical skill of Peter Walker and Ian MacGregor's communications consultants ultimately overtook and overshadowed the persistence and ingenuity of Arthur

Scargill, exposing the fundamental weaknesses within the NUM that I have dwelt on in this book.

Any answer to my question about the emphasis to be placed on public relations would be incomplete without acknowledging the traditional reluctance of the trade unions to employ communications advisers. Within the union movement, an argument has rumbled on for decades over the advantages and disadvantages of publicity, and the desirability or otherwise of seeking a closer relationship with the news media. One Fleet Street labour correspondent who wrote about union communications in the late 1950s and early 1960s described how unions were always saying that everything would have been 'all right' if only the public had understood their plight. He gave this explanation of why the union leaders of his day shunned the art of public relations, even though many members wanted the leadership to acknowledge the importance of public opinion:

> The reasons for this muddled attitude are complex. Partly it is a sort of race memory of the days when unions were illegal and every activity had to be conducted in secret. Allied to that, perhaps going deeper, is the belief, based on generations of experience, that every man's hand is against them. They take a bitter pride in their isolation. They believe that anything they do or say will be distorted. So they must face the inevitable unpopularity and obloquy and rely on their own strength and solidarity, defying the capitalists, the government, the law, the establishment and the press.
>
> (Eric Wigham, *What's Wrong With the Unions?*,
> Penguin Special, 1961)

During the early 1980s there was a major reassessment of traditional trade union responses to advertising and public relations. After three to four million union members had voted for a Conservative government in both the 1979 and 1983 general elections, the movement recognised its inadequacy in conveying information to the membership and in winning the support of the public. In January 1985 a special TUC conference on union communications was told that the average union spent less than 12 per cent of its income on promotion. A year later the TUC published guidelines on the use of advertising, saying that while unions would not want to 'sell themselves like soap powder' they did need to reach beyond the activists and 'talk directly to their members and the public generally'.

The six trade unions representing telephone engineering and clerical workers were the first to seize the initiative, launching a major campaign in October 1982 against the government's plans for the privatisation of British Telecom. Over a period of twenty months, around £2 million was spent on direct publicity. The British Telecom Union Committee believed the campaign was responsible for securing substantial amendments to the

Telecommunications Bill during its passage through Parliament in 1984. The unions were satisfied that their efforts to alert public opinion helped to obtain guarantees for rural telephone services, and did provide protection for thousands of jobs, including the posts of 15,000 telephonists which could have been threatened if British Telecom had been allowed to dispense with a free directory-inquiries service. According to one estimate, the six unions recouped the cost of the publicity within eighteen months, through membership subscriptions which would have been lost if British Telecom had been allowed to make all the redundancies it wanted.

The Telecom campaign coincided with a publicity drive by another union, the National and Local Government Officers' Association, which spent nearly £1 million between April and July 1983 as part of a concerted attempt to warn the public of the consequences of the government's cuts in public services and the welfare state. Out of the total budget, £588,000 went on advertising, mainly in the national press, with the campaign slogan, 'Put People First.' Although NALGO felt the impact of its publicity had been weakened considerably by the government's decision to call the 1983 general election in the middle of the campaign, it concluded that it had made a 'major contribution' towards increasing public awareness on issues like privatisation.

Other unions which have been unable to afford extensive advertising campaigns believe significant results can be achieved through the preparation of a relatively inexpensive public relations strategy. In the 1982 health workers' pay dispute, the TUC's health services committee planned a campaign based largely on regional 'days of action'. The code of conduct for maintaining emergency cover, which had been introduced after the 1979 'winter of discontent', prevented extensive industrial action: instead, the health unions concentrated their limited resources on organising events in each area, which they tried to make as newsworthy as possible in the hope of attracting the interest of the media. Nurses and other hospital workers were told to go to rallies and marches with their pay slips, in order to display them for the benefit of newspaper photographers and television cameramen. This they did, obtaining widespread publicity both in the national newspapers and on television, especially in regional programmes where, day after day, there were reports and pictures of protest meetings and demonstrations outside the major hospitals.

After the strike action of 1979, the health unions had made many complaints about what they said was the unfair treatment that their members had received from the news media. By 1982 the union leaders had learned from their experience: they had discovered there were steps that could be taken to secure publicity, which would help in the presentation of their members' case. The health unions believe the publicity obtained during their 1982 campaign was reflected for some years afterwards in opinion polls, which continue to show that a clear majority of the public thought nurses and other health workers should be paid more.

As we have seen, the option of fighting pit closures through a campaign designed to win public opinion, perhaps by a combination of strike action and publicity, does not seem to have been considered by the miners' leadership. At no point in the section of the union's 1985 annual report reviewing media relations during the strike does the national executive refer to the experience of other trade unions, or make any mention of having examined the possibility of spending some of its own resources on advertising or public relations.

In contrast, the NCB's expenditure of £4,566,000 on newspaper advertisements alone set a new record during a British industrial dispute. When the coal board began placing national newspaper advertisements in the early months of the stoppage, there were discussions between the NUM and the Campaign for Press and Broadcasting Freedom on the likelihood of being able to demand equal space for a right of reply free of charge. However, most newspaper proprietors made it clear, when the printworkers issued their statement of solidarity with the miners, that such messages would be published only as paid-for advertisements – the standard practice of the British press.

As so little information has been released about the NUM's finances, it is difficult to discover whether the union did have sufficient funds to mount its own advertising campaign. Throughout the strike Arthur Scargill refused to answer financial questions, and once the NUM's assets had been sequestrated he simply said the union was 'broke'. However, it did start the strike with considerable reserves, having had assets of £8.5 million to transfer abroad when the dispute began. Miners paid subscriptions of between about £1 and £1.50 a week in the year before the strike, and the money was shared between the individual areas and the national union. In the twelve months ending December 1983, the NUM declared a national income of £7.3 million, of which £6.7 million was its share of the subscription payments.

According to its own estimate, supplied to the TUC in May 1985, the dispute had cost the NUM a total of £35 million at national and area level, setting a new record for a union's expenditure during a strike. Accounts were not published at the 1985 annual NUM conference, so no breakdown was given either on the source of the money or on what it was spent on. However, in addition to the reserves held at national and area level, the miners did, as we have seen, receive large amounts in donations and loans from other unions, much of the money going into separate hardship funds. A large but unknown proportion of direct expenditure of the strike went towards the cost of paying expenses and travelling allowances for the pickets who were sent from areas like Yorkshire to Nottinghamshire and the other working coalfields. Payments varied from area to area, but were a minimum of £1 a day per man and £4 for the use of a car.

Although the leadership did not draw any pay during the strike, the salaries normally paid to the miners' national officers have been well above those of many other unions; the NUM's travelling expenses, its union-owned houses and cars have also been the envy of many other trade unions. In view of the level of expenditure to which the NUM was usually accustomed, it could easily have afforded the cost of employing professional consultants on advertising and public relations, if it had been thought necessary. An assessment could then have been made on the likely cost of publicity.

Early on in the strike there was one unofficial proposal for a publicity campaign on behalf of the miners, which suggested a budget of £2 million on advertising and public relations. That estimate was prepared by Keith Bill, a director of Union Communications, which had advised the British Telecom unions in their publicity campaign against privatisation. Mr Bill believed it would have been possible for the NUM, through a clearly defined communications strategy, to exert considerable public pressure and force the government to appoint a review body, which would have had the independence and authority to overrule the coal board and take the final decision on pit closures. Mr Bill's ideas were discussed at the time in a BBC radio programme, but like the others that came from the communications industry, they were not followed up by the union.

The NUM's failure to adopt an overall strategy for communications and publicity should serve as a warning to the trade union and labour movement – indeed, there is already some evidence that this is happening. The TUC is encouraging its affiliates to recognise the advances that employers have made, both in communicating directly with employees and in influencing the presentation of news during industrial disputes. Several major unions now regularly spend more on public relations and advertising than they do on strike pay. That number could well increase, as more unions weigh up the advantages of using publicity rather than prolonged industrial action.

A strong rebuke for having ignored public opinion was delivered to the NUM afterwards by Bill Sirs, who had been, for most of the strike, general secretary of the Iron and Steel Trades Confederation, and whose union had been involved in bitter disagreement with the miners over attempts to halt steel production during the pit dispute. In his autobiography he claimed that the experience of the steelworkers, who had succeeded in 1981 with the help of public support, in stopping the closure of the Ravenscraig works in Scotland, showed that industrial action on its own would not win the day. Strikes, marches and rallies were useful, but had to be used sparingly. The overwhelming necessity was to win over public opinion:

There was no attempt at all by the NUM to win that support. There was no explanation of their case, only half a dozen phrases repeated parrot-fashion by the NUM leadership when they appeared on television. Where were the booklets, the leaflets, the full-page advertisements in the national and provincial press? Where were the posters and hoardings? The NUM persisted in doing things the old-fashioned way. Any large-scale public relations and advertising campaign costs money – but a campaign of the size necessary to swing public opinion and secure for the NUM effective arbiters would have cost far less than the money the NUM spent on maintaining the strike – and all to no avail.

(Bill Sirs, *Hard Labour*, Sidgwick and Jackson, September 1985)

Within months of the miners' return to work, the repercussions of the NUM's defeat were felt on the railways. On this occasion, unlike the rail disputes of 1982 (see chapter 2), public sympathy seemed largely on the side of the union, as it was management that had failed to communicate. After recording a £408 million loss for 1984–5, of which £250 million was blamed directly on the absence of coal traffic, British Rail was determined to speed up its drive to increase efficiency and introduce driver-only trains on freight services and certain suburban passenger lines. When management pressed ahead with trials of driver-only trains, union opposition increased. During August 1985 there was a series of unofficial strikes, and 251 guards were dismissed. However, most passengers and members of the public sided firmly with the National Union of Railwaymen, which had argued that the added safety derived from having a guard on every train was more important than any saving in costs.

When the dispute seemed on the point of provoking a national rail strike, the NUR agreed to hold a ballot among its 5,500 guards, who, against expectations, narrowly rejected industrial action. British Rail was as surprised as the union at the ballot result: its public affairs department had already prepared a press statement expressing the disappointment of the personnel director, John Pallette, at what he had assumed would be the guards' 'yes' vote. If the NUR leadership had in fact gained a majority for industrial action, those advising the general secretary, Jimmy Knapp, were going to recommend that he should suggest to the executive that instead of calling a strike, the union should mount an advertising campaign designed to retain and expand public support for guards on trains.

British Rail was peeved by the success that the union had already achieved, accusing the NUR of using unscrupulous tactics to create the myth that guards were to be taken off every passenger train, when in fact they were only to be removed from certain freight trains, and new passenger trains with sliding doors and radio-controlled communications, and in conjunction with closed-circuit television on platforms. Perhaps it was not surprising that BR's case had gone by default, as Sir Robert Reid, chairman of British Rail for the previous two years, had always made it clear that he did not see himself as a public performer like his predecessor Sir Peter Parker, who had been ready to appear at a moment's notice on programmes like the Jimmy Young show on BBC radio.

In the six months up to the end of July 1985, the rail board and its subsidiaries spent an estimated £8 million on press advertising. But, it was not until two days after the guards had voted, that British Rail thought to publish a national newspaper advertisement designed to reassure the public that driver-only trains were 'safe to operate and to use'. Five days later, the NUR responded with its own advertisement in the nationals, explaining why the union remained convinced that there was a continuing role for the guard. The advertisement contained quotations taken from letters which were said to be 'pouring' into the NUR's headquarters, supporting the union's case by 'over 40 to 1'. The accuracy of the union's advertising copy was questioned by *The Times*, but when the NUR offered to make the correspondence available, the advertisement department of Times Newspapers withdrew its challenge. The guards' dispute was a major departure for a union that had previously relied on its industrial strength: it has learned many lessons from the miners' strike, and had accepted the importance of preparing a communications strategy before trying to embark on strike action.

During the period examined in this book, management has been in the ascendancy; the fear of redundancy has speeded up the rate of industrial change and weakened trade union resistance. On the other hand, there is one tactical management advantage that has been eroded: the monopoly that employers previously enjoyed of up-to-date personal information about union members, such as their latest home addresses.

The change has been hastened by Conservative legislation for which, in retrospect, the unions might be grateful. Under the government's 1984 Trade Union Act, each union was required by October 1985 to establish a central register of the names and addresses of its members, in case of being ordered by a court to conduct a postal ballot during a union election. A number of unions already possessed computerised membership records, but in view of the legal requirement many more decided during 1985 to compile and maintain up-to-date membership records independent of the 'check-off' system under which union subscriptions are deducted at work.

Two major unions, the Amalgamated Union of Engineering Workers and the Electrical, Electronic, Telecommunication and Plumbing Union, had already been operating computerised membership records for some years, precisely because of their policy of conducting postal ballots in union elections. The EETPU was the first union to install a computerised register, in April 1967, which by mid-1985 was estimated to be 98 per cent accurate; the AUEW's computerised system, in operation since January 1972, was said to contain the correct addresses of 83 per cent of the union's membership.

Because of the heavy financial cost of postal balloting, both unions decided early in 1985 to defy the established policy of the Trades Union Congress – even though it carried the risk of suspension from the TUC – by applying to the government for reimbursement of the postal charges. A state fund of £2 million a year had been established by the government after the introduction of the 1980 Employment Act, in line with the commitment in the Conservative Party's 1979 election manifesto to try to encourage wider participation in trade union voting. The AUEW was paid £1.2 million for postal ballots held between March 1981 and September 1984, which resulted in the TUC general council charging the union in August 1985 with activities which might be 'detrimental' to the interests of the trade union movement and contrary to declared Congress policy.

Despite the criticism of the AUEW and EETPU over their decision to break ranks and accept government money, few in the movement could fault the two unions on the efficiency of their communications systems, which were used to distribute not only ballot papers but also union journals. Britain's biggest union, the Transport and General Workers', was among those which decided after the 1984 Act to invest in a computerised system. Ron Todd, when he became general secretary in July 1985, made internal union communications his first priority. He told me that he wanted the transport union to have as much information about its own members as did any employer. By 1987, Mr Todd hoped, the Transport and General would have a central record of the names and addresses of its 1.5 million members, and the names and addresses of their employers and details of the wage agreements under which they worked.

Shortly after the strike, the NUM did take some steps to improve its internal communications, by preparing a computerised record of the names and addresses of the 4,000 miners in Nottinghamshire who had registered their wish to stay in the national union rather than become members of a break-away union. Progressive steps towards the formation of a separate union for the 28,000 Nottinghamshire miners were taken during the closing months of the strike and the summer of 1985. In May, when there was mounting controversy within the union over the introduction of a new rule book containing revised disciplinary proce-dures, the Nottinghamshire area held a local pit-head ballot. Seventy-three per cent of those who participated voted against accepting the new national rules, even if it meant their area being expelled from the NUM. They feared the national union would impose severe penalties on those who had worked during the strike and who disagreed with NUM policy. In July, after the NUM annual conference had accepted the new rule book, Nottinghamshire area delegates voted by an overwhelming majority to break away.

The final vote to establish the new Union of Democratic Mineworkers was decisive: 72 per cent said 'Yes' in Nottinghamshire, 51 per cent in South Derbyshire and 98 per cent in the small Durham Colliery Trades

Association. On the eve of the ballot, on 17 October, Arthur Scargill issued a fresh warning about further pit closures, but while there seemed a general acknowledgement within the industry that more collieries were likely to be closed, the majority of miners in the dissident areas decided the NUM was not the right union to represent them. The National Coal Board did all it could to help maintain the publicity build-up for the breakaway, notably with a timely announcement of a pay rise for members of the new union. As the rate of pit closures gathered pace in the autumn of 1985 the board's public relations department rarely volunteered information to journalists. The only exception involved statements sympathetic to the new union, and the press officers were told to pass on this information as quickly as possible by telephoning the appropriate news organisations.

The NUM's somewhat belated response in the field of computerised records was in sharp contrast to the approach to communications and publicity that had been adopted by leaders of the break-away Nottinghamshire union. Well before the end of the strike, when a split first seemed likely, Roy Lynk, who was to become the new Nottinghamshire general secretary, sought the advice of a local public relations consultancy, Myles PR, founded by a former BBC television journalist, Bruce Myles. Mr Lynk told me that he first made contact with Mr Myles in December 1984, a month before the Nottinghamshire area approved changes to its own constitution designed to loosen its ties with the NUM. However, according to Mr Myles, it was on 21 January the next year that his consultancy officially began work for the Nottinghamshire area.

Mr Myles' brief was to give the area leaders advice on how to present their case against the NUM's rule changes to the news media, and to make contact with local and national journalists. Myles PR also produced a new area newspaper, *The Nottinghamshire Miner*, which first appeared in February 1985. Mr Lynk and his colleagues hoped the new paper would counter what they believed was Arthur Scargill's 'misleading' propaganda about the Nottinghamshire miners. The new Notts leaders believed that good communications with the membership had been one factor in obtaining such an overwhelming vote of support in the May ballot. Later, in August 1985, when the break-away leaders began campaigning for a second ballot on the possibility of leaving the NUM in order to form a new Union of Democratic Mineworkers with other men in South Derbyshire and Durham, the Nottinghamshire area took advertising space on 124 poster hoardings throughout the Notts coalfield. Myles PR commissioned the cartoonist John Kent to prepare two posters urging the miners to vote 'yes' and leave the NUM. Mr Myles refused at the time to say how much the publicity had cost.

As the campaign gathered pace the NUM took further measures to counter Nottinghamshire's publicity. Bundles of *The Miner* were still being delivered to the Nottinghamshire headquarters, and although they

Plate 17   The first poster commissioned by the break-away Nottinghamshire union as part of its campaign to persuade miners in the area to vote in favour of leaving the NUM appeared in August 1985. It took its inspiration from Arthur Scargill's warning that Nottinghamshire miners would be treated like 'lepers and outcasts' if they failed to support their union. The second poster showed the NUM vice-president Mick McGahey with Mr Scargill, and a ballot box which had been thrown into a waste-paper basket.

were not being distributed to the pits, copies were available for collection by any member who wanted to read what the NUM was saying. Then, in the summer of 1985, the union began publishing a new newspaper, *The Notts Collier*, which was printed free of charge by the Workers' Revolutionary Party. Henry Richardson, who had been dismissed as Nottinghamshire general secretary and who was campaigning against the break-away union, was one of the two publishers. He defended the NUM's decision to take help from the WRP, maintaining that the party had at no time influenced the content or philosophy of *The Notts Collier*. When one Fleet Street Sunday newspaper ran a full-page lead story under the headline, 'Miners' paper printed free by Trotskyists', Mr Richardson replied:

We have no money. The WRP print the paper for nothing. How else do we get our view across when the break-away enjoys support from anti-union newspapers and can employ public relations staff at £200 a week to fight their campaign? I have no money to fight a campaign. Our funds are sequestrated. Every penny I receive goes to support the 24 Notts miners sacked during the strike.

(Henry Richardson, *Observer*, 29 September 1985)

The miners' strike demonstrated, as did no other dispute, the pitfalls of trying to negotiate through the news media. After the 1982 rail strikes, British Rail's industrial relations director Clifford Rose had voiced his concern over the dangers inherent in this process (see chapter 2). He came to the firm conclusion that new proposals or pay offers should always be discussed first at the negotiating table – never aired for the first time on radio or television or in the press. As we saw earlier, Mr Rose's reservations were shared by the coal board's director-general of industrial relations Ned Smith, who also found that the difficulties facing management were only compounded when government ministers started using the news media to prescribe the very conditions for negotiations.

Mr Smith's views seemed to carry no weight with Ian MacGregor, Michael Eaton or government ministers, who like the miners' leaders frequently became engrossed in trying to score negotiating points in public. For union, management and government, presentation had become a matter of overriding importance. As coal board and government inched towards the draft agreements offered in July 1984 and then, after the TUC's intervention, those of February 1985, members of management who were urging compromise feared their efforts would almost certainly prove in vain, because of Arthur Scargill's urge to declare a 'victory' and Margaret Thatcher's determination to deny him at all costs the grounds for making any such claim.

The TUC general secretary Norman Willis, also, had found that his attempts at mediation were hindered by the protagonists' insistence on competing with each other in endless interviews. Whenever he made an approach to one side, he would instantly hear complaints about what the other side had just said. He tried without success to explain that there might be a difference between an official policy statement and an answer given in the heat of the moment in the face of provocative or hostile questions from a journalist.

Another penalty of making so many statements in public was that the negotiators inevitably found their hands could be tied – which hardly promoted an atmosphere of compromise. Although Mr Scargill did seem genuinely distressed by the premature disclosure of the unsuccessful joint initiative by Ned Smith and Peter Heathfield in January 1985, he had, as we have seen, for most of the strike openly encouraged the process of negotiation through the news media. Largely by his own efforts as president, he succeeded in using the perpetual prospect of negotiations as a way of sustaining support for the strike and of maintaining the interest of the news media. Mr Scargill was prepared for the dispute to have continued, despite the conference vote to return to work.

A few months after the end of the strike, some interesting research started into the effects of news coverage on the process of industrial negotiation. As part of an investigation into the conduct of television news during the miners' strike, prepared for the Broadcasting Research Unit by Aston University, an audience survey was commissioned to discover whether people thought the presence of television cameras and personnel influenced the business of coming to an agreement. The research team reached this conclusion:

> Very few respondents (2 per cent) thought that television coverage had made it easier to reach an agreement. The bulk of the respondents were fairly evenly divided between feeling that television coverage had made no difference (47 per cent) and feeling that it had hindered agreement (46 per cent). Even if the presence of television crews had hindered an agreement, this must be balanced against the public's right to know what is going on. Weighing up these competing interests represents a dilemma for broadcasters.
>
> ('Television News and the Miners' Strike' (provisional report),
> Broadcasting Research Unit, September 1985)

After six years as a labour correspondent reporting industrial disputes, I am convinced there have been occasions when settlements have been delayed or frustrated by the growing tendency to negotiate through radio and television. Organisations and individuals who seek publicity, while criticising the news media, should also be able to recognise the value of self-discipline in their attempts to explain their case and win support: the wider public interest must be served – and seen to be served – rather than the more personal concerns of the individuals in the spotlight.

Index

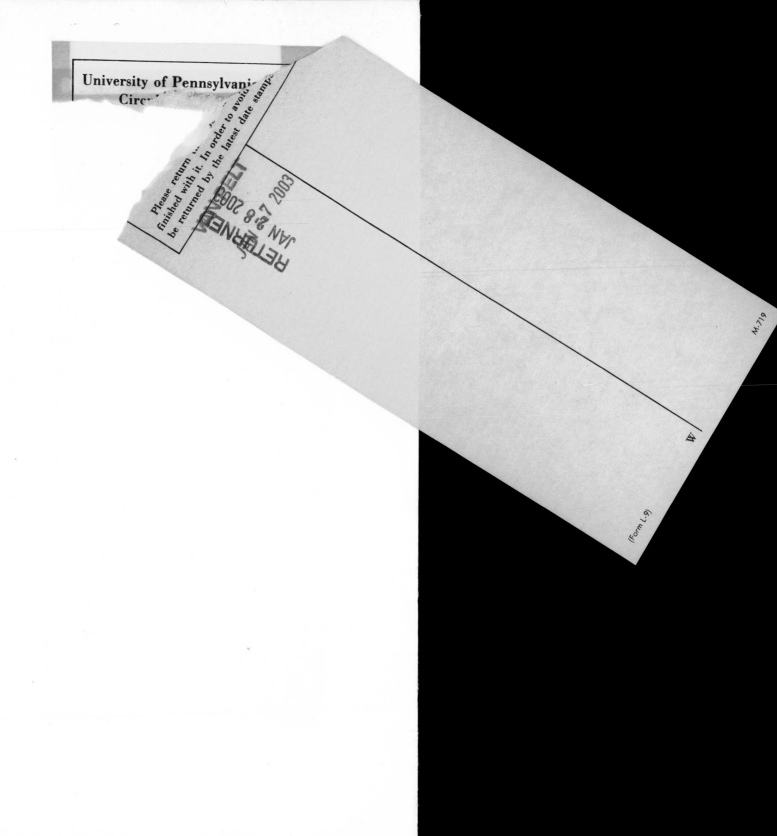